MW00806090

Harold B. Lee Library

WITHDRAWN
11/2/2023
STP

MAY 2 0 1993

170

A SHORT HISTORY OF THE NETHERLANDS ANTILLES AND SURINAM

5579/46

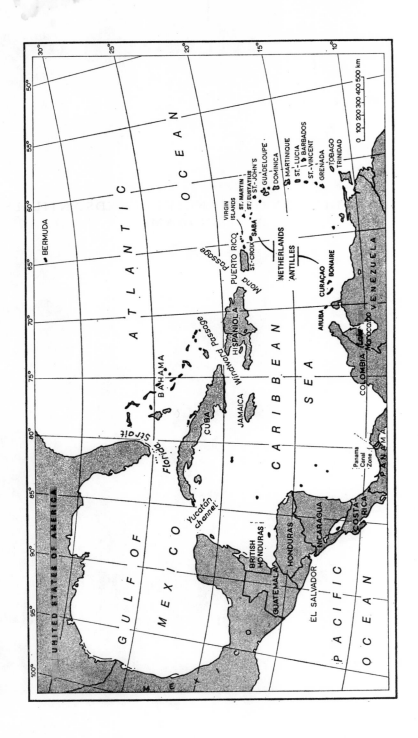

F
2141
.G63
copy 2

A SHORT HISTORY OF THE NETHERLANDS ANTILLES AND SURINAM

by

CORNELIS CH. GOSLINGA

1979

MARTINUS NIJHOFF

THE HAGUE/BOSTON/LONDON

To
CATY, BERNTH, and NILS

© 1979 by Martinus Nijhoff, Publishers bv, The Hague
All rights reserved. No part of this publication may be reproduced,
stored in a retrieval system, or transmitted in any form or by any
means, mechanical, photocopying, recording, or otherwise,
without the prior written permission of the publisher,
Martinus Nijhoff Publishers bv, P.O.B. 566, 2501 CN
The Hague, The Netherlands

ISBN 90 247 2118 0

PRINTED IN THE NETHERLANDS

HAROLD B. LEE LIBRARY
BRIGHAM YOUNG UNIVERSITY
PROVO, UTAH

FOREWORD

To English-speaking historians, the author of this book, a Dutchman who for many years now finds his base at the University of Florida, became well known when his *The Dutch in the Caribbean and on the Wild Coast, 1580–1680* was published in 1972.

At that time Professor Goslinga, who prior to his academic career in the United States, lived for an extended period in Curaçao, Netherlands Antilles, had already acquired a solid reputation among Dutch Caribbeanists by his manifold publications on social, political and maritime aspects of Dutch West Indian history.

By his training, interests and present position, Dr. Goslinga would seem to me to be singularly well-equipped to write a comprehensive history – geared to an English-speaking university public – of what was once known as the Netherlands West Indies.

The present book is the product of this professional equipment and of his long teaching experience. It should go a long way in filling the old and wide gap in historical information on this part of the former Dutch empire, and I hope an equally wide but younger audience will appreciate it.

H. HOETINK
Center for Caribbean Studies
Department of Anthropology
University of Utrecht
The Netherlands

PREFACE

The Netherlands Antilles and Surinam, once integral units of the Dutch colonial empire around the Atlantic, are parts of the Caribbean and Guiana areas the history of which is little known, one of the major impediments to their study obviously being the language barrier. Practically everything written about their history and development is in the Dutch language.

The events of the last decades which brought both these areas an autonomous status within the "new style monarchy" of the Netherlands – also called the "tripartite kingdom" and, in the mid-seventies, independence to Surinam, have stimulated interest in these regions. Both have the dominating characteristics of segmented and plural societies which evolved out of the inheritances from the seventeenth and eighteenth centuries with the master-slave relationships characteristic of the areas. Both, bound by sentiment, political inferiority, and economic dependency, to the Dutch mother country, passed through the colonial phases of exploitation, either benign neglect or a destructive policy of restriction – *versoberingspolitiek* – to emerge in the twentieth century as self-sustaining, financially solvent, and politically maturing dominions which, no longer satisfied with dependency and obeissance broke away from these prescribed, colonial roles to take their rightful places in the Dutch community as well as in their own geographical sphere.

This little book is an account of their history through three centuries of a rather stormy existence. The Curaçao islands and the Dutch Leeward group passed through the complexities of functioning as a slave market and warehouse for the Caribbean and other areas, of a beleaguered rock in a sea infested by privateers, pirates, and hostile fleets of European enemies, through periods of great depression and huge profits, through foreign occupation and involvement in the sweeping changes brought about by Latin American independence, while Surinam suffered all the calamities of a monocultural, sugar-producing society, its prosperity, and its downfall, a post-emancipation recession, and the vicissitudes of contract laborer immigration. The events of the twentieth century revealed the weakness of agricultural monoculture in the case of Surinam, and the inefficacy of illicit trade in the case of Curaçao, only to see these replaced by industrial monoculture: bauxite and oil, which substituted newer dependencies for the old and discredited ones of their colonial past.

They engendered, however, desires for change, for political emancipation and a voice in the destiny of the own native soil. There is nothing unique about this process: many other peoples have passed through the same phase. The twentieth century, especially the last three decades, witnessed most, if not all, of these dreams to come true. But problems multiply like flies, and are lyke Hydra heads which, although cut off continue to sprout at a vociferous rate. While political independence came withing their grasp, unrest, unemployment, local conflicts, racial strifes propelled their societies into a new era in which apparently uncontrollable forces tended to move with irresistible strength in unpredictable directions.

The Dutch West Indies – mixed societies of remarkable composition – play their modest role in the changing atmosphere of the New World. This short history intends to be no more than an introduction to their struggle and problems.

My thanks to John Mugar and my daughter Marian for editing the text.

CORNELIS CH. GOSLINGA

TABLE OF CONTENTS

INTRODUCTION

The Netherlands Antilles are composed of two groups of islands: the Curaçao islands and three islands in the Leeward group (in Dutch and Spanish called the Windward Islands). The Curaçao group includes the islands Curaçao with Little Curaçao, Aruba, and Bonaire with Little Bonaire. The three islands in the Leeward section of the Lesser Antilles are St. Martin (which is half Dutch and half French), St. Eustatius, and Saba.

The island of Curaçao has a land area of 170 square miles, Aruba of 70, and Bonaire of 100. Little Curaçao has less than a square mile and Little Bonaire a little more than two square miles. The capital of Curaçao is Willemstad, of Aruba Oranjestad, and of Bonaire Kralendijk. In 1970, the Curaçao islands together had around 240,000 inhabitants. Of the Leeward islands St. Martin is the largest with thirteen square miles of which six are Dutch. Its capital is Philipsburg; St. Eustatius covers twelve square miles, and Saba has the size of Little Curaçao. The total population of this group in 1970 was around 6500 inhabitants. This means that more than 97 per cent of the population of the Netherlands Antilles lives on the Curaçao islands.

These islands are located in the southern part of the Caribbean within view of the Venezuelan coast, yet outside of the hurricane area. They have a tropical climate with an average annual temperature of 81.4° Fahrenheit. September is the hottest month, January and February are the coolest. The sun is in zenith twice a year: April 22 and August 22. Average yearly rainfall is around 22 inches on Curaçao, 20 on Bonaire, and 18 on Aruba. There are two rainy seasons: one from October to January, and a shorter one in May or June. The divi-divi trees show the direction of the prevailing winds which blow from the northeast to the southwest with a steady velocity of ten miles per hour.

The Curaçao group, like all the islands off the Venezuelan coast have a different geological composition from the continent. The three islands differ in degree of elevation; all three have tertiary chalk formation, quartair coral, and aluvial sediment.

The flora of the islands is predominantly xerophitic and very similar to the

flora of the nearby coast. Its best known specimens are the divi-divi, the
campeche or brazilwood tree, the aloe, the agave, and several varieties of
cactus. Coconut palms, tamarind, guyaba, mango, and papaya trees are
found in cultivated areas. Halophitic or salt-loving vegetation is represented
by the manzanilla tree.

The fauna of the islands is still being inventoried. There are no big native
animals, although Curaçao boasts a small deer. Goats, horses, and cattle
were imported by the Spaniards, as were probably also rats, mice, and
rabbits. More than one hundred different types of birds are found, the best
known being the flamingo of Bonaire, the *tortolica*, a small pigeon, and the
pelican which roams the coast in great numbers. There are no poisonous
snakes, but many varieties of lizards, of which the largest is the iguana.

Although Indian traits are still visible, at least on Aruba, the Indian
population has long since disappeared. During most of the colonial period
society was composed of a white upper-class, a black slave class, and, in
between these two, a mulatto class called *hende di coló* (colored people),
which gradually gained in importance.

The three Dutch Leeward islands are perched on the northern rim of the
Lesser Antilles, in the area of both the trade winds and the hurricanes. They
have a tropical climate with a temperature steady at 79°. Average yearly
rainfall is between 40 and 46 inches.

The Dutch half of St. Martin has good salt pans. Saba is a high hill and is
therefore somewhat cooler than the other two while St. Eustatius lies lower
and is warmer. The population is white and the people speak Leeward
English, although Dutch is the official language.

Surinam, or Dutch Guiana, is located on the northern coast of the continent in the region between the Amazon and the Orinoco which, in earlier
centuries, was called the Wild Coast. It is separated from English-speaking
Guiana (now Guyana) to the west by the Corantine River, and from French
Guiana, or Cayenne, to the east by the Marowine River. The southern
border is shared with Brazil. Surinam's area, with the exclusion of disputed
territories about which no agreement has yet been reached, is almost 55,000
square miles or 4.4 times the size of the Netherlands. The population was,
in 1970, approximately 350,000 with 100,000 of these living in the capital,
Paramaribo.

The country is crossed by many rivers the most important of which are the
Surinam, the Commowine with its tributaries, the Cottica, the Coppename,
and the Saramacca. While greatly contributing to the exploration and development of the interior, the rivers have also constituted almost insurmounta-
ble obstacles to the east-west traffic, for they all flow in a south-north
direction.

From the coast to the Brazilian border, the country can be divided into three zones. Along the coast are the lowlands of clay soil covered with swamps. It is in this area, 15 miles wide in the east, increasing to 40 miles in the west, that 95 per cent of the people live.

Next follows an area about 25 miles in width, which is mainly savannah with scattered scrubs and low-growing trees. South of this is the third region, the highlands. Here we meet dense tropical forests intersected by a variety of streams of different sizes. This is the home of the approximately 30,000 so-called Bushnegroes, and of perhaps 5000 remaining Indians.

Surinam has a tropical climate. The coastal area, the hottest, varies from 73° to 88° in the course of a day, with an annual average of 81°. The northeast trade winds make themselves felt during the whole year. Annual rainfall is 92 inches for Paramaribo and somewhat less – 76 inches – in the western part of the country. There are two rainy seasons, the main one lasting from April through August, and the other from November to February.

CHAPTER I

THE CURAÇAO ISLANDS. THE INHABITANTS

When, in 1499, the Spanish *conquistador* Alonso de Ojeda discovered the islands Bonaire, Curaçao, and possibly also Aruba, he found them to be inhabited by peaceable Caiquetíos, a coastal tribe of the Arawak Indians occupying the nearby mainland, which together with the Jirajiras controlled the western shore of Lake Maracaibo eastward to Puerto Cabello and deep into the interior along the river valleys.

The Caiquetíos lived in numerous small communities under a chieftain, the *cacique*, who might also be a *boratio* or priest, since the priesthood was not a closed class. The *cacique* divided the daily workload and the harvest among the tribe. Their homes were rectangular huts with thatched saddle-roofs, and in the Lake Maracaibo area, were constructed on wooden poles to provide some protection against animals and rising waters.

The insular Caiquetíos were primarily fishermen, fish, and particularly shellfish forming the mainstay of their diet, but they also did some cultivating, and brewed an intoxicating liquor from the agave. To supplement their monotonous bill of fare the islanders bartered with their coastal neighbors for fruit, vegetables, and manioc, in exchange for whelk shells and *carcos*, or edible snails. They also frequently visited the nearby island of Little Curaçao to hunt the *bubis*, or sea gulls, and sea turtles living there in great numbers. A continuous flow of traffic between the islands and the coast was carried on in not too seaworthy dugout canoes called *piraguas*, *cayucos*, or *jangandas*. Judging from the number of these found in the area, commercial ties between the various branches of the Caiquetíos must have been fairly close.

The domestic utensils found on the islands, dating from this period, were in the petaloid form characteristic of the Arawaks. Axes, chisels, and knives were usually made of basalt or nephrite, although jasper was not uncommon. In time of war, these rather primitive implements also served as weapons. Fish hooks and combs were made either of wood or the bones of large fish. Nephrite stones were popular religious talismans and body ornaments. Small ceramic female figures, with openings between the arms and chest, were presumably parts of necklaces.

The women wove textiles from which they sewed the brief *taparita* which served the adults as clothing. They also made a primitive pottery without the use of the wheel yet with a natural affinity for color and style. Jars, bottles and dishes used for cooking as well as the preservation of food, are frequently found, and, especially on Aruba, huge quantities of spoons.

Water storage was an important problem on the islands as rain was scarce and restricted to certain months of the year. It has been suggested that prior to the arrival of the Spaniards the ground was covered with a lush growth and occasional forests but this seems unlikely. It is known that the Caiquetíos dug wells all over the islands, not only to reach ground water, but also to accumulate it; they likewise stored water in natural reservoirs, one of which, the so-called cave of Shingot located on Curaçao between Hato and San Pedro, still functions as such today. By these measures, the Indians maintained a water supply for a population of perhaps 2000, plus an unknown number of animals such as deer and rabbits.

That the Caiquetíos also knew how to extract salt from seawater is evident from the remains of a salt pan, known to the natives as Charomba, north of Asension on Curaçao. The salt here must have been for local use exclusively as the pan is located too far from the sea.

The religion of the Caiquetíos was animistic. They worshipped their ancestors, the sun and moon, and some animals, such as the frog; but the central figure, according to Oviedo y Baños, was the evil spirit *Hurakane*. The word hurricane is derived from this Indian god who played a dominant role in the lives of the Caiquetíos, was honored at all important events, and was consistently consulted on all matters of significance to the tribe.

The *boratio* or priest was, at the same time, medical doctor and diviner, and was sometimes of more local importance than the *cacique*. Under the intoxicating influence of tobacco, agave, and *pita* juices, the *boratio* tried to predict the harvest, answer questions relating to the fertility of the soil, and solve matters of personal concern. Prognostications were made by interpreting the figures made by ashes on either corn or tobacco leaves.

Spanish authors of the discovery provide us with a description of prevailing medical practice on the mainland which can reasonably be extended to the islands. When called in, the *boratio* would first order the family of the sick person to fast. Next, he would symbolically "dust" or "suck" away the illness in one sweeping motion. If this one attempt was not successful, the case was declared hopeless.

Closely related to the religious beliefs were the Caiquetíos' burial practices. Both on Curaçao and Aruba the dead were buried in urns, ordinarily in a squatting position. However, the discovery of occasional narrow-necked urns suggests their alternative use as depositories of bones. Some have been found to contain only parts of the skeleton, usually the skull, the rest of the body presumably being discarded, or cremated without much ceremony. Traces of charcoal collected from these burial grounds seem to indicate that the Indians burnt all personal possessions of the individual at the same time.

Geographically, the Caiquetíos were distributed over several communities or villages. On Curaçao, for instance, there were settlements at St. Ann Bay, Asension, and St. Barbara. Remains of Indian villages on Aruba have been found in the vicinity of the Hooiberg, the island's highest hill. The exact village locations on Bonaire are not known. As testimonies of their presence, on all three islands the Indians have left cave and rock drawings of undetermined age, done in red, or sometimes in black.

There appear to have existed strong political as well as cultural bonds between the Indians of the coast and of the islands. The *cacique* of Paraguaná, the Venezuelan peninsula east of the Lake of Maracaibo, was recognized as the highest authority of all the Caiquetíos, and the local *boratios* or *caciques* were, ultimately, subordinate to him.

The language of the Indians is still a matter of speculation. Dutch investigator De Goeje suspects that they spoke an Achagua dialect, similar to that of the Arawak-Maipure tribes, but has found no confirmation of this hypothesis. The diary of a Spanish priest who lived on Curaçao in the early eighteenth century, does mention the fact that the island and coastal Indians had no apparent difficulty understanding and conversing with each other. A catechism in their language, published by this same priest, has unfortunately disappeared without a trace. In 1880, another Dutch investigator compiled a list of contemporary Indian words and expressions which is still very valuable where all three islands are concerned.

The Spanish invasion of the Caribbean introduced a third party to the fierce struggle for survival between the militant Caribs and the peace-loving Arawaks. The former had already occupied many of the Lesser Antilles, forcing the Arawaks to flee northwestward, from the mainland to the Greater Antilles. Since the Curaçao islands lay outside the range of Carib conquest, their inhabitants had escaped being enslaved or killed by fellow Indians. However, shortly after the arrival of the Spaniards, many Caiquetíos were forcibly removed from the islands to be encomended on Hispaniola. A century later, with the occupation of the Dutch, most of the remaining Indians scattered to the mainland. Those who did not were gradually absorbed into the black and white population until in 1795 only five full-blooded Indians could still be found on Curaçao, and at the beginning of the nineteenth century none. On Aruba and Bonaire, the Indians maintained their identity almost a century longer, but in the twentieth century, as a result of the process of miscegenation, there are no full-blooded Indians on any of the islands.

CHAPTER II

HISTORICAL BACKGROUND AND DISCOVERY

In 1495 the exclusive rights of the Great Admiral Columbus, as granted by the *capitulación* of 1492, were revoked by Queen Isabel and – with certain restrictions – navigation to the Indies was thrown open to all Spaniards. Among the first to take advantage of this opportunity was one Alonso de Ojeda.

Ojeda was born in Cuenca, Spain, a scion of the exalted family of Ojeda y Ojeda and cousin to the inquisitor of the same name. Young Alonso, who cut quite a dashing figure, succeeded in catching the eye of the Queen with a reckless dance on top of the Giralda tower. By his kinsman, the inquisitor, he was introduced to the influential Juan Rodríguez de Fonseca, archdeacon of Seville, father confessor of the Queen and later foremost adviser to the Catholic kings. Due to these connections, Ojeda, at twenty-six, became a participant in the second Columbus expedition in 1493.

Immediately upon his return, Ojeda, a born leader, obtained royal permission to fit out a fleet of four ships under his own flag. Another veteran of Columbus' crossings, Juan de la Cosa, was enlisted as cartographer and general scientific expert. A third man, still unknown but soon to acquire world fame, was Amerigo Vespucci of Florence, Ojeda's *piloto mayor*.

On May 16, 1499, the small squadron left Cádiz for the New World. No accurate record of the journey exists, but there are two general sources which, although contradicting each other, nevertheless throw some light upon the entire operation. The first of these, the so-called *Lettera* written by Vespucci to one Tomasso Soderini of Florence and dated September 4, 1504, is generally believed to be less trustworthy than the other: some documents containing the testimony of various crew members presented at the trial in which the discovery of the Gulf of Paria was disputed by the heirs of Columbus.

Since the original Vespucci letter has vanished, any conclusions drawn from it would be dubious. Nevertheless, a Latin translation was discovered in 1507, and an apocryphal edition dating from 1580 is also in evidence, both of which refer to the discovery of Bonaire, the "brazilwood island" and Curaçao, the "island of giants."

Vespucci writes that after leaving Margarita behind, the expedition sighted another island at a proximate distance of fifteen miles from the mainland. The inhabitants were ignorant savages living off fish and turtles, and chewing leaves dipped in a strange white powder. For a day and a half the Spaniards searched the island for fresh water without success. Although the natives proved friendly, they had no wells, quenching their thirst with the dew of plants. They also had no huts and were accustomed to taking shelter from the sun under the leaves and branches of trees.

Thus far Vespucci's account of Bonaire. Of Curaçao he writes:

We found the island to be inhabited by a race of very tall people. As we disembarked to search for fresh drinking water, at first we saw nobody and imagined the island to be deserted. But on the beach we soon came upon some human footprints of gigantic dimensions; this fact induced us to conclude that the natives of the island must be very tall indeed. A little further on, we discovered a path leading inland and nine of us decided to follow it. After about one mile, we found ourselves in a secluded valley and saw five huts; upon coming closer we met five women – two old ones and three girls – who were all so tall as to arouse our curiosity. Although they were badly frightened, they did not run away but stood their ground in awe of us After a while, the two older women regained their composure and started to talk to us, bringing food and leading us into the shade of their huts. While we were contemplating the seizure of the three girls in order to bring them back to Castile as evidence, thirty-six men – stark naked and armed with bows and arrows – entered the compound. They were so tall and handsome as to be a pleasure to behold. As soon as they detected us, they started to talk among themselves and from their gestures we concluded they meant to attack us. We hurriedly left the hut we were in and made for the ships, the natives following closely on our heels but unable to catch up with us. Once aboard, we could see them throwing themselves into the ocean and venting their anger by sending a storm of arrows our way. Confident of our impregnability, we responded by firing two of our cannons to scare rather than kill them As soon as they heard the terrible noise of the explosion, they fled in all directions and have not been seen since. I call this island the Island of Giants after the size of the Indians.

Although no one can dispute the loquacity of the Italian on this subject, some well-founded doubts have arisen as to the veracity of these and subsequent statements. Vespucci writes, for instance, that he arrived at the brazilwood island – this must be Bonaire – after having been at sea for approximately one year. According to present calculations, this would be May of 1500. Yet further on he specifically mentions May 5 of that same year as the day of his arrival on Hispaniola. If, according to his own testimony, land was first sighted on June 27 of the previous year, this would pose a serious question as to Vespucci's whereabouts during the intervening period.

There is some uncertainty whether the leaders of the small squadron continued to navigate together or decided instead to try their luck separately. The well-known French biographer of Vespucci, Henri Vignaud, assumes on some grounds that Ojeda and Cosa continued their journey together, leaving Vespucci behind to explore the area more thoroughly. According to this historian, Ojeda thereupon headed straight for Hispaniola. Bartolomé de las Casas, basing his opinion on hearsay, wrote many years later that Ojeda arrived at Yaquimo (or Jacmel), Hispaniola, on September 5, 1499.

Again according to Vignaud, Vespucci spent his time cruising along the coast, past the islands of Margarita, Bonaire, and Curaçao respectively, winding up in the Gulf of Maracaibo, from which he made intermittent trips to the various islands in an effort to establish trade. In this version, he is not supposed to have arrived on Hispaniola until the beginning of May, 1500.

The Vespucci version is strongly contradicted by eyewitness accounts given during the Columbus trial. Ojeda himself, makes no mention of any separation as the fleet proceeded westward and northward, along the coast to Margarita, discovered but never actually set foot upon by the Great Admiral. Ojeda alludes to the landing of some of his men in order to explore the island, and confirms the fact that he was accompanied by Juan de la Cosa and Amerigo Vespucci. He states that they continued their voyage – passing en route the hitherto unknown Frayles Islands, and disembarking on the Island of the Giants to question the Indians.

There are few grounds to cast any doubts on these statements, made under oath at a time when Ojeda was still young enough to recall such an event vividly. Las Casas accepted his version, and more recent historians have also, among them two prominent Venezuelans, Guillermo Morón and Pedro Manuel Arcaya, both of whom without question grant Ojeda the honor of the discovery of the Curaçao islands.

While the exact date on which this took place has never actually been ascertained, it is safe to assume that it was either at the end of July or the beginning of August, 1499.

In 1500, Juan de la Cosa, himself an eyewitness to the discovery, sketched a map known as the *Mapamundi*. Although far from accurate, this document already includes the outlines of the *Isla de Palo de Brasil* (Bonaire) and the *Isla de los Gigantes* (Curaçao). Another map, drawn by Vesconte de Maiollo in 1519, for the first time refers to the latter island as Curasote while, seven years later, Juan de Ampués, the first Spanish representative on the island, officially reports on Corazante or Coraçante. Spanish maps dating from after 1525 refer to the island as Curaçote, Curasaote, and Curasaore. Other more or less similar names continue to appear occasionally; however, by the seventeenth century the island was generally known as Curaçao or Curazao.

As to the meaning of the word Curaçao, several interesting theories exist, none of which can be proven conclusively. The word may have been derived from the long since extinct Caiquetío language, or it may have evolved from the Spanish *corazón* or the Portuguese *curazon*. As depicted on the earliest maps, the shape of the island indeed resembles a heart. A popular interpretation claims that the word Curaçao is a contraction of two Spanish words – *cura* or priest, and *asado* or *asao*, roasted. Father Labat, designating the island as Corossol, seeks to trace the origin of this name to the corossul fruit, which French colonists imported from there. Yet the name Curaçao had become a familiar one long before the first French settlers had set foot in the Caribbean.

Aside from these various hypotheses, the fact remains that the first syllable of the word occurs in many Venezuelan names. At the same time, neither is the ending *ao* alien to the Spanish tongue. The similarity of the dialects of the insular Indians to those on the continent, makes an Indian origin of the word Curaçao plausible. Further corroboration comes from Spanish sources themselves. At the beginning of the seventeenth century the Spanish governor of the area, Francisco Núñez Melián, wrote to the king that he had sent a canoe with *Curaçaos*, Indians belonging to the Caiquetíos tribe, to the island, at that time occupied by the Dutch. This particular group is also mentioned in a declaration made in Caracas in 1635 by a local baptized native, one Juan Mateo of Curaçao.

At the southeastern tip of Curaçao lies a smaller island now called Little Curaçao but formerly known as *Adicora* or *Nicula* by Indians and Spaniards alike. An Indian origin of these names is also highly probable.

The apellations used for the other two major islands are similarly surrounded by controversy. On the earliest maps, Aruba is spelled Oruba, Ouraba, and by other variants. It has been suggested that the word is formed by a contraction of *oro*, gold, and *hubo*, past tense of the verb *to be*. The roots of the word seem, however, of Indian origin. Possible joinings include *ora* and *oubao*, meaning shell island. During the eighteenth century, when there were still Indians living on the islands and their language had not yet completely disappeared, inhabitants of Aruba proper thought that the word meant "well situated," in terms of the coast. The well-known Dutch historian J.H.J. Hamelberg's thesis that in the Guaraní idiom Aruba or *Oirubae* simply means companion (in other words companion of Curaçao) is deserving of attention.

With Bonaire the difficulties are identical. To explain the name on the basis of the island's good, clean air is no longer acceptable. Although the island was first known as the *Isla do Brazil* or *Isla de Brasil*, this name was soon replaced by the present one, with many variants: Boynare, Buinare, Bonari, Banari, Bonaira, etc. Hamelberg thought it to be derived from the Caribbean word *banara*, also meaning companion. Thus in two different tongues the words Aruba and Bonaire would mean the same. Later Hamelberg introduced a new interpretation derived from the Guaraní Indians: low land. Up to now, no air-tight argument has been made to support any of the suggestions.

On older maps, the Lesser Antilles are grouped together under the common name of *Islas Canibales* or *Islas Comarcanas*. The first refers to the man-eating habits of the Caribs, the latter literally signifies "surrounding islands," probably of the Greater Antilles or Hispaniola. The three Curaçao islands, however, were not included in this description but formed an independent entity with the other islands along the Venezuelan coast. Hence their name *Islas adyacentes a la Costa Firme*, i.e. islands adjacent to the continental coast. As such they were politically united with Coquibacoa or Coro – the latter name dating from some years later – and in 1502 put under the factorship of Alonso de Ojeda.

At the time of their alleged discovery, the sea north of these islands was already called the Caribbean Sea. Deep into the eighteenth century, the sea south of them was known as the Sea of Venezuela – at least to the Dutch who also referred to the entire area between the Greater and Lesser Antilles and the coasts of Venezuela, Colombia, and Central America up to the Strait of Yucatán as the *Kraal*, a derivation of the Spanish *corral* or Portuguese *curral* meaning an enclosed space. Not until well into the nineteenth century was the entire body of water surrounding the islands known by the common name of Caribbean Sea.

CHAPTER III

THE SPANISH PERIOD

The history of the Curaçao islands under Spanish dominion is closely related to that of Venezuela and cannot be considered separately. With a *real cédula,* a royal decree, of June 8, 1501, the Catholic kings united the coastal regions of Coquibacoa (Coro) and Guajira with the recently acquired islands and appointed Alonso de Ojeda as *factor* or royal representative over the area. Among the instructions it was specified that settlements be made along the entire coast, presumably also on the islands, although this was not mentioned outright.

Previous to this decree, the area had been tentatively explored by Cristóbal Guerra (1499), a slaver and pearl fisher, and Rodrigo de Bastidas (1500), a former notary public of Seville and father of the future first bishop of Venezuela. In 1501 Guerra again visited the islands, bringing back some Indians from Bonaire to sell as slaves.

In January of 1502, Alonso de Ojeda left Cádiz for the third time, now in command of another squadron. After a short stop-over at Jamaica for provisions, he sailed directly to Curaçao where the Spaniards stayed for a brief period. No giants were reported. Soon Ojeda was on his way again, to found on the nearby Tierra Firme coast a settlement, which was, however, shortly afterwards abandoned. On his return to Spain, Ojeda was summoned before a court to explain this failure and the errors of judgment and cruelty which had characterized this expedition. After a hearing, he was condemned to surrender all his earthly goods and to be banished from among the ranks of his peers. Although this sentence was not executed to the letter – due to the timely intervention of his benefactor, Bishop Fonseca – Ojeda was never able to regain his former prosperity. In 1515, or thereabouts, he died a pauper in a Franciscan convent in Hispaniola, requesting to be buried under the treshold of the main entrance as a token of humility.

In 1504, the island of Curaçao was visited by Juan de la Cosa, who had sailed to the west with a small fleet of four ships much like Ojeda had shortly before, and returned with a substantial cargo of brazilwood from the islands. Although expeditions for this dye wood became fairly regular, nothing but gold could hold the Spanish interest for very long. Consequently, in 1513 Diego Colombus, viceroy of the Spanish empire in the New World, declared these islands to be *islas inútiles* or useless islands. By this decree the trade of the familiar and dreaded *indiero*, or Indian hunter, seemed for the first time officially sanctioned. Almost before the ink had dried on the vicerocy's decree, Diego de Salazar fitted out a fleet with the express purpose of evacuating the entire population of the Curaçao islands to Hispaniola, to relieve there a critical labor shortage caused by sickness and rebellions. Around 2000 people, nearly the entire population of Aruba, Curaçao, and Bonaire were taken prisoner and sold into slavery on Hispaniola.

In those days the *factor* of Hispaniola was Juan Martínez de Ampués appointed by a *real cédula* of May 19, 1511. A noted military man, veteran of many foreign campaigns, Ampués had enjoyed the right to supervise and control all of Hispaniola's economic activities before his appointment as *factor*. Within a relatively short period of time, and needless to say at the expense of the Crown and the people, Ampués managed to become a wealthy man, with a number of houses, a watermill, several sugarcane fields, numerous cattle and slaves, among whom were a few natives from the Curaçao islands.

It is not known what prompted Ampués to petition the Crown to send some of these island Indians back to their former homes. He may have realized that these Caiquetíos were not the man-eating Caribs so feared by the Spaniards, and have come to the determination of protecting them from annihilation. But whatever his motives, they are not likely to have been alltogether philanthropic. Even in the heat of his humanitarian arguments he was more than likely aware of the profits to be reaped from Indian labor. After all, somebody had to do the heavy work to which the Spaniards would not stoop, and without which the islands would indeed be worthless.

It is a well-established fact that during the years 1516–1517 the first missionaries of the Curaçao islands – the Hieronymites – had complained bitterly to Cardinal Cisneros about the abuses and deprivations suffered by the Indians on these islands, and had recommended that Cisneros make an official investigation. Just previously, Las Casas' now famous plea on behalf of the Indian had likewise urged the king to take definite steps to protect the natives from the cruelty of the *indieros;* and the sermons of Father Montesinos in the Franciscan church of Santo Domingo added to the outcry.

In order to by-pass the slow Spanish bureaucratic machinery, Ampués, informed of the Hieronymites' complaint, immediately addressed himself to the *Audiencia* of Santo Domingo, requesting provisional permission and the means to carry out his contemplated plan. He was a rich and influential person in the budding colonial society, and knew the members of this august body personally. The fact that *indieros* were continuing to ply their trade under the very noses of the Spanish officials must have irritated not only Ampués, but also Rodrigo de Figueroa, the new *juez* or judge sent to Hispaniola to conduct the inquiry. Figueroa soon realized that there would be no end to the raiding until there was some visible sign of Spanish authority on the islands. His proposal to send Ampués as representative of the Spanish Crown to the Curaçao islands coincided with the latter's ambition to save them from depopulation.

In November, 1525, Ampués received the *Audiencia's* provisional authorization to follow up his ideas and to reinhabit the islands. This appointment was confirmed by Charles V in a *real cédula* which specifically stated that the three Curaçao islands were to be put under the protection of Juan de Ampués, it being forbidden under penalty of death for anyone to land on any of the islands without his express permission. The few surviving Indians – it is not known how many – were given to him in *encomienda*. In a later decree Charles V not only reiterated his former statements but expanded these to give his consent to the suggested repopulation.

One of Ampués' first official acts was to organize an expedition to the nearby mainland, presumably to establish good relations with the well-known *cacique* Manaure. He trusted his mission to meet with some success, since he had previously returned Manaure's daughter and some other Indian hostages who had been sold on Hispaniola. Under the command of Lázaro Bejarano, Ampués' son-in-law, a ship left Curaçao, and, on July 26, 1527, dropped anchor off the coast of Tierra Firme. As was customary, a town was founded at the landing site and given the name of Santa Ana de Coro – Coro being the Indian word by which the area was known. Some time later, Ampués himself arrived with some soldiers and concluded a peaceful treaty with Manaure.

In this treaty, the Caiquetío chieftain was vouched the protection of the Spanish Crown against the *indieros* in return for surrendering to Ampués his *indios guerreros* or Indian prisoners of war. In this way, Manaure could sell his enemies to the Spaniards, and, at the same time count on Spanish support against Indian hunters. To see this pact in its true light, it must be recognized that this document was never valid, as Ampués had absolutely no rights on the mainland.

Toward the middle of 1528, Ampués was back on Hispaniola where among other difficulties he became embroiled in a divorce proceeding against his wife Florencia. One of these proved even more damaging to his career than the divorce. Although the members of the *Audiencia* had silently approved of Ampués' journey to Coro, his subsequent efforts to expand his ventures to the mainland were frustrated by Charles V's flamboyant fiscal policy. The emperor, in order to finance his election campaign in the German countries, had borrowed a huge sum of money from the banking house of Welser in Augsburg, and was gradually running out of excuses for not repaying it. The Welsers, weary of Charles' evasiveness, had sent some of their representatives to Santo Domingo to find out whether the overseas empire was bringing in any substantial returns. While there, the Welser agents had heard the legend of *El Dorado*, the Gilded Man, and his fabulous hoard of gold somewhere in the continent's heartland, and they suggested that pressure be brought to bear upon the emperor-king to grant the Welsers a slice of the continent. The area they had in mind stretched from the Orinoco to the Gulf of Maracaibo – what is now Venezuela.

Ampués, hearing of this turn of events, asked the *Audiencia* of Santo Domingo in September, 1528, to recognize his claim to Coro forthwith. At the same time, the Council of the Indies requested the *Audiencia* to investigate more clearly the pretentious demands of Ampués. Meanwhile, negotiations with the Welsers went ahead as planned.

Ampués, sensing the outcome was not going to be in his favor, organized a new expedition to Curaçao toward the end of 1528. Ostensibly it was to be a visit to his recently constructed *rancho*, but since he took some sixty soldiers along, he seems to have been planning an armed invasion of Coro from Curaçao. As events turned out, however, by the time of his return to Coro in January, 1529, the matter had already been settled and an armed attack must have been the furthest thing from his mind.

In the fall of 1528, Charles V had sealed the fate of the territory by signing a grant irrevocably confirming the rights of the Welsers to Venezuela. In February, 1529, Ambrosius Ehinger, one of the banking house's directors, landed with a small army at Coro to take possession of the new domain. A brief skirmish between the two military parties is not out of the question. At any rate, Ampués, aware that he was clutching the losing end of the straw, withdrew to Curaçao, and then to Hispaniola, suing Ehinger in court for impeding his cutting of brazilwood.

Ampués died soon afterwards, probably in 1533. Outside interference and domestic politics both, had hampered his efforts to acquire control over the Venezuelan coast. His other professed aim, the repopulation of the Curaçao islands, had met with more success. He had not only brought some 200 Indians back to the main island, but he had also promoted the importation of European cattle, horses, pigs, and goats, and the introduction of many seeds, in particular of fruit trees.

In spite of these untiring efforts, Ampués was no longer a rich man. On the contrary, at the time of his death, he was deeply in debt, owing a small fortune to the Crown and to private persons. His repeated attempts to foment a red slave-trade with the mainland, the object of his treaty with Manaure, had never gotten off the ground. His name has been preserved for posterity for other reasons, among these his humane treatment of the Curaçao Indians. One Venezuelan historian refers to him as John the Good; it is, perhaps, not an ill-chosen name.

Ampués was succeeded as *factor* of the islands by his son-in-law, Lázaro Bejarano, a sugarcane planter from Hispaniola, who was also a satirist and a great student of the Dutch humanist Erasmus. Bejarano did not remain on Curaçao very long. After the death of his only child, he left the island in the company of his fellow poet Juan de Castellanos, who had come to visit him in 1540.

Upon Bejarano's departure, the three Curaçao islands returned to the supervision of the *Audiencia* of Santo Domingo, and shortly afterwards, a *real cédula* prohibiting settlement on the islands without previous permission helped to erase them from the official Spanish memory, and to make them *islas olvidadas*, forgotten islands.

Although the organization of the Spanish governmental machinery on the islands is not too clear, it is known that the *mayordomo* and *administrador* in charge of Bonaire and Aruba were responsible to the governor of Curaçao, whose headquarters were in St. Ann, at the entrance of the bay of that same name. The Indians had their own chief, the *boratio* or *piache*, who after the baptism of the Indians was called a *cacique* and was, of course, responsible to the governor.

It must be stressed at this point there was never any question as to who ruled the islands. The Indians were allowed their own form of government under their own chieftains but under Spanish supervision. Nowhere in the Caribbean were the native officials allowed to occupy other than subordinate positions vis-à-vis their Spanish rulers.

Not long after the Curaçao islands had reverted to control from Hispaniola, the regime of the Welsers in Venezuela ended rather abruptly and that entire territory was restored to Spanish rule. During the Welser interlude, many Indians of the Tierra Firme had fled to the Curaçao islands to escape the harsh German taskmasters. The influx of continental refugees caused small villages to spring up on the main island. Virtually nothing is known about Indian migration to the other two. This movement of peoples slowed down noticeably after the Welsers had been replaced by Spanish officials, and as a consequence, the ties with the continent gradually loosened and the *caciques* of Curaçao became more and more independent of the coastal chieftains.

During most of the Spanish period, the Indians of Curaçao continued to live as their forefathers had centuries before, fishing and hunting, and collecting salt from the Charoma saltpan near Asension for their barter trade with the coast. Toward the end of this era of tranquility, however, foreign invaders, English, French, and Dutch, came swarming into the Caribbean waters. After 1621 the Dutch especially were frequent visitors to the islands, attracted by wood and salt. To avoid any contact with these heretic outsiders, the Spanish officials gathered and concentrated all the Indians into two villages: Asension in the northeast and St. Ann in the center, both places situated close to water-wells and under firm Spanish control.

During the first three decades after their discovery, when the islands formed part of the ecclesiastical realm of Santo Domingo, little or no effort was made to convert the inhabitants or instruct them in the Roman Catholic faith. But in 1526, with the appointment of Ampués as *factor* it was stipulated that he take with him two priests to assume spiritual leadership over the Indians. If the natives refused to accept the Christian doctrine and clung to their former cult, they were to be sold forthwith into slavery.

In 1527, or thereabouts, a small chapel of clay and stone was built at St. Barbara on Curaçao, which probably served the added purpose of a Spanish bastion against the Indians. It is quite possible that later on Bejarano ordered the construction of another chapel, this one of stone, with its façade in the prevailing *mudéjar* style. However, no remains of this chapel have been found.

When Charles V signed away part of his domain to the Welsers, they asked that he use his influence with the pope and request the establishment of a separate Venezuelan bishopric in order to free the German colony from any ecclesiastical intervention by Santo Domingo. Although under the *patronato real* the pope reserved the right to create bishoprics, Charles V, claiming the prerogative of *presentación*, was entitled to select the bishop, who received papal confirmation as a mere formality. In a papal bull of 1531, entitled *Pro Excellencia Praeeminentia*, Pope Clemens VII acquiesced to the imperial demand and created the bishopric of Venezuela with its seat at Coro, a bishopric which officially included the Curaçao islands. This created a strange situation: politically, the islands remained under the rule of Ampués, Bejarano, and finally the *Audiencia* of Santo Domingo; ecclesiastically, however, the Curaçao islands formed part of the growing Venezuelan colony.

At the time of the bull's promulgation, a young priest named Rodrigo de Bastidas, dean of the cathedral of Santo Domingo and son of the well-known *conquistador* of the same name, was visiting Madrid. Young Bastidas was, presumably, born in Spain before his father girded himself with the sword instead of the pen (he had been a notary public in Seville) and left for the New World to make history. Other sources contend that Rodrigo was born on the island of Hispaniola, and was thus the first creole bishop. As the preferred candidate of the Welsers, Rodrigo de Bastidas, in 1532, was raised to the high office of Bishop of Venezuela and Coro.

It is obvious that he bore no great love for either Venezuela or his new career, which was characterized by absenteeism, unconcern, and willful neglect. He never bothered to visit the Curaçao islands, and, if we may believe Castellanos, the religious situation there deteriorated to the point that laymen performed all the Church functions. In spite of this, the entire population of the islands had been baptized by the time the Dutch arrived in 1634.

In 1542, with the appointment of Bastidas to the bishopric of San Juan de Puerto Rico, his former see was occupied successively by ten other bishops, several of whom fell into the same habit as Bastidas and were absent from their post most of the time. The lingering religious ties between the islands and the mainland were severed by the Dutch conquest as abruptly as the political relationship.

CHAPTER IV

THE DUTCH CONQUEST

Neither gold nor the lust for adventure ultimately brought the Dutch into the forbidden waters of the Caribbean. It was their need for salt which forced them to penetrate Spain's *mare clausum* in open defiance of Philip II. The prosperous Dutch herring industry, steadily expanding since the middle of the fifteenth century, grew at an even faster rate after a Zeelander invented a method of curing the fish. This required salt; hence the fate of the Dutch was intimately bound up with locating this commodity.

The Dutch had been accustomed to acquiring all their salt from the Iberian peninsula, particularly from Setúbal, in exchange for the goods they brought from the Baltic Sea area. But with the Dutch rebellion against Spanish domination – the famous Eighty Years' War – the advisors of Philip II urged him to put a stop to this trade. In 1585 the first of the so-called *arrests* took place, in which hundreds of Dutch merchantmen and saltcarriers were seized in Spanish ports and their crews imprisoned.

After this, the Dutch thought twice before entering an Iberian port. As their herrings lay rotting in the warehouses, their need for salt grew desperate. Finally, a fisherman from Enkhuizen returned from an exploratory journey to the Cape Verde Islands (the so-called Salt Islands) with a shipload of salt, and soon this region was swarming with Dutchmen. But the Salt Islands were Spanish territory and not too safe.

Forced by necessity, the enterprising Dutchmen ventured further and further south, sailing along the African coast and even daring the journey across the Atlantic to Brazil, where some saltpans were indeed discovered, although they were soon abandoned due to the poor quality. From Brazil, it was not much of a leap to the Tierra Firme, where the Dutch arrived before the turn of the century. At the lagoon of Punta de Araya, not exploited by the Spaniard but well known to him, they found salt of excellent quality and in inexhaustible quanties.

Repeated complaints from the governors of Cumaná and Margarita to Madrid resulted in the dispatching of a fleet under Luis de Fajardo to intercept the foreign saltcarriers and to put an end to their illicit traffic. This attempt met with only limited success, however. Once the Dutch had recovered from the scare, they resumed their voyages overseas, not to be interrupted again until the Twelve Years' Truce. When after the Truce the Dutch discovered that the Spaniards had fortified the pan, they had to relinquish their stake in the salt of Araya.

Immediately after the resumption of hostilities the Dutch founded the West India Company. Like its sister company in the East, the WIC was a joint-stock corporation organized by private merchants and individual shareholders. Unlike the other company, however, the WIC was an explicit instrument of war and privateering against Spain. This was to be, at all times, its main objective; commerce and colonization came second – a choice of priorities which would eventually lead to the Company's downfall in 1674.

With the founding of the WIC, private enterprise thus took over some of the responsibilities of the state and waged war beyond the line of amity, in other continents, for the fatherland and the Company's shareholders. War was, essentially, the *raison d'être* of the WIC. Spain now had one more reason to regret her former neglect of the *islas inútiles* as they fell, one by one, to the foreign interlopers disputing her haughty claims.

After 1621, Dutch affairs in the Caribbean were officially under the supervision of the WIC, whose charter, in addition to the east and west coasts of America, included the west coast of Africa, and all existing Dutch settlements on both continents. The Company's executive board was called the *Heren XIX* or simply the *XIX*, and was composed of eight representatives from Amsterdam, four from Zeeland, two apiece from the three other districts, and the last member, number nineteen, representing the High and Mighty Lords of the States General. The *XIX* soon became the organizer of a dangerous series of attacks on the Spanish colonial empire in the West.

As before, numerous private salt carriers of Dutch origin, and smugglers, who in so-called *barcos de rescate* traded with the Spanish settlers, continued to scour Philip's colonial domain. Over and beyond these, the Dutch West India Company gradually assumed a leading position in the struggle for colonial hegemony in the Caribbean. In contrast to the English and the French, equally desirous of obtaining a foothold in the new market, the aim of the Dutch was not so much the occupation and colonization of the many easily available islands, as the gathering of information concerning the movements of the Spanish treasure fleets. Two of these regularly sailed each year from Spain; the *flota* with Mexico as its destination, and the *galeones* headed for the ports of Cartagena and Porto Bello. After loading their precious cargo, these two fleets would meet in Havana around July or August and sail home under a united command.

In 1623, the first official fleet of the new WIC, a small squadron of only three ships under the command of Pieter Schouten, left for the Caribbean to prowl and pillage the Lesser Antilles and the Yucatán peninsula. One of the ships even managed to waylay a Honduras galleon, bringing home an extremely rich booty to whet the appetite of the *Heren XIX*. A few years later, in 1625, a Dutch fleet of seventeen or eighteen ships under the command of Boudewijn Hendriksz sailed into the Kraal from Brazil after an unsuccessful attempt to wrest Bahia from the united Iberian fleet in its port. Hendriksz arrived in the Caribbean with explicit instructions to occupy both Puerto Rico and the island of Margarita, and to take the *flota*, of whose movements the Dutch were fairly well informed. He failed to capture either Puerto Rico or Margarita, and his sudden death, while he waited north of Havana for the arrival of the silver fleet from New Spain, frustrated the third aim.

In 1626, while Hendriksz' fleet was returning to the United Provinces, Admiral Piet Heyn, with another WIC fleet, was crossing the Atlantic in the opposite direction, intending to join Hendriksz and proceed together. When this failed, Heyn followed the second part of his instructions, namely to sail to Brazil. Two years later, in 1628, in command of more than thirty ships, he was successful in his attempt to lure the fleet of New Spain into Matanzas Bay and seize it – the only time that a Spanish silver fleet was ever lost to an enemy.

After this year the WIC realized the importance of a military foothold in the Caribbean. In 1630 this became the island of St. Martin in the Leeward group of the Lesser Antilles. When in 1633 a Spanish fleet retook the island, Dutch attention was redirected, this time toward Curaçao.

As far as is known, the earliest Dutchman to set foot on the Curaçao islands was Captain Jan Jariksz of the West Frisian town of Stavoren in Friesland. Surprised by the local Spanish authorities on Bonaire while cutting wood and loading salt, Jariksz was nevertheless allowed to go free, and returned to the United Provinces with a valuable cargo. No clue remains as to whether the Schouten expedition even sighted the Curaçao group. It is known, however, that on Easter of 1626 Boudewijn Hendriksz landed on Bonaire to rest his men for a few days after their abortive attempt to conquer Margarita. A year later, a small squadron under the command of Hendrik Jacobszoon Lucifer passed the Curaçao islands, but the Dutch did not go ashore. In 1628, Joost van Trappen, Piet Heyn's rear admiral in the adventure of Matanzas, visited Bonaire. In 1629, another agent of the WIC, Adriaan Janszoon Pater, passed the Curaçao islands without disembarking, although on his return voyage a year later he did stay for a few days on Bonaire.

In the following years, the Curaçao islands were regurlarly patronized by Dutchmen. Among these, special mention should be made of the many ships which, after providing newly conquered Pernambuco with men and materials, wanted a return cargo for the long voyage home. A load of salt was the obvious answer, and since the lagoon of Araya was now strongly defended, the Dutch turned their attention to the saltpans of Tortuga off the Venezuelan coast, St. Martin, the Curaçao islands, and the coastal area around the Uribe River in Venezuela. Contemporary Spanish documents abound with complaints and accusations concerning these supposed intrusions.

As early as 1628 or 1629, the Dutch had begun obtaining salt regularly on Tortuga. The Governor of Venezuela, Francisco Núñez Melián, destroyed the pans and took some Dutchmen prisoners, using them on the way back to Spain to cut some brazilwood at Curaçao. Here one of the Dutchmen, Jan Janszoon Otzen, took careful stock of the island's excellent harbor and profitable saltpans, information he communicated to the *Heren XIX*.

The Amsterdam Chamber of the West India Company, well aware that the Dutch were losing their battle for salt in the Caribbean and that the war against Spain required the acquisition of a base in these waters, studied these items of information and in the spring of 1634 advised the *XIX* to take immediate possession of Curaçao. The *XIX* approved the suggested conquest, and soon active plans were being made to accomplish it. Johannes van Walbeeck, an agent of the Company well known for his excellent record of service in Brazil, and just happening to be in the United Provinces at the time, was appointed commander of the expedition and future governor of the island. As military leader, the *XIX* named another veteran from Brazil, Pierre le Grand. Two weeks later both men swore their allegiance to the States General in a solemn ceremony.

With the commissioning of these two officers the first step was taken toward the realization of a bold plan: to occupy Spanish territory very close to the mainland. The *XIX* did not spare expenses in its actual preparation. All five chambers of the Company contributed their share – of money as well as men – and the expedition was indeed an example of effective collaboration, resulting in six ships and at least 180 sailors, plus 225 soldiers. Furthermore, one of the ships carried in its hulk food supplies sufficient for five to nine months, plus arms, ammunition, pikes, leaping poles, and materials for the construction of a fort.

At the beginning of May, 1634, a bare four weeks after Otzen's information had reached the *XIX*, the fleet set out. On June 23, it arrived at Barbados; the next day it dropped anchor off St. Vincent, from which Van Walbeeck sent the yacht *Brack* on a separate exploratory venture along the coast of

Venezuela. On June 29, the other ships set sail for Bonaire, where they arrived four days later and were rejoined the next day by the *Brack*.

On the night of the seventh of July the Dutch fleet sailed along the southern coast of Curaçao, the *Brack* with Otzen aboard leading the way westward. At noon the next day they passed a huge cross standing embedded in the rocks. Otzen hesitated, uncertain whether he had reached the entrance to the bay. When he finally decided, it was too late; the strong current and the heavy breeze had driven the ships far beyond the entrance and Van Walbeeck discovered to his annoyance that it was impossible to turn back. The fleet had to continue its course along the entire southern coast and detour to Hispaniola, before it could return to Bonaire.

On July 26, the Dutch again dropped anchor off the coast of Bonaire. Once again Van Walbeeck and his war council sat down to draw up a strategy of attack, this time without Otzen, who had lost Van Walbeeck's confidence. On the night of July 28, the Dutch left Bonaire for the second time and sailed to Curaçao. Around noon Van Walbeeck again sighted the cross, and shortly afterwards the ships, one after another, except for one left to guard the entrance, entered the St. Ann Bay, the narrow mouth to the Schottegat, where they dropped anchor.

Van Walbeeck then dispatched a few sloops to reconnoiter. No enemy naval force seemed to be near. However, the Spaniards were not long in showing up in the person of the governor, Lope López de Morla, who politely came to inquire whether the Dutch were there to trade or to fight. He discovered their intention soon enough when Van Walbeeck landed his troops. They found the little village of St. Ann deserted, with the well poisoned. Proceeding methodically in both directions from St. Ann with the support of a cavalry company made possible by the many horses roaming near by, the Dutch were able to bring the island under control within three weeks. On August 21, De Morla capitulated on condition that he and his men be allowed to leave unharmed for the mainland. Van Walbeeck agreed to this request but, apparently not trusting newly converted Roman Catholics, insisted that the Indians – with the exception of 20 families – accompany their former masters.

All these refugees were put ashore fifteen miles from Coro, with nothing but their personal belongings. Among them were 32 Spaniards, including the 12 children of Juan Mateo, the governor's right hand man. As soon as De Morla arrived in Coro he submitted a written report to Núñez Melián. The news, together with Melián's views on the subject, was conveyed to the king and the Council of the Indies, and was probably received in Madrid before the end of the year.

The Dutch leader likewise informed the *Heren XIX* of the successful conquest. In this report he reveals that one of the first areas to fall to the Dutch was the Point, or *Punda*, upon which the Dutch constructed the Waterfort, with building materials which they were fortunate enough to find in abundance.

Accompanying the report was the first Dutch map of the island, remarkably accurate and already delineating the southern coast's vulnerable points. Van Walbeeck stressed that the island had only sparse vegetable growth, limited wood, and poor saltpans. If the *Heren XIX* wished the island to remain in Dutch hands, he strongly advised them to send an additional 300 men with the corresponding guns and ammunition. This report was supplemented by that of Le Grand, who was particularly outspoken about the need for fire arms and a strong garrison.

The testimony of both Dutch leaders was pessimistic and seemed to suggest abandoning the island. A committee was therefore appointed by the *Heren XIX* to study the matter and report to the States General. Notwithstanding the previous testimony, this committee urged that the Dutch keep the island, for its strategic location but also on account of the salt. In December, 1634, the States General decided to support the *Heren XIX* and to retain the island, voting a sum of 264,000 guilders to be spent for this purpose. No doubt, Curaçao's strategic location between Pernambuco and New Amsterdam and within the local Caribbean setting influenced this decision. The Schottegat was much too advantageously located for the Dutch to let it go.

CHAPTER V

CURAÇAO AS WAR BASE

With the occupation of the Curaçao islands, the Dutch acquired a firm foothold in the Caribbean for their empire around the Atlantic Ocean, to which the crucial slave depot of Angola, São Paulo de Loanda, was soon added, sparking a bitter struggle with the Portuguese over control of the slave trade. In 1636 the conquest of the northern part of Brazil – New Holland – was reinforced by the appointment as governor of Count Johan Maurits of Nassau-Siegen. Extremely competent, Count Maurits not only consolidated the Dutch position at the expense of Portugal in that part of the world but consistently worked to increase the influence of the United Provinces elsewhere abroad. New Netherland likewise appeared to be flourishing. The *Heren XIX* kept their eyes on the Caribbean, intent upon establishing a strong naval base to promote privateering, and after Piet Heyn's exhilarating success, to aid in the future capture of Spanish treasure fleets.

To this end, the good as well as the bad points of Curaçao were carefully reviewed. Its proximity to the Tierra Firme was, obviously, a major disadvantage: any suspicious movement by the Dutch could be instantly detected by the Spanish *veladores*. A naval base on Tobago seemed a more logical choice. There the arrival of Dutch ships would pass largely unnoticed by the Spaniards; the rich and fertile soil could be used to grow foodstuffs, while closer relations with the Guianas would benefit both colonies. Nevertheless, the *XIX* were reluctant to assign such importance to Tobago, and stubbornly insisted upon making the Curaçao islands the WIC's Caribbean base.

Van Walbeeck was therefore instructed to consolidate his position on Curaçao and to conquer Bonaire and Aruba. A rumor that the Spaniards were preparing a vast counterattack caused a short delay, but this danger failed to materialize.

Bonaire, more important in those days than Aruba because of its salt, had almost no inhabitants. Spaniards came annually to pick up sheep- or goat-skins from the Indians. English, Dutch, or French ships frequently stopped by unmolested for wood and salt – as many as fifteen foreign ships at one time – according to Spanish reports of the early thirtees.

Bonaire had been singled out for the next Dutch campaign. Van Walbeeck had an accurate map drawn and dispatched a ship to reconnoiter. Its captain reported that the island was inhabited by a few cattle and six Indians. The occupation took place in April of 1636 and was marked by nothing at all. Van Walbeeck ordered the construction of a small fort in a place called Barbudo (the Poos di Vaca of today), and equipped it with some guns and a garrison of around forty men.

Aruba was occupied a month later, after its few Spanish residents had hastily departed for the mainland, taking the Indians with them.

Of course, Spain could not be expected to accept these repeated defeats in her colonial domains without retaliation. Venezuela's governors, in particular Ruy Fernández de Fuenmayor, were much disturbed at the loss of the Curaçao islands, lying so near the *galeones*' route to Cartagena and Porto Bello. In response to his incessant admonitions, Fuenmayor was finally authorized to re-conquer Curaçao. A few ships and *piraguas* were forthwith fitted out and made ready for battle, and in 1642 the Venezuelan governor left La Guaira for Bonaire, accompanied by approximately 300 men, mostly Indian allies. Once Bonaire was restored to Spanish hands, Curaçao was expected to be an easy prey.

Fuenmayor planned, after arrival at Bonaire, to divide his army into three groups, to attack the fort, take the saltpans, and defend the harbor. The Spaniards, however, erred and landed more to the south than they had planned. The sea was rough and the night moonless. Fuenmayor almost drowned in the surf, and some of his men actually did. On shore at last, the Spaniards found the small wooden fort in flames, and no trace of the Dutch occupants, who had apparently decided to surrender the island without a fight and, after setting fire to their settlement, had sailed away to inform the governor at Curaçao.

Fuenmayor remained on Bonaire for an entire week, discussing the perplexing situation with his war council. The majority opinion of this body was that the Spanish forces were much too weak to attack the main island, and, although Fuenmayor accused some of his officers of piercing holes in their own ships in order to prevent action, he was ultimately forced to give in. Besides, many of the Spaniards were sick, supposedly from the drinking water, thought to have been polluted by the Dutch before they left. To avenge the poisoning of the wells, Fuenmayor ordered the slaughter of all the cattle and horses on the island.

Not really reconciled to relinquishing his plan for the conquest of Curaçao,

Fuenmayor deliberately fired a defiant volley when passing the Dutch fort at the Point on his way back to La Guaira. He also left a spy who, protected by a white flag, rowed into St. Ann Bay in a *piragua* and was cordially received by Peter Stuyvesant, current governor of the islands. Stuyvesant invited the Spanish spy to his table and joined him in a hearty toast to Spain and the Prince of Orange. Although well aware of his visitor's purpose, the Dutch governor made no move to confine the Spaniard's movement, and the spy realizing the strength of the Dutch forces on Curaçao, returned to the mainland to convince Fuenmayor of the utter folly of any attack. From that time on Curaçao was beyond the grasp of the Spaniards, and firmly in the hands of the Dutch.

Under Van Walbeeck a formal government had been organized for the new colony. From 1634 to 1639, Van Walbeeck himself assumed the duties of governor with full authority in civil matters, while Le Grand supervised military affairs. This division of power at the top was a cause of friction, and probably the reason why Le Grand laid down the office in 1635 and returned to the United Provinces. In time, both functions were united in one person, and Van Walbeeck's successor, Pieter Jacobszoon Tolck, could wield an undisputed scepter.

Van Walbeeck also organized an advisory council – the *Raad* – consisting of Le Grand and other functionaries. At first, only employees of the WIC were eligible for membership on the *Raad;* gradually, however, the ranks were expanded to include Jews and other prominent citizens as well. All appointments were made by the governor and were subject to the approval of the *XIX*.

While the lines of authority were thus clearly delineated from the beginning, the vacilating attitude of the *XIX* with respect to the islands caused much uncertainty. Although it had been decided to retain them and the States General had apportioned a huge sum for their defense and general upkeep, the WIC found this new commitment a strain on its financial resources, already being slowly drained by Brazil, and some voices were raised protesting the additional liability. Notwithstanding these objections, the *XIX*, in a meeting in 1635, voted to keep the island – to the satisfaction of the Amsterdam Chamber, which had been entrusted with their administration from the first. This resolution was in force until 1674 when the old Company expired.

A persistent problem for the Dutch on Curaçao was the attachment of the natives to their former masters. Of the remaining twenty families of Indians, not one person could be trusted. Van Walbeeck, fearing the possible consequences of an alliance between the Indians of the island and the mainland with the Spaniards pushed forward the construction on the Point, of the Waterfort, a temporary defense, and of Fort Amsterdam, also on the Point, to protect the entrance to the Schottegat. The Waterfort was soon a reality, in spite of the threat of mutiny among the soldiers, who several times refused to cooperate or demanded more pay. The circumstances under which they labored were indeed far from easy. Exposed to the blistering sun, the men had to walk with their buckets more than an hour back and forth to a well in order to draw water for drinking and making mortar. Not until June, 1635, did they finally use a small boat for this purpose.

By January 1636, the Waterfort was finished and ready for occupation. Ten cannons were placed facing the bayfront, five facing the sea, and eight inland. Within the stockade, a few houses had been built: small ones for the officers and soldiers, and a larger one for the governor. In the following years more buildings were added, such as a warehouse for the Company, called the West India House. Van Walbeeck's successor, Tolck, was to protect the town north of the fort with a fifteen foot high wall.

Shortly after the completion of the fort, Van Walbeeck planned a similar structure at the strategic and unprotected St. Barbara Bay after an attempt to barricade the bay with sunken ships had proven to be impossible. This was not built, however, until Tolck (1639–1641) held the reins of government; hence its name Tolcksburg.

Once the Dutch felt themselves and their property securely entrenched behind these bulwarks, a busy traffic developed between the new colony and the recent settlement in Pernambuco. Dutch ships, after unloading their wares on Brazilian shores, were more than anxious to drop anchor off the islands and fill their holds with a valuable cargo of wood and Caribbean salt, the latter far superior in quality to the Brazilian. Meanwhile, the island of Curaçao was also being used as a permanent base for armed excursions against the enemy. As early as 1635, Cornelis Corneliszoon Jol received specific orders from the *XIX* to remain on Curaçao, to assume command of all the Company's ships in the area, and to collaborate closely with Van Walbeeck in all matters of military significance. During the fourteen years in which Curaçao functioned as a naval base against Spain, the Schottegat always harbored a few men-of-war kept ready for action at all times, and belonging to what may be referred to as the Curaçao Squadron.

If we are to believe the testimony of Governor Iñigo de la Mota Sarmiento of Puerto Rico, directed to the Spanish king in 1639, the Dutch on Curaçao not only enjoyed an impregnable defense system but swarmed out in all directions to infest the Caribbean waters. Jol, for example, carried out several highly successful raids against the Spaniards, making his name nearly as dreaded as that of Francis Drake fifty years earlier.

Indeed, the Dutch had become so strong that Mota Sarmiento resigned himself to the fact that it would be impossible to drive them from their stronghold. Not only had Curaçao become a notorious sally port for privateering operations, but the governors of the island, beginning with Tolck, did not hesitate to attack the Spanish settlements on Tierra Firme, organizing expeditions which roamed, burned, and pillaged the length of the Venezuelan coast. In 1640, Tolck even planned a campaign against Coro and Maracaibo; although this scheme could not be carried out because Jol, promoted to admiral, needed all available ships for his last attempt on the Spanish treasure fleets. In this, Jol was unlucky again: a hurricane caused so much havoc among the Dutch that no effort could be spared for adventure. In addition, the power of the WIC was now decidedly on the wane, and its shareholders were growing more and more reluctant to engage in great designs.

In 1641, the Dutch did launch an attack on Tierra Firme from Curaçao. A small squadron under Hendrick Gerritsz (in Spanish Enrico Giraldo) sailing from the Schottegat into Lake Maracaibo, bombarded that town of about 500 inhabitants. The Spaniards were unimpressed. Their losses were minimal, and as they refused to pay any levy the Dutch had no choice but to retreat. At the same time, however, Dutch ships sponsored by the Curaçao government were plundering other parts of the Venezuelan coast, venturing as far away as the coastal towns of Puerto Rico.

In 1641, Tolck was replaced by Jan Claeszoon van Campen (1641–1642), who had been commander of St. Martin up until 1633 when the Spaniards had claimed this island. In 1635 Van Campen had been sent to Curaçao as an expert on salt but it is not known whether he made any improvements to the pans. He died either at the end of 1641 or at the beginning of 1642, to be succeeded by a man who was to leave a deeper mark on history: Peter Stuyvesant (1642–1664).

Stuyvesant was a native Frisian, born in the northern province of the Netherlands, and the son of a minister of the Dutch Reformed Church. His father had sent him to the University of Franeker to receive a higher education, but young Peter had become romantically involved with the daughter of his landlord and as a result had been forced to leave the university. Thereupon, he had entered upon a life of scrupulous service to the West India Company. His first position as a junior clerk took him to the island of Fernando de Noronha, where he had to check the cargoes of all incoming and outgoing ships. In time he was transferred to Pernambuco in the same category. While Stuyvesant was on leave in Holland in 1638, the Chamber of Amsterdam appointed him Company agent on Curaçao where he was to be in control of all incoming goods and booty, and responsible for their safe removal to Amsterdam. So trustworthy an employee was Stuyvesant that four years later the same Chamber promoted him to governor of the Curaçao islands.

In the first months of Stuyvesant's rule, the Spaniards under Fernández de Fuenmayor attacked Bonaire as the first step toward their objective of taking Curaçao. When the soldiers of Stuyvesant arrived after the Spaniards had left, they found all houses and landing stages destroyed, and most cattle and horses killed as revenge for the alleged poisoning of the wells. Stuyvesant's reaction was immediate and direct. He sent a squadron to Puerto Cabello with orders to sink the four Spanish frigates in the harbor, while he himself sailed to Cape San Román where the Dutch went on a looting spree which lasted for two weeks and from which they returned to Curaçao with enough goats and horses to replace the losses at Bonaire twice over.

Stuyvesant's aggressive governorship becomes all the more evident in the 1644 expedition to recover the island of St. Martin. Since the Spaniards had taken the island from the Dutch in 1633, the conditions had grown from bad to worse. The Spanish garrison, which in 1634 had counted almost 300 men, had, in ten years shrunk to less than 120, many of whom suffered from disease. A proper Spanish settlement had never developed, while the former prosperous Dutch colony, near the saltpans, had disappeared. No ships had entered the bay to load salt since the Dutch had left. Indeed, shortly before Stuyvesant's campaign, the Spanish governor wrote that in the past three years he had received provisions only once, and then just enough for one month.

This letter was written in March, 1644, three days after Stuyvesant had left Curaçao with a fleet of eighteen ships. He dropped anchor at St. Eustatius to receive reinforcements, and when the Dutch left this island, their fleet had swollen to about thirty-five ships.

By Stuyvesant's calculations, the conquest of St. Martin should be relatively easy, not requiring more than four or five days. The Dutch arrived at their destination early in the morning of Palm Sunday, March 20. While many of the smaller ships circled around the island to prevent outside interference, six or seven of the larger ships sailed into Kay Bay and disembarked troops beyond the range of the Spaniard's guns.

Commanding the island was one Guajardo Fajardo, who immediately had all available supplies as well as most of the cattle brought within the walls of the fort. Stuyvesant, having decided to direct the first blow against this stronghold, planted his men on the crests of the surrounding hills from where they had an unrestricted view of the entire area, controlled all points of access to the wells, and could cut off the Spaniards from escape into the neighboring wilderness.

On March 22, after the Spanish commander had refused a formal request to surrender, the Dutch began to bombard the fort. In the return fire, a cannon ball struck Stuyvesant in the right leg, wounding the Dutch governor so badly that he was forced to withdraw from the field. During the following days, nevertheless, the shooting continued unabated. Fajardo succeeded in contacting the Governor of Puerto Rico and a promise of reinforcements emboldened him in his stubborn defense.

At the end of March the Dutch launched their infantry of about 400 men against the fort, and were repelled. A few days later the attempt was repeated with the same result. A change of tactics was deemed advisable; all actual combat was stopped, and the roads to the fort were kept under strict sur-veillance in a last, concerted effort to starve the garrison into surrender. Still the Spaniards gave no sign of weakening. Discouraged by the entire turn of events and demoralized by the injury to their leader, the Dutch lifted the siege, and sailed back to Curaçao. Stuyvesant himself went on to Holland where his wounded leg was amputated. The attempt to recover the St. Martin saltpans appeared to have failed dismally.

There was, however, a very curious and unexpected aftermath. The Spanish War Council, informed of the casualties suffered and the damage done to Spanish property, reconsidered St. Martin's minimal value to the Crown and voted for its abandonment. This occurred in the beginning of 1648 when peace with the United Provinces was about to be concluded. Shortly afterwards, Abraham Adriaanssen, the Dutch commander of St. Eustatius, occupied the island. Simultaneous French claims led to a subsequent partition in which the Dutch retained the coveted saltpans.

Back in the United Provinces, the *Heren XIX* were casting their eyes about for a new governor (the title was director-general) of New Netherland to take the place of the inept Willem Kieft. Stuyvesant, recently arrived in Holland for treatment of his wound, seemed to all of them the right man for the position. Even as a cripple Peg-leg Stuyvesant remained an imposing figure, inspiring his subordinates and impressing his superiors. The fact that he had previously advised a change in the government of the Curaçao islands also helped to propel him into the higher rank. At the time, the not yet famous Frisian had proposed that the ties to New Holland be cut, and the govern-ment of the islands be linked instead to New Netherland, for various reasons, not the least one being the relative ease of communication between New Amsterdam and Curaçao. In their meeting of 1646, hence, the *XIX* formally designated Stuyvesant as the next governor of their North American colony and attached the Curaçao islands to the latter.

In December of 1646, Stuyvesant departed for Curaçao, where a Lucas Rodenburch had been left in charge. From there, he sailed to New Netherland. Although for more than seventeen years he ruled his former domain from far-away New Amsterdam, he never saw Curaçao again. During that long period he visited the Caribbean area only once, travelling as far as Barbados in an attempt to rescue eight Dutch ships caught by the English during the first Anglo-Dutch war. He did not succeed, nor did he engage in any further journeying.

It would be utterly misleading to judge Stuyvesant without taking into account the period in which he lived and the norms to which he adhered. If it is true that he was authoritative, self-possessed, stubborn to the point of being obnoxious, and well-deserving of his nickname "stiff-necked Peter," he was, nevertheless an honest, hard-working, and trustworthy servant of the West India Company. He sacrificed private advantage to the good of the Company; yet without ever losing sight of the welfare of the common people entrusted to him. He encouraged trade wherever in his power, and the great prosperity enjoyed by New Amsterdam even after the surrender to the English was mainly due to his untiring efforts. History owes him a word of praise.

Stuyvesant's interest in the Curaçao islands, on the other hand, was light and lukewarm. During his governorship he did organize some expeditions against the Spaniards, as is mentioned before, and he also tried to promote Curaçao as a slave market, but he was soon convinced that the Company would never extract any great profits from the islands. He therefore was not long in urging the *XIX* to get rid of them without delay. With peace with Spain in the offing, the islands were rapidly losing their significance as a military base. What Stuyvesant overlooked was that Curaçao, in spite of his experience to the contrary, might have great possibilities as a center of the Caribbean slave trade, and thus as a source of wealth for the Company.

The Peace of Westphalia signalled the end of the Eighty Years' War of the Dutch against Spain. In 1648, the latter country not only recognized the *de facto* independence of the United Provinces, but also accepted the fact that the Dutch held territory in the East and West Indies. Curaçao found itself robbed of an important source of income: her revenues from privateering. At that time, there were approximately 500 Dutch or European inhabitants on the island, of whom some 350 were soldiers. Most of the other 150 were employees of the WIC, but there were also a few merchants, and a handful of farmers struggling with the barren soil. It is difficult to estimate the true number of blacks; the great years of the Dutch slave trade were still to come.

Within the first months of the conquest by the Dutch, a minister of the

Dutch Reformed Church had arrived on Curaçao, and henceforth, this branch of Calvinism was the recognized religion for the new colony, a law of 1629 explicitly stating that "no other religion would be allowed to be exercized ..." The Roman Catholic faith was strictly taboo. But practice was far more tolerant than the laws implied, and persons having other faiths were never molested. The Jews, who soon began to arrive in numbers, received a charter guaranteeing the same freedoms enjoyed by Jews in Amsterdam. Against a background of medieval religious traditions and intolerance, this liberal attitude stood in sharp contrast to the rigid line adopted by Spain.

CHAPTER VI

THE STRUGGLE FOR SURVIVAL

The thirty years separating the Peace of Westphalia of 1648 and the Peace of Nijmegen of 1678, were years of crisis for the Dutch Antilles as well as for the entire Caribbean region. By 1648, the Curaçao islands had lost their *raison d'être* as a military outpost, while Stuyvesant's well-meaning project to strenghten the ties between the islands and New Netherland had not resulted in great advantages for either. The governor had been of the opinion that the two colonies could supplement each other's output and combine their resources: New Netherland would furnish all foodstuffs in exchange for slaves from Curaçao, horses from Aruba, and salt from Bonaire.

But Stuyvesant had not reckoned with the existence of rivalry between the two colonies, a rivalry which made them unable to cooperate efficiently and profitably. The Dutch on Curaçao preferred to sell their black merchandise to other Caribbean islands where they could command a higher price rather than to trade with their fellow country-men to the north. In addition, the islands were actively engaged in illicit barter with the Spanish mainland, and were most reluctant to exchange this for a legalized commerce of the kind New Netherland had to offer. Governor Stuyvesant desperately needed slaves to build up the defenses of New Amsterdam. Yet all he received, especially after the end of the first Anglo Dutch war, in reply to his incessant clamor, were the so-called *mancarrons* or invalid slaves, those too old or too sick for work, while the better cargo went elsewhere to a higher bidder.

On the other hand, the colonists of New Netherland were not given to altruistic motives or patriotic sentiments either, and refused to renounce their commercial intercourse with the neighboring French, English, and Swedish settlers across the border. Only in times of dire need did the bond of a common ancestry transcend pecuniary commitment: for instance when, after a few dry seasons, the islands were suffering from famine, and Stuyvesant, in the nick of time, saved the population by sending a ship with provisions.

The unhappy liaison between the Curaçao islands and New Netherland ended abruptly in 1664 when, at a time when war between England and the

United Provinces had not yet been formally declared, an English fleet under the command of Richard Nicolls, demanded the surrender of New Amsterdam. Although the colony was briefly restored to the Dutch in 1673, the following year it was used as a pawn to convince the English of the perils inherent in their alliance with France.

Throughout the seventeenth century the real enemy of the Dutch was neither Spain nor France but England as evidenced by the three wars the Dutch fought against this country. Contrary to the first Anglo-Dutch War (1652–1654), the second (1665–1667) had a lasting effect in the Caribbean. By that time, great changes had been brough about in the area, in particular after the Dutch had lost New Holland to the Portuguese and a war of attrition with this nation had ended in an unsatisfactory settlement. Dutch refugees from Brazil, converging upon the area after 1654, not only added to the growing population but brought with them the know-how of the sugar industry Sugarcane soon became the leading crop on most of the islands, replacing tobacco, while Dutch capital helped French and English planters to purchase the necessary processing equipment. In the late thirties and early forties, all the important Portuguese slave depots on Africa's west coast had successively succumbed to the Dutch, assuring them of ready access to black labor, and Dutch control over the slave trade was well-nigh absolute. Dutch merchants would buy the sugar crops and, in turn, provide the French and English colonies with food, hardware, slaves, and other commodities throughout the years when civil strife and other problems at home prevented their governments from contributing to their support or enforcing existing laws against trade with foreigners.

Alan Burns observes that the Dutch could not have gotten away with this breach of contemporary mercantilism under normal circumstances. Neither France, with the rebellion of the Fronde on her hands, nor England engaged in a bitter civil war and its cruel aftermath were in a position to enforce prerogatives and to prevent contraband. The colonists of both nations, needless to say, wholeheartedly endorsed Dutch trade.

The several French companies of the West Indies, charged with sole responsibility for the French settlements in the Caribbean, were plagued by a constant lack of funds and never mustered the force to expel the Dutch. In 1650, the French sold their colonies to individual *seigneurs*, thus creating an equivalent to the English and Dutch patronships. A year later, Philippe de Louvilliers, Sieur de Poincy, one of the more influential members of the Malthese Order, acquired St. Christopher and some other French islands, including the French part of St. Martin, as *seigneur* or patron. De Poincy himself had furnished 120,000 francs of the total cost, and it was agreed that he should act as governor until his death. At that date, the French Antilles were reorganized by Colbert under a *Compagnie des Indes Occidentales*, and stricter laws to exclude foreign trade were rigidly applied.

The relationship of the English colonies with the Dutch was both more complex and more provocative. The passage of the first Navigation Laws in 1651, aimed to smother Dutch competition and circumscribing all commercial intercourse with the Hollanders and Zeelanders, not only became the main reason for the outbreak of the first Anglo-Dutch war, but was interpreted, at least in the English Caribbean, as a direct blow by the Cromwell regime at the colonies' very existence. The English colonists were driven to take a stand against the mother country in protest, and Francis Lord Willoughby, Governor of Barbados, issued a spirited declaration denouncing the English Parliament and assuring the Dutch that "they might continue, if they please, all freedom of commerce and traffic with us."

The governors of the other English islands similarly made public their gratitude to the Dutch for having provided them, over the years, with arms, ammunition, and other commodities in exchange for sugar. The English planters also gave their assurance that this trade would continue and claimed not to believe "our number so contemptible nor our resolution so weake to be forced or persuaded to so ignoble a submission."

Despite these proclamations, it was not long before Parliament had restored order in the English settlements in the Caribbean. The Navigation Laws were put into effect without further delay. Nor did the restoration of Charles II bring a revocation of the restrictive laws, much to the dismay of both the Dutch merchants and the island planters. Indeed, soon after Charles had regained his father's throne, he added the well-known "enumeration clause" making certain products such as sugar and tobacco exportable only to England or to other English territory.

Smuggling intensified in the English domains, while dissatisfaction continued to mount. Yet, with a few minor changes, the spirit of the Navigation Laws directed English colonial policy for almost two centuries. Backed by strict surveillance, they were eventually to succeed in bringing about, as expected, the utter collapse of Dutch trade with the English bases. The Dutch found bitter irony in the fact that their skill, enterprise, and money had created a closed market for the enjoyment of their adversary.

Cromwell's pretentious Western Design, calling for the consolidation and expansion of England's overseas territories, although it was an engaging plan and did result in the conquest of Jamaica, still floundered, partly because of the reluctance of the Dutch to make their country a sloop behind the English man-of-war. Although the Protector's successors, the restored Stuarts, tried once more to accomplish the same end, their means were quite different. The primary authors of this new bid – trying to dislodge the Dutch from their advantageous positions on Africa's west coast, the Caribbean, and New Netherland – were the vainglorious Charles II, his crypto-Catholic brother James, Duke of York, and their cousin Rupert, son of the Winter King. At the service of the three royal *brasseurs d'affaires* was the inestimable George Downing, English minister in The Hague.

The harassments of the royal adventurers began in 1661 when an English squadron under Sir Robert Holmes boldly raided the Dutch settlements on the West African coast. A year later, a royal charter issued by Charles II generously bequeathed American territory which included New Netherland to his brother James. James did not delay and on September 8, 1664, before any war had been declared, New Amsterdam was occupied by English forces and renamed New York. As Commander Richard Nicolls put it to Peter Stuyvesant: "The right and title of His Majesty to these parts of America are indisputable."

Similar tidings from the Caribbean made it clear that the Dutch were also to be driven unconditionally from the West Indies. English ships were reported in the vicinity of Curaçao, commissioned by James to stop and overpower any ships with Spanish goods aboard – an empty pretext since the English were no more at war with Spain than they were with the United Provinces.

Spurred by continuous reports of English perfidy, the Dutch ultimately resolved to use armed force to redress the losses inflicted upon their West India Company. Vice-admiral De Ruyter, who happened to be in the Mediterranean at the time, was ordered to reconquer the forts and factories occupied by the English under Holmes.

As De Ruyter's fleet proceeded along the African coast all former Dutch forts and factories now occupied by the English surrendered to him. At Elmina the Dutch admiral was instructed to cross the Atlantic and attack the English in the Caribbean. His exploits in the West Indies were not as successful, however, and no permanent results were obtained.

Although Europe was the center stage for the conflict among the two powers, repercussions of the tension were felt all over the Caribbean. Even before De Ruyter had set foot in the area, Francis Lord Willoughby of Barbados had already requested aid against what he termed the aggressive policies of the Dutch. At about this time, moreover, Governor Thomas Modyford of Jamaica was suggesting that the English employ Caribbean buccaneers before the latter could side with the enemy. This was accoomplished with the commission of Lieutenant-Colonel Edward Morgan, whose fleet of buccaneers was to seize the islands of St. Eustatius, Saba, and Curaçao, hopefully demolishing the Dutch position in the Caribbean once and for all.

Morgan's fleet of 10 ships and 500 men departed for the attack on St. Eustatius. During the fight, Morgan died from overexhaustion but Colonel Carey, the next in command, succeeded in forcing the surrender of the Dutch fort. All Dutch colonists who refused to take the oath of allegiance to the English king were summarily auctioned off as "white slaves" to planters of the English Antilles. The booty gathered by the buccaneers amounted to 840 slaves, a large supply of guns and ammunition, and 300 cows, sheep, horses, and pigs. Distribution of the spoils caused much dissension among the men and was a primary factor leading to the dissolution of this unnatural alliance.

Some three weeks after the surrender of St. Eustatius, Carey took the nearby island of Saba where he captured 70 blacks. The English, for whom the future seemed bright indeed, now prepared to proceed to Curaçao for an intrepid raid on this strongest fort in the West Indies. At the same time, incidentally, Willoughby was laying plans for his campaign to Tobago and the Wild Coast.

It was not long, however, before Carey realized that his ruthless followers, all of whom had agreed to "cash on the barrel" terms, would now refuse to obey orders unless properly paid. Faced by their insubordination, he reluctantly abandoned the project, and after appointing Thomas Morgan as governor of St. Eustatius and Saba, departed for Jamaica. Although plagued by storms en route the majority of his ships eventually reached the island, with most of their crews and some 400 slaves.

Some time later, in January of 1666, another fleet of buccaneers left Jamaica for an attack on Curaçao. This group included many Dutch and French pirates, and was led by Edward Mansfelt and Henry Morgan – both famous names in the history of the buccaneers. Sailing southward toward Curaçao, it occurred to Mansfelt that his haul would be much larger if he were to strike at the Spaniards instead. Consequently, the fleet altered course and headed toward the Spanish island of Providence off the Nicaraguan coast. The garrison offered only nominal resistance and was easily convinced to surrender. Leaving the protection of Providence the buccaneers continued their pilgrimage along the coast of the Spanish mainland, spreading havoc in the colonies of Honduras and the Mexican Gulf. Curaçao, fortunately, thought to be impregnable, was saved from their attention.

Meanwhile, the war continued. English buccaneers had won some islands for their king but had added very little to the royal treasury. Dutch ships, on the other hand, were conducting such a successful campaign against the

English that a royal order was issued for all English ships to travel in convoys.

On Barbados, Governor Willoughby had managed to equip some ships and recruit 350 men for his anticipated assault on the prosperous Dutch colony on Tobago. Arriving in late 1665, he was surprised to find that Governor Modyford had already captured the island in question a few days earlier and that his privateers were in the act of dismantling the sugar mills. An agreement was reached whereby Willoughby assumed official control and a fifty-man garrison of English troops was stationed on the island.

Thus, during their first year of war in the Caribbean, the Dutch had lost two of their Leeward islands as well as Tobago. But the Dutch position remained strong, the retention of Curaçao amply compensating for these minor set-backs. Curaçao, growing in importance as the slave trade burgeoned, was a strong competitor for the English companies, counterparts of the Dutch West India Company. As Commander Nicolls, the victor of New Amsterdam, wrote to his home government, the Dutch island remained "a thorn in the foot of the Leeward Islands."

In January 1666, Dutch prospects were brightened by France's entry into the war against England. Although Louis XIV had been a nominal ally of the United Provinces since 1662, the French king was more anti-English than pro-Dutch. When he eventually did commit his nation to war, it was with the intention of converting Dutch losses in the Caribbean into French gains. Furthermore, the English were refusing to renew existing neutrality agreements on the French Antilles and had brazenly occupied St. Lucia.

With the entry of France, a new dimension was added to the war. A Franco-Dutch alliance posed a formidable threat to the English position in the Caribbean. Although the English dreaded the Dutch as dangerous competitors, they actually shared many traits with them, not the least of these being an aversion to Roman Catholicism. Feeling between the French and English, however, ran on a quite different level. No matter how cordial official relations might appear to be, a strong undercurrent of hostility and mistrust was never far below the surface. In general, and in spite of much propaganda to the contrary, the Dutch and English would treat each other honorably in combat, in violent contrast to French comportment with either.

An immediate result of this unfolding of the war was the loss of the English part of St. Christopher to the French, the first in a series of English defeats. They caused great alarm in London. The French had gained the initiative with the Dutch as pleased bystanders. From then on, the English islands were subjected to daily annoyances by French naval forces. The Dutch frequently accompanied their comrades in arms, but they also contrived to expand the radius of their clandestine activities in the Caribbean and to conduct a booming business. Furthermore, the English fleet intended for an attack on Curaçao had been dispersed and the buccaneers had taken up their former vocation. Led by Governor Willoughby, English officials in the area badgered their home government with requests for aid to cope with the mounting threat. London, however, moved slowly.

From an almost unassailable position in the Caribbean in 1665 and the beginning of 1666, England's strength had dissipated until by the summer of 1666 she was clearly on the defensive. The employment of buccaneers to further national goals had been a grievous mistake. The French, aiming to consolidate their holdings in the area, continued to push the offensive. Colbert set up another French West India Company, and initiated a new colonial policy for the French Antilles by which new governors, following new orders, imposed rigid restrictions on trade with all foreigners, including the Dutch ally. Exceptions to the rule of generally incompetent French administrators were to be found on Martinique and Tortuga. The governor of the latter island, Bertrand d'Ogeron, distinguished himself as one of the ablest French officials in the Caribbean, and made the island of Tortuga, north of Hispaniola, the center of French authority in that part of the West Indies.

With a desperate attempt in mind to regain the initiative, Governor Willoughby left Barbados on June 18, 1666. After brightening the trip with a little piracy, he sailed toward the Leeward Islands, where he intended to join forces with his brother William. However, the fleet was severely battered in a violent hurricane and only a few English ships managed to reach the relative safety of the Leeward group. Willoughby's own ship was lost and the governor never seen again. The English were understandably morose upon hearing of this stroke of fate; the Dutch and the French rejoiced. The entire Caribbean now beckoned to the allies, and they were not slow to respond.

Tobago was the first island to be recaptured by the French when, in August of 1666, its English garrison surrendered to French planters from Grenada. In November, the French attacked Antigua. At first repulsed, they returned the next month with more men, and successfully occupied the island. At the same time the Dutch from Curaçao, under Gerrit Bogaert, defeated the numerically superior English on St. Eustatius, to be manoeuvred out of their victory by the French. Only after months of tortuous negotiations did the latter reluctantly return the island to the Dutch.

Early in 1667, the island of Monserrat was forced to surrender to the French under Admiral Antoine Lefebvre de la Barre, recently arrived in the Caribbean. Of the Leeward Islands only Nevis now remained in English hands, and this island was overrun by starving refugees from St. Christopher and elsewhere. To the west Jamaica was still English, as was Barbados to the southeast.

Meanwhile, the Dutch, inspired by the victorious French to be sure, but unwilling to allow their ally to harvest all that Dutchmen had sown, moved to an offensive of their own. The Province of Zeeland had long regarded the Wild Coast as a valuable possession and a proposal was accepted to outfit a Zeelandian expedition to the region. A fleet of seven ships was put under the command of Abraham Crijnssen, scion of a highly respected dynasty of seafarers, and a fellow countryman of De Ruyter.

Crijnssen left Zeeland on December 30, 1666, and arrived on the Wild Coast early in February, 1667. He set sail for Cayenne, at that time in French hands, but resolved, for the time being, to leave the colony in the hands of the unreliable ally, and to proceed to Paramaribo.

Surinam, at that time, was an English colony. The English were invited to surrender, but the commander, William Byam, informed Crijnssen that honor obliged him to fight. The fighting which followed was indeed intense, but Byam was soon forced to lay down his arms.

The reconquest of Surinam had been so fortuitous that over-confidence led the Dutch commander to neglect the most important part of his instructions, namely speed. Instead of aiming for the Caribbean, he dallied at Berbice, strengthening Dutch control over that area. Consequently, it was not until April that he finally set sail for Tobago.

Unaware that the island had been deserted for quite a while, Crijnssen was delighted to find no resistance. Before leaving, he rebuilt the fort and stationed a garrison of 25 men on the island.

While the Zeelander was setting sail for Martinique the news reached him that an English squadron under Sir John Berry had made its appearance in the Caribbean – the supposed forerunner of a bigger fleet. Crijnssen immediately decided to consult the French at Martinique. De la Barre proposed a joint undertaking, which was catapulted into action by the news that Berry's fleet was blockading St. Christopher. On May 17, the combined Franco-Dutch fleet left for Nevis, accurately pinpointed by the French admiral as the key to English hegemony in the Leeward Islands. The so-called Battle of Nevis ensued, the only sea battle of the second Anglo-Dutch war in which the Dutch and the French fought jointly against the English. But De la Barre's incompetence caused a retreat, and Crijnssen departed in disgust, setting his course for Virginia, and only returning to Flushing after peace had been concluded at Breda.

There is no question that after the Battle of Nevis control of the Caribbean again shifted, now in favor of the English. Antigua and Monserrat were soon recaptured, and nothing remained to prevent Berry from attacking St. Christopher, as English prospects continued to brighten.

After Crijnssen left the Caribbean, the larger English fleet of Sir John Harman arrived, and the ensuing battles were fought between the English and the French exclusively. Harman succeeded in disabling De la Barre's fleet, and with it French naval power in the Caribbean. English supremacy had been effectively restored. Berry continued the blockade off St. Christopher, resulting in the capture of this island, while Harman and Henry Willoughby, William's son, set sail to wrest Cayenne from the French and Surinam from the Dutch. But when the English returned to Barbados after having successfully completed their mission, they learned to their dismay that peace had been concluded, and that according to the articles of the treaty both Cayenne and Surinam had to be returned to their former owners.

As far as the Dutch were concerned, the war proved to be a heavy blow to their West India Company. Although the WIC had never claimed any exclusive rights in the Caribbean, it had built up a commercial empire embracing French, English, and Spanish colonies. The Peace of Breda put an end to this Dutch supremacy. Hereafter, the English Navigation Laws were rigidly enforced, while French colonial policy actively restricted trade with the French Antilles. Although Dutch ships were still numerous enough five years later, to unite the English and French in an anti-Dutch campaign, the ensuing struggle gave the coup de grâce to the moribund West India Company.

But there was one other consequence of the 1667 peace which should be noted here. The Breda settlement among England, France, and the United Provinces marked the final distribution of colonial possessions in the Caribbean. Exchanging territory, the game which had plagued the area for so long, now came to an end. For the next centuries, there would be virtually no change in colonial holdings. After 1667, therefore, the islands returned to prosperity and peace, to be flustered only slightly by the third Anglo-Dutch War of 1672 and the Nine Years' War of 1688. When, at the end of the century, buccaneering received severe blows, true political stability at last held sway in the Caribbean.

CHAPTER VII

THE LAST DUTCH STAND

The Peace of Breda reaffirmed the United Provinces' international position and proclaimed the fact that the Netherlanders were still a force to be reckoned with. Under pressure of the Medway disaster, England had agreed to Dutch ownership of Surinam, and had promised to mitigate the most offensive clauses of her Navigation Laws. The Dutch, it is true, had had to relinquish New Netherland, but at that time the colony was considered of much less importance than Surinam, and the Dutch footing had been maintained, both in the Caribbean and on the African coast.

With the occupation of New Netherland by the English, the ties between this colony and the Curaçao islands were, as a matter of course, severed. Mathias Beck, Stuyvesant's former vice-governor, continued to head the government of the islands until his death in 1668, at which time the *Raad* provisionally nominated his brother William as successor. The Chamber of Amsterdam, however, refused to confirm this appointment and sent a candidate of its own to the post. Unfortunately, this person died within a week after his arrival on the island and William Beck continued to rule the colony until the end of 1670, when the second appointee of the Amsterdam Chamber, Dirck Otterinck, arrived. Otterinck died in 1673 during the French attack on Curaçao; his successor, again appointed provisionally by the *Raad*, was one Jan Doncker.

The five years between the Peace of Breda and the outbreak of a new war in 1672, were years of setbacks for the Dutch, particularly in the Caribbean. A more rigorous interpretation of the Navigation Laws, in direct violation of the peace treaty, irritated the Dutch and caused endless friction with the English. Although smuggling persisted, regular trade relations with the English islands became almost impossible. Relations with the French were similarly deteriorating, since they, more so than the English, were now following a pronounced anti-Dutch policy. In accordance with Colbert's exclusivist mercantilism, regular squadrons of the French West India Company were sent to the Caribbean to curtail Dutch infringement upon French laws and territory. On one occasion, the French captured some

Dutch ships trading in the northern coastal ports of French Hispaniola, but these harassments were more like recurrent needle pricks intended "to hurt without breaking openly." Jean Charles de Baas, governor-general of the French Caribbean possessions, was advised by Colbert that he could not please Louis XIV more than by "hampering their [the Dutch] trade" and driving the Hollanders from their islands "if this were possible without encroaching directly upon the treaties His Majesty has with them." In the meantime, the Dutch alliances with Sweden and England, sanctioned as recently as 1668, were being undermined by French gold; and in 1670 a treaty aimed squarely at the Dutch was concluded between the French and English kings – the pact known as the Secret Treaty of Dover.

As a preliminary to war, French customs tariffs were altered to the detriment of the Dutch for the third time since 1664. The Dutch responded with reciprocal increases, culminating, in 1672, in an absolute prohibition of French imports.

The Dutch, although realizing that war with France was inevitable, were unaware of the alliance between France and England. England's declaration of war, coming even before France's, was a shock, and one of the main causes of the downfall of Johan de Witt, leader of the United Provinces.

From the outset of the war, however, the Dutch were fully aware of their vulnerable position in the Caribbean and on the Wild Coast and sent reinforcements to these areas as soon as they could. After their decisive victory in Solebay in June of 1672, the Dutch felt able to mount offensives of their own outside European waters, the location of each to be determined by the admiralty boards of the various provinces. The Zeelanders, well pleased with this arrangement, soon decided to outfit a fleet, both for the protection of Dutch colonies in the Western hemisphere and for the discomfiture of adjacent French and English ones. Privateering commissions were handed out and in both Holland and Zeeland people were quick to offer generous contributions to what had become a just cause. When ready, the Zeelandian squadron of six ships was placed under the command of Cornelis Evertsen the Younger, since Crijnssen had died a few years before. He carried on a tradition of seafaring and service like that of the other Zeelandian family, the Crijnssens. Although the Amsterdam admiralty declined to support the Zeelandian adventure outright, it equipped a squadron of its own under Jacob Binckes.

Evertsen arrived at Cayenne in March of 1673, and from there, after voting against a dispersal of his meager forces, set sail for Surinam, still in Dutch hands. Late in May, the Zeelandian ships continued to Martinique where they were about to engage in battle with a small fleet of six ships flying the French flag, only to discover that the enemy was none other than Binckes' Amsterdam squadron. With Evertsen and Binckes alternating in command on a weekly basis, the two squadrons merged for combined action. The odds now seemed to favor the Dutch, and the two commanders agreed to head for Barbados in the hope of catching the English by surprise. It was a futile action for the winds were unfavorable, and the enemy ships were anchored too near their own fort. The Dutch therefore sailed to the north, taking a few French and English prizes in passing, and, in time, arrived at St. Eustatius.

This island's English governor refused to surrender until the Dutch had opened fire and landed troops. The fort was razed to the ground, all other buildings demolished, and the island abandoned.

The combined Dutch fleet now left the Caribbean, having lost its booty in the storms, and deserted its only conquest, St. Eustatius. No effort was made to attack any of the other French or English islands, nor was an investigation even begun of the situation on Tobago. The fleet's major accomplishment was attained later and involved New Netherland rather than the West Indies.

As for the enemy, in March of 1673, De Baas, left Martinique to launch the long-planned attack against the Dutch on Curaçao. Accompanying him were some men-of-war sent by Colbert, whose idea the expedition had been. Counting on the assistance of Governor D'Ogeron and his buccaneers, De Baas had arranged for a rendez-vous at St. Croix, but D'Ogeron never arrived. While the French governor stood helplessly by, all his ships went to the bottom of the sea off the northern coast of Puerto Rico, and most of his men drowned. D'Ogeron himself barely managed to reach Hispaniola.

When, after waiting for a few days, De Baas learned of his ally's fate, he resolved, nonetheless, to proceed as planned with the forces at his disposal, plus a few hundred men to be drafted on St. Christopher and Guadeloupe. Half March he was sighted by the Dutch off Curaçao, with a fleet of at least 7 and perhaps as many as 22 ships, and from 1200 to 2000 men.

Meanwhile, the Governor of Curaçao, Jan Doncker (1673–1679) had been organizing the island's defense by calling all its citizens to arms and by sending part of the militia to Tolcksburg, the small fort at St. Barbara on the eastern end of the island, where the French were expected to land. They did indeed land their troops there and sent out scouting parties, who discovered that their commander had grossly underestimated Curaçao's strength. Doncker refused a summons to surrender. Instead, the Dutch kept a close watch on all enemy movements and waited for their provisions to run out. Four days later the success of this strategy became apparent when a dispirited army and a humiliated French leader quietly left Curaçao.

Peace with England came in 1674. It not only alleviated the financial strain on the Dutch, but enabled their new leader, young William III of Orange, to gather his strength for a renewed attempt to dislodge the French from the Caribbean. The States General had already ordered the admiralty boards, in late 1673, to study a new naval action against the French.

From the very beginning, the conquest of the French Antilles had looked like the most feasible scheme for needling the enemy, and Martinique, the most suitable starting point. More than any other of the French islands, Martinique had been a perpetual menace to the Dutch possessions in the Leeward group. This island was the base, for instance, from which De Baas had launched his attack against Curaçao; it was also the key to controlling the buccaneer strongholds in the West Indies. Besides, the capture of this island would facilitate the seizure of Cayenne and eventually Dutch control of the entire Wild Coast. Finally, the Dutch counted on receiving the support of the population, whose rebellion some years before against Colbert's anti-Dutch policies seemed to indicate a propensity to side with the Hollanders.

At the end of May, 1674, a sizable Dutch fleet under the command of De Ruyter passed through the English Channel en route to the Caribbean. It consisted of 17 large and 3 smaller men-of-war, some fireships, and 18 transport and provision vessels. The fleet was manned by 3400 sailors, 4000 soldiers, and had 1100 pieces of artillery.

The Dutch admiral crossed the Atlantic, and by July 19, had anchored off the coast of Martinique. The French were not unprepared, for the island's defenses had recently been groomed and put in good shape by the addition of troops and provisions from France. The two main forts of the island, Fort St. Pierre and Fort Royal, promised strong resistance to the aggressor, and the population, as well as the garrison, had been trained in defensive tactics. A shore party sent by De Ruyter brought back the disturbing news that the Dutch had been expected for over a month. Despite this discouraging information, the admiral, in view of the great power at his disposal, decided to attack.

After a few hours, with no progress in sight and faced with heavy losses, the Dutch took the wiser course and retreated. Where they had expected an easy victory, they had encountered an unassailable citadel. For some time De Ruyter remained at Guadeloupe, licking his wounds and gathering supplies, before sailing back home. The enterprise had been a costly failure for the Dutch.

During the next two years the States General and the provincial governments alike were incapable of undertaking any other action of importance in

the West Indies. Furthermore, the Dutch West India Company was faced
with imminent dissolution. In 1674, at long last, the old company was
disbanded and a new one created, bearing the same name, but never able to
attain the same heights of power and influence as its predecessor. Totally
dependent upon the slave trade, the new company, after three decades of
prosperity, led a dreary and unremarkable existence. It could, however, still
issue letters of marque to Dutch privateers preying upon French shipping in
African as well as in American waters. A detailed history of their ventures
cannot be reconstructed for lack of data. One of the more spectacular sailors
in those years about whom little is known, was Jan Erasmus Reining, who
was involved in staging an attack against the French on St. Eustatius, and a
frustrated assault on the island of Grenada.

In 1676, the new West India Company was able to persuade the government to underwrite a new expedition to the Caribbean. It was put under the
command of Jacob Binckes, with Reining as an important officer. Binckes
went straight to Cayenne, an area hotly disputed and regularly exchanged
between the Dutch and the French. Within two days the colony was once
more under Dutch authority. Leaving Quirijn Spranger in charge at Cayenne,
Binckes departed for Surinam, and after making sure that it, too, was firmly
in Dutch hands, sailed north, to launch an attack against the French on
Marie Galante.

In buoyant spirits, the Dutch took possession of this island without opposition and continued their journey. An attack on St. Martin, occupied by
the French since the outbreak of hostilities, successfully returned that island
to the Dutch. Binckes then sent part of his fleet with settlers and booty to
Tobago, while he detoured to Hispaniola where his attempt to rally the
French population of the western part "to shake off the unbearable yoke of
the king" failed, but he did defeat a French merchant fleet. He then followed
the rest of his ships to Tobago, arriving there in September. Knowing the
French would probably counterattack, Binckes hurriedly organized the
defense of the island.

In February, 1677, word was received that the French were approaching,
and soon a strong French fleet under the Count D'Estrées entered the Bay.
At sunset, after many hours of fighting, the count reluctantly retreated with
his badly battered fleet. The Dutch fleet was almost completely destroyed.

While Binckes' frantic pleas for assistance made their way through
governmental and Company red tape, Louis XIV, humiliated by D'Estrées'
pyrrhic victory, acted quickly. In December, 1677, D'Estrées again approached the island, and in the ensuing battle Binckes and the greater part of
his men were killed. The French took possession of Tobago, but only for a

short while. Still determined to extinguish Dutch power and prestige in the Caribbean, D'Estrées thoroughly overhauled his fleet, and began to lay plans for an attack on Curaçao.

In May, 1678, five months after the conquest of Tobago, D'Estrées judged his forces strong enough for the anticipated assault, and left Martinique with a fleet of eighteen sails setting their course toward the Dutch colony.

On the evening of May 11, near their destination, some of the French ships stranded on a reef. Other ships trying to cope with this calamity struck the hidden coral themselves breaking their keels in two. No land was in sight and heavy clouds overhead added to the gravity of the situation. It became, indeed, an unparalleled disaster. By ignoring the advice of his more experienced captains, D'Estrées had unwittingly grounded his fleet on the submerged archipelago known as the Aves Islands, stretching from Bonaire to Orchilla.

Marooned on this hidden reef formation, the French admiral could only blame himself. When high tide finally came, the ships were thrown up, broken in two, and their crews drowned or dismembered on the cutting edges of the treacherous atoll. Seven huge men-of-war, three transportation vessels, and some smaller ships were destroyed without the Dutch having to lift a finger. Of the entire French fleet, only a few ships survived the catastrophe and enabled an abject D'Estrées to sail home with the sad tidings.

What the French considered as a national tragedy, the Dutch interpreted as an act of divine intervention on their behalf. The Peace of Nijmegen, signed in August, 1678, added to their rejoicing. France gained undeniable advantages in Europa, but the Dutch did not lose a single square foot neither there nor in the Caribbean, with the exception of Tobago, which lay uninhabited until the English moved in at the end of the century. In addition, William of Orange had earned the hand of Mary Stuart, daughter of the Duke of York, the future James II. This marriage was to elevate the Dutch *stadholder* to the English throne and strengthen the bond between the United Provinces and England.

The free Netherlands had suffered the loss of several posts on the West African coast, which gave the French some control of the trade in that region. On the other hand, the Dutch had wangled a suspension of the high French tariffs which had precipitated the war, and they had also achieved a certain measure of free trade with France – in flat contradiction of Colbert's protective system. Moreover, the Dutch had survived, quite a feat in itself.

All in all, however, the Peace of Nijmegen signalled the end of Dutch commercial hegemony in the Caribbean. They were not defeated by the French, but by the English, who, smarting from Dutch competition had finally succeeded in crippling the ability of the United Provinces to launch naval offensives and, at the same time, in truncating their commerce. Henceforth, while the Caribbean would remain a theater of potential struggle and national rivalry, the Dutch were to be political neutrals, reduced to the role of interested, but helpless bystanders.

CHAPTER VIII

THE END OF THE SEVENTEENTH CENTURY

Immediately after the Peace of Nijmegen, the new West India Company enjoyed an initial period of relative prosperity based upon the slave trade. With the turn of the century, however, the Company's financial prospects began to look less bright, especially after 1715 when, with the Peace of Utrecht, England acquired the right of *asiento*.

With the Peace of Nijmegen, the Dutch could lay claim to six islands in the Caribbean. Beside the three Curaçao islands: Aruba, Curaçao, and Bonaire, they had three smaller ones in the Leeward group: St. Eustatius, Saba, and half of St. Martin. The Dutch had definitely lost Tobago and, in 1678, the small island of Tortola, but the Danish island of St. Thomas, settled in 1662, was *de facto* Dutch, since the Danish West India Company was being financed by Dutch capital.

The charter of the new West India Company was far more limited than the old Company's had been. Responsibility for the Caribbean islands and part of the possessions on the Wild Coast was assigned to the Company's Board of Directors, the *Heren X*, rather than to the Amsterdam Chamber as previously. There was no significant change in the situation on the Curaçao islands to go along with the change in administration. The position of governor was made more attractive, not so much because of the annual salary of 1200 guilders plus a representation allowance of 1000 guilders (later raised to 2000), but because of the fringe benefits. For each slave brought to the islands, the governor received half a piece-of-eight (1,20 guilder). Fines added to his income, and he also pocketed 4 percent (later 5 percent) of all sales on fruits and vegetables.

Not only did the governor enjoy benefits of this type, but many of the Company's employees did as well. Paid very meager salaries – from 240 to 300 guilders annually to a physician for the slaves, and from 300 to 360 guilders to commanders of the islands of Aruba and Bonaire – they received additional income either from the revenues of the Company's plantations, or from the slave trade. The commissioner for slaves, for instance, kept 2½ per cent of the slave's value for himself; the secretary received what was known as "placard money"; the fiscal pocketed part of another tax; while the commanders kept 5 per cent of the revenues on salt. In addition, all Company employees from the governor to the lowest clerk were entitled to free housing and supplementary food rations. Since the islands' desert climate made it difficult to do any gardening, food, brought by Company ships, frequently sold for exorbitant prices on the black market.

The executive power of the governor both before and after 1674, was almost absolute, the *Raad* serving mainly in an advisory capacity, although the governor needed its consent to hire, fire, or suspend an employee in the higher echelons of the governmental hierarchy. The *Heren X* functioned as a court of appeal in these matters, subject at all times to Their High Mightinesses, the Lords of the States General. The *Heren X*, or course, controlled and supervised the governor's prerogatives.

Because of the concomitant slave trade profits, the governorship evolved into a highly coveted position, and after the Peace of Nijmegen it was often held by one of the directors of the WIC themselves. Although the latter were officially required to resign from the Company (or Chamber) Board, a bit of nepotism and a few influential friends here and there made it fairly easy for them to retain their power and to regain their directorship. Doncker's successors, Nicolaas van Liebergen (1679–82), Joan van Erpecum (1682–85), and Willem Kerckrinck (1686–92) were all three directors of the Chamber of Amsterdam before being appointed Governor of the Curaçao islands.

Van Liebergen achieved a certain notoriety by his flagrant neglect of Company affairs and his dedication to his own welfare. An existing dossier testifies how the governor used Company funds for personal transactions and accepted bribes from slave traders who wanted to sell their human cargoes privately, in clear violation of Company regulations. He furthermore extorted money from lawabiding skippers, and was known for his cruel treatment of slaves. In due time, these and other accusations were painstakingly investigated by the *Heren X*, who found the governor guilty on many grounds and, in 1682, relieved him of his post. He was succeeded by another director, Van Erpecum, who had been among the first to denounce Van Liebergen.

Although as a director Van Erpecum had loudly acclaimed the Company's compensations and salaries, as governor he soon found these benefits far from sufficient and protested to the Amsterdam Chamber that he had nothing to put aside for his old age. Before long, the resourceful governor had begun to look for loopholes in Company regulations. Not content with appropriating one third of the Company's fines, he allowed his wife to barter in food and supplies for slaves, as well as to deliver wine and liquor to

Company employees and private individuals. It was even said that the governor extracted profit by not reporting shortages in gunpowder, in order to sell to the Company from a private, overpriced stockpile. In short, he defied Company regulations wherever he could, even those he had helped to formulate himself. The directors of the Amsterdam Chamber made a few feeble attempts to bring their governor back into line when, in 1685, Van Erpecum unexpectedly but very conveniently died.

Another ex-director, Kerckrinck, was appointed to succeed him. During Kerckrinck's term, an increase of population due to the prospering slave trade caused the island's economy to thrive. The new governor repaired the crumbling city walls and extended them eastward to accomodate the influx of people. In spite of these achievements he, like his two predecessors, was accused of neglecting the public cause and of being engrossed in his own well-being. Kerckrinck died in 1692. The Nine Years' War which began during his term did not affect the Dutch possessions.

Curaçao's next governor was Bastiaan Bernagie, a former commissioner of the slave trade. During his eight-year term (he died in 1700) the Chamber of Amsterdam realized that the golden days of the slave trade were drawing to a close, and urged the governor to reduce the expenses of the colony. "We fear that henceforth the expenses of Curaçao will exceed the revenues by far." The annual budget, comprised of the salaries of the Company's employees, the maintenance of the garrison, and the expenses for slaves, came to around 100,000 guilders. In 1697, the *Heren X* repeated this admonition and called the governor's attention to the fact that the Curaçao islands' expenses had skyrocketed over the past years. Twenty years earlier, they pointed out, monthly expenditures for the 63 Company employees on all three islands had amounted to only 26,000 guilders. In 1695, this figure had risen to almost 58,000, and there were more than twice as many on the payroll.

As an immediate measure, Bernagie was ordered to raise the poll tax from six *reales* to one *peso* per slave. Furthermore, it was suggested that the Dutch Reformed minister, the schoolmaster, and the Bible reader might all three subsist on private donations. Finally, the governor was invited to propose some new, moderate taxes to augment the Company revenues.

Soon after the WIC had assumed control over the Curaçao islands, it had conceived a vigorous agricultural program. When the slave trade had begun to prosper in the sixties, the Company had ordered its governors to establish a network of plantations over the entire island of Curaçao, and on these to produce food for the great numbers of slaves accumulating in the island's warehouses. These expectations ignored altogether the island's desertlike climate. Besides, the administration of the Company plantations turned out to be sadly inefficient. It was often mentioned that during the period from 1686 to 1693, the eight plantations of the WIC on Curaçao – mixed enterprises of stockraising and agriculture – had cost the Company 31,080 guilders to operate, while their yearly income had amounted to 31,970 guilders. After subtracting from this sum the 5 percent for the governor, and the $2\frac{1}{2}$ per cent for the commissioner of the slave trade, the net income came to 29,572.25 guilders, or a loss of 1507.75 guilders. Frequently, the losses were even larger, as in 1697 when, because of a long dry spell, a large number of horses and cattle perished. During that distressing year, the *Heren X* were forced to consider selling the Company plantations, along with the almost 600 blacks working on them. It was decided to sell five of the holdings, but there were no buyers. A few years later the plantations were again put up for sale, with the same negative result; whereupon the Company found it better to lease them out for a small but steady revenue.

The call of the *Heren X* to frugality was not received with enthusiasm. Although in obedience to his orders, Bernagie dutifully fired some of the higher employees and increased the poll tax, he did nothing to implement the other regulations. A direct confrontation between the governor and the angry Board of Directors was only avoided by Bernagie's death not long after receiving his latest rebuke.

Salt, one of the main reasons for the occupation of the Curaçao islands, had been the subject of many concerted experiments to enhance both its quality and quantity. The efforts of Van Campen to foment a salt industry on Curaçao, however, had met with failure, and what was subsequently sold in Amsterdam as Curaçao salt really came from Bonaire. In 1668, while the war between Spain and Portugal made Spain unwilling to buy Portuguese salt, the salt pans of Bonaire attracted the attention of one Jan Delian, who quickly requested permission of the Amsterdam Chamber to carry salt from that island to Spain.

Scenting profits in this proposal, the *X* denied Delian's request and chose to investigate the same possibility for the Company. Before long, salt was again a regular component of cargoes from Curaçao. A bare four years after Delian's rediscovery, the supply of salt stored in Company warehouses in Amsterdam was valued at approximately 100,000 guilders.

Other products, such as tobacco, sugar, cotton, and brazilwood, were also being exported to the United Provinces on a regular if modest basis. While tobacco had considerable attention as early as 1635, sugar is not mentioned until 1670. It never amounted to much since the quality was poor, and sugar cultivation stopped altogether in 1688.

Jan Doncker effectively broadened the base of agricultural exports by encouraging the cultivation of oranges, lemons, and other citrus fruits. So pleased were the *Heren X* with the results of Doncker's program, that they ordered his successor, Van Erpecum, not to abandon it under any circumstances. Van Erpecum himself introduced the growing of cotton, for which the Company, in a flare of optimism, sent him one hundred spinning wheels. Succeeding governors likewise catered to cotton until, in the nineties, the entire crop was devastated by caterpillars and production was abandoned once and for all.

Any colonist interested in migrating to the Curaçao islands could expect to receive, upon arrival, a plot of land. Although the grants were for the use of the land, rather than outright property deeds, this policy served the dual purpose of enlivening the island's agriculture and multiplying its population. Jan Doncker, in particular, concerned himself with attracting prospecting immigrants.

As early as 1651, the Company gave a charter to one João de Ilhão to colonize the islands and, not quite a full year later, did the same for another Portuguese-Brazilian Jew, Josef Nuñes da Fonseca, alias David Nassy. This charter has survived, together with its reissue of 1659, when a Jewish-Brazilian colony was established on Curaçao. Briefly, its articles authorized Nassy to bring an unlimited number of colonists to the island. Upon arrival, they were required to take an oath of allegiance to the Company, after which they received as much land as they could reasonably cultivate, excepting the *salinjas* or salt pans and the wooded areas. It was stipulated that the land had to be in cultivation within one year after the initial date of transfer. Furthermore, the colonists were to be exempt from recognition fees for a period of ten years and to enjoy full freedom of religion.

When De Ilhão left the United Provinces he carried letters of recommendation from the States General to Stuyvesant in New Netherland and Beck on Curaçao. He likely did not receive much cooperation from Company employees, probably because the directors had let it be known that he came to trade rather than to cultivate the soil. David Nassy had better luck. His Jewish-Brazilian colony survived. In 1660 it consisted of more than seventy persons, or twelve families, living in the Jewish Quarter with a synagogue and a cemetery, Beth Haim (meaning House of the Living). The first immigrants seem to have busied themselves mainly with the cultivation of sugar and tobacco until 1664, when, due to increased Anglo-Dutch friction, regular exports became impossible. Consequently, they turned to smuggling and privateering. With the conclusion of peace more Jews, mostly from Amsterdam, arrived on the island and were immediately absorbed by the hustle and bustle of commercial Willemstad. Before long, a new synagogue gave visible proof of a flourishing Jewish community. The first rabbi may have arrived on the island as early as 1674.

In addition to Jews, other colonists flocked to the Curaçao islands. On certain conditions, members of the garrison could remain in the colony after the expiration of their contracts and receive land themselves for agricultural purposes. This liberal policy, coupled with the steadily growing population, caused some problems. In the absence of an official property register, it frequently happened that planters fenced in larger pieces of land than were rightfully theirs, while others given permission to graze their cattle on Company land, misinterpreted their license and regarded the pasture as their property. By 1680, the Company had begun to be conscious of serious misappropriations of land, and ordered Van Liebergen to regulate property holding on the islands.

Sensing the turmoil such an undertaking would create, Van Liebergen confined himself to reissuing an older regulation limiting the possession of cattle. Even this mild measure met with poor results. In 1693, the X reiterated their order, while a year later Governor Bernagie was instructed to buy up all cattle held in excess of the quota, and to tell the guilty planters that henceforth the services of Company slaves would no longer be available to them.

Bernagie, however, made no real effort to enforce the law, and his successor made even less. Because of the far-reaching legal implications, the governor and his *Raad* were of the opinion that unravelling the knot would be more trouble than it was worth, and would cause unrest in the insular society's upper strata. In the end, the *Heren X* reluctantly accepted that view, and restricted themselves to introducing some kind of land tax, starting in 1714. This tax produced some results and met with minimal opposition.

The Company's attitude was at least partly inspired by its concern for the food situation. Cattle raising required very little outlay, and provided relatively inexpensive nourishment for the islands' inhabitants. In addition, the hides shipped home brought in a handsome profit.

Although there was some trade in cattle between the Curaçao islands and Jamaica, some of the Leeward Islands, and the Venezuelan coast, the Company did not look with favor upon this exchange for reasons of defense, and repeatedly urged its governors to tighten the controls.

With the conquest of the three Curaçao islands, the Roman Catholic religion was no longer countenanced, and its place was taken by the Dutch Reformed Church. However, the islands enjoyed an atmosphere of religious tolerance which was much more lenient than that on the British isles, and unheard of in either the French or Spanish possessions. Even if this flexibility was partly inspired by commercial motives, it remains undeniable that the Dutch, at least in the religious field, were far more broad-minded than their contemporaries. The restrictive placards issued from time to time against Roman Catholics, in particular Spanish priests, should be interpreted as conforming to a general historical trend rather than as an example of persecution. When, in 1635, the Zeeland Chamber, less tolerant than their Amsterdam counterpart, prohibited the public exercise of the Roman Catholic religion, they did not restrain its observance in the privacy of one's home. Employees of the Company were forbidden to attend such private services, and membership in the Roman Catholic Church was severely proscribed, yet it is questionable whether this harsh Zeelandian placard was ever enforced. The commercial interests and the very nature of the Netherlanders would have impeded the rigid application of this or subsequent laws of its sort. Only rarely does one come across any mention in the minutes of the *Heren XIX* or *X* of the expulsion of a Roman Catholic priest, and even then, the reason always lies outside of his religious activities.

While Roman Catholics were distrusted and their religion disapproved (the same happened, and worse, to Protestants in Roman Catholic countries), Jews were consistently honored as ranking citizens, and guaranteed the same freedom of worship enjoyed by their counter parts in Amsterdam. Some problems occasionally arose. Vice-Governor Beck, for instance, wanted to use the Jews' slaves, along with those of other slaveowners, to work on the new fort on Saturdays. The Jewish community, addressing to the Amsterdam Chamber, violently objected to what was to them a serious religious offense. The Chamber forthwith responded by ordering the governor to refrain from harassing their Jewish subjects, and expressed their surprise at Beck's order because "the Jews, in times of danger and distress have yet to shirk their responsibility."

The tax system in the Dutch colonies resembled the one in use in the United Provinces. The oldest tax was probably the *tenth*, collected by the Company annually on the produce of the islands: tobacco, maize, indigo, fruits, and other items. This tax seems to have been gathered with some difficulty. More than once, one comes upon the republication of the very same placard exhorting the population, under threat of heavy fines, to pay their dues. The *tenth* was finally abolished in 1695, to the relief of all concerned. In its place, a new tax was adopted, the *poll tax* on slaves. Originally four *reales* per slave, this tax was eventually raised to six *reales* and later to one *peso*.

Another tax was the *family tax*, introduced by Bernagie, and levied annually on all heads of family with the exception of soldiers and sailors.

Intended to relieve the Company from having to pay the salaries of the minister, the Biblereader, and the schoolmaster, in due time the family tax became just another of the many WIC levies.

At the end of the seventeenth century, the *placard tax* was instituted. Each ship entering the harbor was henceforth to pay two *pesos* for the privilege of carrying a placard nailed to the mast with the warning that it was strictly forbidden to throw waste into the water or to start a fire aboard. Another tax was the *weighage*, which the Company assessed on all shipped commodities of more than 25 pounds. At first, this toll amounted to 1 per cent of the value of goods worth less than six pennies, and ½ per cent of the remainder. Before long, however, a universal 1 per cent tax was charged on all goods regardless of their worth.

Also on the books was an *export tax* of 2 per cent on slaves, sugar, brazil-wood, and other items. Another source of income was the *import tax* of 8 per cent on woven textiles, flour, cheese, wine, beer, bread, beans, rice, and other foods, except bacon and meat, on which the tax was 4 per cent.

Besides these taxes, the Company raised money from harbor dues and transit permits. In a resolution of 1675, it was decreed that all ships entering the harbor of Curaçao from foreign ports should pay incoming dues of 8 per cent on the value of their cargoes, and exit rights of 5 per cent. Commodities from the Dutch East Indies were exempt. Dutch ships paid a tonnage duty of 30 guilders per ton as acknowledgment of the Company's right to 10 per cent of their tonnage. However, as the latter assessment was always paid in the United Provinces, it did not really pertain to the revenues the Company grossed from the three Curaçao islands. All these taxes together were never sufficient to pay the governmental expenses of the Company and had to be supplemented with profits from the slave trade and other commercial activities.

CHAPTER IX

THE EIGHTEENTH CENTURY

Since the beginning of the Nine Years' War, or King William's War, in 1688, William III, Stadholder of Holland and King of England, had been forging Europe's anti-French forces into a strong coalition under his own leadership. During the War of the Spanish Succession, or Queen Anne's War, which heralded the eighteenth century, these politics almost brought Louis XIV to his knees, although William himself died at the outbreak of hostilities. As the Dutch were now siding with England against France and Spain, there were, in the Dutch Antilles, many more repercussions of this conflict than there had been of the last war.

As soon as war had been declared, the Dutch West India Company authorized Nicolaas van Beek (1701–1704), the newly inaugurated Governor of the Curaçao islands, to issue *kaperbrieven*, or privateering commissions. Soon thereafter, however, the *Heren X*, apprehensive lest the actions of Dutch privateers imperil their trade with the Spanish colonies – continuing in spite of the war – ordered Van Beek not to hand out any further permits. But the English minimized the benefits of this measure. From their stronghold in Jamaica they preyed upon all Spanish shipping, and Dutch commercial intercourse with the enemy was severely hampered by the jealous ally.

At the end of May, 1701, Van Beek received word from the Amsterdam Chamber to strengthen Curaçao's defense system for possible attacks. Consulting with his *Raad*, the governor took appropriate measures, and, to protect the inlet of St. Ann Bay, requested the *X* to send an iron chain. The islanders contributed more than 3500 *pesos*, or approximately half the amount required for this end and other projects which included the restoration of the town wall.

Successful though he was in his dealings with the *Heren X*, Van Beek was less fortunate in affairs of internal administration. He soon became extremely unpopular among his subordinates, who filed a formal complaint with the States General, accusing the governor of usurpation and fraudulence. In 1704, Van Beek was relieved of his duties and replaced by Jacob Beck.

Almost immediately upon his arrival in Willemstad, the latter dispatched an urgent communication to the X with another proposal to fortify the town. In view of the rapidly developing European conflict, the X hastily approved his suggestions while two men-of-war, equipped by the Admiralty Board of Amsterdam, were stationed at Curaçao for the purposes of defending the islands, protecting Dutch trade with the Spanish colonies, and escorting Company ships back and forth across the Atlantic. It was also under Beck that the town of Willemstad spread to the other side of the St. Ann Bay, called Otrabanda, with the condition put by the X that construction be limited to one-story houses and an open field be left for the fort's cannons.

In order to compensate for the additional war expenses, Governor Van Beek had proposed, in 1702, an extra tax of 1 per cent on all Spanish goods brought to the island by privateers. His successor established a special privateering fund – *kaapvaart kas* – into which this tax was deposited to cover the equipment of men-of-war as needed. Furthermore, to meet the growing expense of the recently established convoy system, the Admiralty Board of Amsterdam instituted an extra 3 per cent tax on all commodities entering the United Provinces and an additional $2\frac{1}{2}$ per cent duty on all goods from the home country regardless of their destiny.

War frequently abounds in contradictory phenomena, and this particular conflict was no exception. So it was that although a state of war had been declared between Spain and the United Provinces, the two countries continued to be partners in trade, a situation already mentioned and benignly sanctioned by the *Heren X*. The latter even went so far as to convince the States General that Van Beek's privateering licenses were detrimental to the national interest, as a result of which all were abrogated. The English were more consistent in their practices – to the great dissatisfaction of their Caribbean merchants and planters. Evidence exists that the English colonists, however, did not altogether heed their government's official stand and there are well-known examples of their trade with the enemy, at times via Curaçao.

As commercial relations between the United Provinces and Spain's colonies in the West grew more and more lucrative, Dutch merchants, or their agents, began to settle in Caracas, La Guaira, and Cartagena. At the same time, Spanish and creole inhabitants of the coastal regions regularly crossed the narrow stretch of water to Curaçao in order to shop and buy supplies. As an inevitable concomitant of warfare, the island steadily rose in importance as a trading base for the adjacent coastal regions, and many a fortune was made by unscrupulous Dutch businessmen. Even Spain herself, cut off from her overseas empire but reluctant to forego the recently discovered delicacy of cacao, was more than willing to buy this commodity from the Dutch on Curaçao, who in turn acquired the beans from the Venezuelan colonists. Indeed, it is even known to have occurred more than once that Spanish ships laden with cacao bought on Curaçao fell into the hands of Dutch privateers, who returned it to Willemstad where it was again sold to Spanish merchants.

In reality, the Dutch suffered far more at the hands of their allies, the English, than at those of their enemies. After less than three years of continuous warfare in the Caribbean, they had lost a mere 3 ships to the Spaniards and 21 to their grudging comrades in arms. Not infrequently, Dutch privateers armed with English commissions which the governors of Jamaica were only too happy to hand out, seized their own countrymen's ships, as was the case in 1704 when one Reynier Tongerloo summarily appropriated 5 Dutch ships and confiscated their cargoes. England's ascending power paralyzed any Dutch retaliation against the ally, except for empty paper protests leading to long drawn-out trials. Regular sea battles along the Venezuelan coast between Dutch merchantmen or smugglers and English privateers were not uncommon.

The first ten years of the war had caused only minor ripples in the general atmosphere of peace prevailing on the Curaçao islands. Despite some occasional harassment, caused by friend more than by foe, few changes had been wrought in either their political or social structure. By 1712, however, the French had somewhat recovered from the devastating defeats they had suffered in 1709 and 1710. Profiting from the fact that Queen Anne of England wanted peace in order to aid her half-brother, the Pretender James III, to the English throne, the French organized a new West India Company, openly designed to plunder English and Dutch possessions in the Caribbean. The semi-official institution was financed by a group of wealthy merchants, the most prominent of whom was Jacques Cassard of Nantes.

Under the command of this merchant-mariner, one of the first fleets of the new Company sailed in 1712 to the Caribbean to harass the enemy. In January, 1713, the inhabitants of Curaçao were shaken by signs of an impending assault. Immediately, Governor Jeremias van Collen (1711–1715) ordered a state of siege and issued a decree forbidding any ships to leave the harbor. Vessels sailing along the coast were ordered to return forthwith, and armed guards were mounted on strategic points along the shores. Nevertheless, the governor's efforts to prepare the island's defense were hampered by a severe shortage in ammunition, guns, and men, reflecting the state of neglect characteristic of his and prior administrations.

To ward off the French Van Collen had at his disposal approximately eight hundred men, counting both professional soldiers and a hurriedly mobilized motley group of whites. The French had just scored a decisive victory over the Dutch settlements on the Wild Coast, and on the way to Curaçao had collected 3000 *pesos* in ransom from the island of St. Eustatius. Curaçao was buzzing with rumors and the people were, not unreasonably, filled with apprehension.

In February, 1713, the French fleet of twelve ships passed Fort Amsterdam to drop anchor in the Bay of St. Cruz on the western end of the island. The few troops stationed here stood by helplessly while the French disembarked and prepared to march on Willemstad. Held up by minor skirmishes, Cassard was able to reach Otrabanda after ten days where he mounted his artillery and sent a negotiator to Van Collen with a summons for surrender and ransom. The Dutch governor replied that since their two countries had recently agreed to a truce of two months, a siege was pointless. Cassard retorted that the alleged truce was merely a rumor. Still, Van Collen delayed, declaring the only ransom he could offer the French was gunpowder and lead from his cannons.

Haggling over the amount of ransom continued for more than six meetings. Only 400,000 *pesos*, the French insisted, would satisfy Cassard. The Dutch, on their side, were equally insistent upon lowering the price of their deliverance. After some time, the French dropped their demand to 300,000 and then to 250,000 *pesos*, upon which the Dutch raised their ceiling to 60,000. Ultimately, both parties agreed on 115,000 *pesos* to be paid in commodities, slaves, and ready cash, with the condition that if a truce had indeed been concluded in Europe, the amount would be refunded. When, at the end of March, this ransom had been duly paid, the French fleet left the Bay of St. Cruz.

So prosperous had Curaçao's merchants become that even this enormous sum made only a slight dent in the island's economy. When, the following year, the governor issued a plea for money to build several forts along the vulnerable south shore, the necessary 20,000 *pesos* were readily available.

Under Van Collen's successors, the island continued to prosper for some time, until years of unabated fighting against foreign privateers and pirates finally began to catch up with the economy. No longer content with stealing slaves and cattle from Aruba and Bonaire, in 1722 these outlaws murdered the Commander of Aruba in cold blood. Upon learning the news, the Governor of Curaçao, Jan Noach du Fay (1721–1731), former magistrate of Amsterdam, resolved to end this kind of outrage once and for all. Yet, when he put out heavily armed cruisers to guard the coast, complaints and accusations began to come in from the neighboring Spanish authorities that the

Dutch were violating the existing peace between their countries by boarding Spanish ships and forcing Spanish subjects into *rescate*, under pretense of enforcing the law. At the same time, many Curaçao Dutch were equally displeased with the new measure, as they saw profits reduced on their own privateering. Notwithstanding this adverse reception, it seems, nevertheless, that Du Fay did succeed in limiting the evils of piracy on the islands. The islands' years of prosperity, however, were rapidly ending. With the *Asiento Treaty* of 1715, Great Britain had assured herself of the coveted monopoly, and Dutch participation in this lucrative business was dwindling. A main source of revenue for the Company came to an end.

In the late thirties, after a lengthy European peace, there were indications that the precarious balance of power between the various European nations was again in danger. The United Provinces, no longer a power to be reckoned with in the political and military field, still remained the world's most important financial center; an alliance with the Dutch, therefore, was not only craved but ardently pursued – especially by the English.

In 1741, war again erupted (Great Britain fought since 1739) and was soon felt overseas in an abrupt decline in the volume of Dutch trade. The previous year Isaac Faesch had been promoted from Commander of the Dutch Leeward Islands to Governor of the Curaçao group (1740–1758), and immediately proclaimed a state of emergency, mobilizing every able-bodied white male. This mass conscription, coupled with the economic depression, resulted in an exodus which soon reached such alarming proportions that the colonial government was compelled to prohibit any unauthorized departures. A few years later, as the war continued, even boys of sixteen and free blacks were drafted. Although the Curaçao islands remained outside the theater of conflict, the swarms of war-fevered pirates and privateers who converged upon the area prevented all but the bravest from leaving the safety of the Schottegat. In 1745, for example, Feasch wrote the *Heren X* that five richly laden merchantmen had been captured by pirates just off the Curaçao coast, and complaints such as these were soon common. Yet the island was never actually attacked, and some prosperity returned when the peace of 1748 reestablished a semblance of normality.

Peace did not last long, however, for the tranquility of Curaçao was next threatened by a slave revolt. As early as 1740, lawlessness and recurring unrest among blacks had caused Governor Faesch to impose a 9 o'clock curfew and to limit their gatherings to no more than six persons. Even so, theft and robbery were almost a daily occurrence; by 1747 not even the town's cemetery was safe from the black grave robbers.

The slaves of the Curaçao islands originally came from the West African coast (Guinea and Angola), and traced their heritage to some of Africa's fiercest and proudest tribes. In 1750, refusing to submit to their white masters any longer, they rose in rebellion.

The revolt proper began at the plantation of Hato on the north coast of Curaçao, where a number of slaves armed themselves with rifles, axes, and knives, descended upon the neighboring houses, killed some loyal blacks, and burnt a few buildings. They were about to march on Willemstad when Governor Faesch, informed of the situation, sent a small military detachment of white soldiers and free blacks to wipe them out. The rebels, badly organized, had no chance against this disciplined opposition, and after a short time order had been restored. Some blacks preferring death to slavery, jumped from the high cliffs of Hato into the sea. What makes this first attempt by Curaçao slaves to regain their freedom so remarkable is the fact that the Dutch governor pitted blacks against each other.

In 1756, another European war broke out, the Seven Years' War or the French and Indian War, in which the Dutch suffered heavy trading losses everywhere, even though the United Provinces remained neutral. Many of their merchantmen were confiscated by the English, who were close to being masters of the seas. West India Company insurance premiums soared sky high to compensate for the enormous risks. The agreed cost for insuring a ship in convoy from Curaçao to Amsterdam climbed to as high as 9 per cent of its cargo.

After eighteen years in office, Governor Faesch died and was succeeded by Jacob van Bosvelt (1761–1762), who himself died before his firm program against piracy and privateering on Dutch ships could be carried out. Van Bosvelt was followed by Jean Rodier (1762–1782), whose name has become linked with one of Curaçao's most prosperous periods, although this affluence was not so much a consequence of Rodier's wise statesmanship as it was the inevitable sequel to the revolt of the North American colonies.

At this time Curaçao and St. Eustatius, already the central merkets for privateers of all nationalities, also became the foremost suppliers of European products to the American rebels – a lucrative source of income. Not only private merchants, but also the colonial government benefited greatly from the increase in trade. Furthermore, the war, in the sixties, between England and Spain, led the Spanish authorities on Tierra Firme to favor closer trading ties with Curaçao in order to have the protection of the Dutch flag for their own merchantmen. Thus, the island became not only a commercial center for the entire Caribbean, but a cosmopolitan meeting place where pirates, American rebels, not too respectable Dutchmen, upright Spaniards, and creole grandees from the coast rubbed shoulders.

Spain was evidently impressed by the might of Curaçao, but Rodier was not. The governor reported his disdain for the existing defense system to the *Heren X*, who agreed and approved his proposals to strenghten the defenses. Rodier wasted no time, and, in 1764, was able to submit an impressive list of his accomplishments to date. By that time, however, the initial fervor of the *X* had cooled. Arguing that both the fort and the town would succumb rapidly to attack, regardless of costly reinforcements, they discreetly discouraged any further reforms.

With the outbreak of the fourth Anglo-Dutch War in 1780 – provoked to a great extent by the United Provinces' open sympathies with the American rebels – proposals to improve the defenses were again taken up. From a report of that year we know that Rodier's views on this matter had changed over the years, and he now favored a more comprehensive strategy, which involved a citizen militia, furnishing more horses to the cavalry, and replacing the older soldiers with able-bodied younger men. His concern even extended to those houses – including the gunpowder house – which had been built so dangerously close to the fort that they could easily be attacked from the sea.

In spite of the governor's fears, Curaçao was allowed to watch the war actions from a distance, without becoming directly involved. Just prior to the war, a serious accident had occurred in St. Ann Bay when a recently-arrived Dutch man-of-war unexplainably exploded killing more than two hundred members of the crew, as well as an unknown number of civilians. A few years later, when a French fleet under Admiral De Grasse was badly beaten by the English under Rodney near the island of Guadeloupe, Curaçao saw other badly damaged men-of-war limp into the Schottegat. A year after that, Curaçao was visited by another French fleet under Rochambeau, which, having left France in 1781 to aid the Americans, was now returning to the mother country. At least twenty-eight French men-of-war dropped their anchors in the Schottegat at one time, and the presence of so many ships and men could not but make an impact on the island's social and economic life. All the excitement ended, however, with the coming of peace in 1783.

The Dutch conclusion of peace in 1784 came only shortly before the suspension of the West India Company which had, by now, long outlived the reasons for its existence. The colonists on the islands were dissatisfied with many aspects of WIC rule, not the least being the trade regulations arbitrarily set by the *Heren X* and their overseas representatives. The same feeling of unrest had also been brewing in the Dutch settlements on the Wild Coast: Surinam, Essequibo, and Demerara. Since Rodier's successor, Johannes de Veer (1782–1796), was unfit to ease the rising discontent, their High Mightinesses, as a last resort, took the unusual step of asking the *Stadholder*,

Prince William V of Orange, in his alternate capacity as Governor-General of the West India Company, to send an investigative commission to the colonies. This commission was to be composed of Squire William Grovestins, deputy of the States of Friesland to the States General, and William Cornelis Boey, sheriff of the town of Haarlem. A third member acted as secretary.

After brief stops at Demerara and Essequibo, the commissioners arrived at Curaçao at the end of August, 1789. They stayed for more than three months, handing in their report in February of the following year, – a document which remains one of the richest sources of information about the prevailing conditions on the Curaçao islands. As a result of their recommendations, and despite some efforts to the contrary, the West India Company was at long last disbanded in 1791, after a life span of 170 years.

The Grovestins and Boey report focused upon a critical period in Curaçao's history. Criminals and vagrants were on the loose. The more prominent citizens considered themselves properly exempt from any kind of contribution, and a new law had been passed under which the common man was to bear the lion's share of island taxation. Tension had mounted, and in 1785 a repeal of this measure was demanded and consented to by the governor after due deliberation with his *Raad*. The report concluded that in this matter the governor and the *Raad* had overstepped their authority and should be removed without delay. At the same time, the *Heren X* were accused of negligence and incompetence in their supervision of colonial affairs.

Prior to the dissolution of the WIC, Their High Mightinesses organized a Council of the Colonies and Possessions in Africa and America, which assumed responsibility as soon as the WIC was liquidated. This change of organization, limited as it was to the higher echelons of administration, had no apparent effect upon the internal life of the Curaçao islands. A much more significant aftermath of the fourth Anglo-Dutch War was the growing awareness among virtually all population groups of the new forces of freedom and enlightenment rapidly spreading across the globe. The influence of the new ideology was especially far-reaching among the slaves. An insurrection, more serious than the crisis of 1750, was the inevitable result (see chapter XV). Hardly suppressed, the Napoleonic wars began and the Curaçao islands once more suffered the fate of their dependency upon the mother country.

CHAPTER X

THE ENGLISH INTERREGNUM

During the last years of the eighteenth century the population of the Curaçao islands, and especially of the main island, had been divided on many issues. The philosophy of the French Enlightenment had been received by many people with great enthusiasm and was the subject of many a heated discussion in various clubs and social gatherings. Nor were the colored and black classes immune to this feeling of excitement; they grasped the new ideas with all the fervor their limited status would allow.

When, in 1793, it became known that the United Provinces and France were at war with each other, many of Curaçao's inhabitants openly manifested their French sympathies, forcing the Government to make it punishable to attack "the honor and reputation of the House of Orange." In May, 1795, the news arrived in Willemstad that the *Stadholder*, Prince William V, had fled to England and that the Dutch populace had hailed an invading French army as liberators.

Clashes between the pro-French "patriots" and the garrison now became a daily occurrence as the former, emboldened by this recent French success, strove to press their advantage to the fullest. A second slave insurrection temporarily united the opposing factions, but after the slaves had been brought back into subjection, animosity again erupted between the patriots and the Orangists or pro-*stadholder* group.

As an additional complication William V, from his exile in England, wrote letters (the Letters of Kew) to all Dutch overseas governors ordering them to consider the English as friends and the French as enemies. At the same time the governors received instructions from the pro-French States General to the contrary. On Curaçao, Governor De Veer tried to remain uncommitted to either of the factions. However, on August 10, 1796, it was learned that the *stadholder's* position had been liquidated, and that with the Treaty of The Hague the Batavian Republic – as the United Provinces were rechristened – had entered into an official federation with France. De Veer resigned, to be succeeded by the pro-English Jacob Beaujon, but the latter was opposed on every issue by the very pro-French *Raad*, and in turn made way for Johann Rudolf Lauffer, captain of the civilian militia and leader of a conspiracy against Beaujon. Lauffer enjoyed the support of the pro-French group and was also the favorite of French agents from Guadeloupe who strongly desired a closer alliance with the Curaçao islands against the British colonies.

Yet after his appointment – provisionally by the *Raad* and later officially confirmed by the States General – Lauffer had a change of heart and, turning a cold shoulder toward his former friends, decided to remain strictly neutral. With this collapse of solidarity from the top, the pro-French party disintegrated, making it possible for Lauffer to restore some semblance of domestic tranquility to the island. Suspecting the French agents of intrigue against his regime, Lauffer had them deported, after which he settled down to the business of government.

In 1800, in accordance with the Treaty of The Hague, five French ships asked permission to enter St. Ann Bay. Although his assent would have been perfectly legitimate, Lauffer, weary of all the trouble the French had caused him hitherto, wisely refused. There were some moments of tension, especially when the French were reinforced by a fully equipped man-of-war, but Lauffer remained cool and ordered the cannons of Fort Amsterdam to be in readiness. Fort Republic, built on top of the Sablica hill dominating the Schottegat as well as the St. Ann Bay and surroundings, was also put on the alert.

Upon witnessing these preliminaries, the French, who had already disembarked some troops, judged their plan too risky and decided to retreat. But before abandoning Curaçao altogether they chose the Bay of St. Michel as their target for one more attempt to occupy the island. Although the governor was able to rally a substantial defense in that area, he could not prevent the French from landing and marching on Willemstad. Otrabanda had to be evacuated and the enemy entrenched himself in the houses along the Bay facing Fort Amsterdam.

Lauffer was far from intimidated, yet even he had to concede that his forces would not be able to hold out much longer against the opponent's numerical superiority. At this time, an English war-frigate appeared off the coast and Lauffer managed to communicate his predicament. In return for the English captain's aid, the Dutch governor, authorized by the *Raad* and the Letters of Kew, signed a treaty with him on September 13, 1800, surrendering the colony to England. So began the first English period on the island, lasting until January 13, 1803.

Although the French were now clearly placed on the defensive, they were not actually forced to withdraw until a few days later, on September 22, when the defenders of the fort joyfully hoisted the Dutch and English flags. But it did not take long for trouble to arise again, this time with the English as the source of difficulties. Relations between the allies had become more strained daily, partly because neither Lauffer nor any of his subordinates could speak English, but also because the governor realized only too well that with the September 13 treaty he had signed away all real power. Watkins, the English commander, alienated the influential Dutch merchants by insisting they hand over the keys of their storehouses to convince him of the absence of contraband. A few days later, without consulting the Dutch authorities, he abducted the island's French inhabitants and kept them aboard his ship as prisoners of war. But when he broke into the warehouses, and encouraged his men to take whatever suited their fancy from the merchants' private homes, tensions reached a dangerous level.

In October, before matters could come to a head, Lord Hugh Seymour, the English Governor of Jamaica, arrived to put an end to any further pretensions of Dutch sovereignity and to take over the reins of government in the name of the King of England. The Dutch flag was lowered from Fort Amsterdam and, for the time being, disappeared from the island.

Although Lauffer was asked to remain in charge of civilian affairs, military control was effectively transferred to the English with Seymour himself as commander-in-chief. Upon the latter's return to Jamaica after six weeks, Captain Walter Tremenheere was left in charge of the troops pending the arrival of an English governor. On August 11, 1801, Lieutenant-Colonel William Carlyon Hughes arrived on Curaçao to head the new government; he was replaced in 1802 by Arthur Whetham, whose term of office was to last less than a year.

In 1802, the Peace of Amiens was concluded between France and England, as a result of which England was obliged to return the Curaçao islands to the Dutch. In January, 1803, the English formally departed and the area was restored to Dutch rule. Abraham de Veer was appointed governor by the government of the Batavian Republic, and on January 13, 1803, he set foot on Curaçao. De Veer immediately called the *Raad* together and fired Lauffer, sending him off to the home country to answer for his actions.

After years of uninterrupted warfare and privateering, the island was on the brink of economic ruin. Since 1795, not one man of war had entered St. Ann Bay, while the surrounding waters teemed with hungry privateers. Curaçao's merchants had suffered tremendous losses, and many were near poverty. To make matters worse, the treasury was empty, with no prospect of earnings in sight. Yet rumors of a new war were soon circulating again.

De Veer's first concern was with defense, and the public was enjoined to meet the cost of an expanded military budget. Needless to say, this appeal met with little enthusiasm, and only the most basic reforms were endorsed by popular vote. It was, among other things, decided to reorganize the civilian militia and to form a separate Corps of Dragoons headed by one of Curaçao's better known residents, Pedro Luis Brion. But as enlistment was optional, the Corps turned out to be a failure: of the hundred men solicited, only fifty-six were found willing to join.

In June, 1803, a member of the *Raad* received word that war had been renewed in Europe, and, grateful for this warning, Governor de Veer ordered the militia to cooperate with the garrison and to man the forts and several other strategic points. Hardly was this measure taken when Curaçao was visited by an English squadron. The *Raad*, hastily assembled, refused a demand to surrender, whereupon the English disembarked about 120 men at Piscadera Bay, found the local garrison of thirteen men to have fled, and advanced on Otrabanda. Meeting with no resistance here either, the English next proposed to march around the Schottegat but were prevented from doing so by a group of civilians led by one Manuel Carel Piar, to be remembered as a precursor of Venezuelan independence. Reluctantly, the English abandoned the campaign and, a few days later, departed. Yet, as they continued to control the surrounding sea and to keep the islands under a heavy blockade, Curaçao's economic predicament was unalleviated.

Just as detrimental as the English blockade, was the persistent threat posed by privateers, particularly those licensed on the neighboring French Antilles. As a result of these two factors, the arrival of ships from the home country became severely restricted, and acute shortages developed in many basic necessities. Prices soared and many an unscrupulous merchant made huge profits without regard for the sufferings of the poor and the slaves.

In March, 1804, Pierre Jean Changuion was appointed governor of the islands and, at the end of August, arrived on Curaçao. Before he had time, however, to settle down to the business of government, he was unexpectedly confronted by the frigate *La Franchise*, carrying an English flag, which, under pretext of exchanging prisoners, demanded entry into the harbor. Despite this critical situation, with only enough food for one more month, Changuion refused to be intimidated and denied the request. Catastrophe was only adverted by the timely arrival of some supply ships from the home country. The enemy withdrew.

In April, 1805, the English again menaced Curaçao, this time by landing troops at Portomari, on the western end of the island and out of reach of the imposing forts. After giving his men a chance to loot to their heart's content the English commander dispatched a firm demand for surrender. Once more, the Dutch refused. The English now partially shifted their attention to the east, disembarking some men near Fort Beekenburg. However, upon attacking this fort, they were repelled; nor was their other front in the west more successful. This stalemate lasted until June, when events for the English suddenly took a turn for the worse. Brion forced their troops in the east to retreat; moreover, their leader, Lord Murray, suddenly died. Again the English withdrew, although they persisted in their efforts to patrol the surrounding waters. Curaçao's position, however, improved so substantially that Changuion even felt free to dispatch some troops in order to rescue the other islands of the Curaçao group which the enemy had often occupied even though they were utterly useless without the main island.

The lessening of the English peril coincided with an increase in French activity on the island, with Curaçao's four hundred or so French inhabitants carrying on a vigorous program of propaganda and spying.

In 1806, rumors of peace were adrift again and the imminent demise of the Batavian Republic was predicted. Indeed, at the end of November the news arrived that Napoleon had decreed the country a monarchy to be ruled by his brother Louis Napoleon as King of Holland. But France and England remained at war, and in the Caribbean the English blockade continued to extract heavy tolls. The occasional arrival of a solitary Dutch ship came to be viewed as a godsend.

Toward the end of the year, a heavily armed fleet of seven English ships, under the command of Sir William Bolton, appeared off Curaçao's coast, and Changuion was again summoned to surrender the island. As expected, he refused and the English fleet ostensibly sailed away. On nearby Aruba, however, they were joined by additional ships and men, and the overall command was transferred to Sir Charles Brisbane.

Meanwhile, the Dutch at Curaçao had been lulled into a false sense of security. Governor Changuion cheerfully set out on the evening of December 31 to spend New Year's Eve at home with his family, leaving Frederik H. Pfeiffer in command.

The evening was celebrated, as usual, with all kinds of elaborate fireworks. Many Dutch officers were guests of Curaçao families, and the air was filled with merriment. Indeed, Pfeiffer, by refusing to abandon his post at Fort Amsterdam, was among the very few who took their orders seriously.

Unknown to the revelers, the English fleet was stealthily approaching around the eastern tip of the island. Early in the morning of January 1, the lieutenant in charge of Fort Beekenburg detected the enemy ships and fired warning shots to alert both Fort Amsterdam and Fort Republic. Brisbane realized that he had been seen and that the town was on guard, but in the end resolved to go ahead as planned.

The guard at Fort Amsterdam reported the warning shots from Fort Beekenburg at 5 a.m. Soon afterward, the enemy was sighted proceeding along the southern shore of the island. A state of emergency was immediately declared and the forts sealed off from the outside. As had been arranged before he had left for his plantation at Blenheim, Governor Changuion was notified with still another alarm shot.

With a recklessness not customary for one of his responsibility, and totally unexpected by the Dutch, Brisbane sailed directly into St. Ann Bay aboard the *Arethusea*, bearing the white flag of truce and passing under the very nose of Fort Amsterdam. Too late the fort opened fire, and the Dutch were forced to stand by helplessy while Brisbane, out of reach of their cannons, lowered landing sloops and brazenly occupied both the town and the fort, entering it from the undefended landside. It was the first time that an alien force had set foot in famous Fort Amsterdam.

Brisbane's boldness guaranteed an English victory. When Governor Changuion finally returned to the fort, he was confronted by an accomplished fact and found himself a prisoner. Fort Republic remained in Dutch hands, however, a continuous a threat to the English as its artillery reached as far a Willemstad, Fort Amsterdam, and St. Ann Bay. The Dutch men-of-war – the *Kenau Hasselaar* and the *Surinam* – had been put out of combat when a fortunate shot by the enemy had killed their commanding officer.

Changuion requested that he be allowed to confer with his *Raad* on the terms of surrender. The ensuing deliberations lasted the whole day, being twice interrupted by an impatient Brisbane. As presented, they contained the following points:

1. The surrender of Fort Republic.
2. The retention of all government employees in their respective offices.
3. Recognition and respect for all private property, including the merchandise in the warehouses, and all merchantmen, whatever their nationality.

Changuion then ordered the garrison of Fort Republic, the sole remaining Dutch stronghold, to lay down their arms. The transfer of power was soon accomplished, and from January 1, 1807, to January 16, 1816, the island was again under English rule.

Brisbane asked Changuion to remain as governor, but the latter refused to become a puppet of the English. Upon his return to Holland, he was brought to trial and condemned to death, a penalty, however, which was never executed. Under King William I, the former governor was restored to all his honors to serve in other high positions. He died in 1820 in Surinam.

After Changuion's resignation and subsequent departure, the English appointed Sir James Cockburn as the new Governor of Curaçao. He was succeeded, in 1809, by John Hodgson, who governed until September, 1814, to be followed in turn by John LeCouteur. In 1816, the Curaçao islands were formally returned to Dutch Governor-General Albert Kikkert according to the agreement reached between the new Kingdom of the Netherlands and Great Britain.

The second English period, unlike the first, left a deep impact on the history of the island, not only for the political innovations introduced at the time, but, seen in retrospect, for the English success in effecting a maximum of change with a minimum of dislocation.

During this period the English strengthened their precarious hold over the island by revitalizing all existing defenses. From the first, Brisbane fully recognized the strategic value of the new possession. Fort Republic – now rebaptized Fort George – and Fort Amsterdam were staffed with sufficient men and provisions to outlast any possible siege. In spite of the articles of surrender, Englishmen were put in key positions, and before long, the governmental bureaucracy was entirely in English hands. Laws and official proclamations, at first accompanied by their Dutch translation, were soon issued in English only.

It cannot be denied that the new regime did everything in its power to avoid friction with a hostile population. In doing so, the English exhibited a rare degree of tolerance, especially during the initial period of adjustment. A principal problem was the increase in taxes which the government felt compelled to levy, but this form of protest was not strange to the island, as taxation had been a source of constant discontent even during the days of the WIC. In general, as long as trade and commerce prospered, the merchants, who formed the most influential clique among the inhabitants, were willing to accommodate themselves to the new situation.

And indeed, fortune seemed to beckon once more. With the lifting of the blockade, the volume of trade soon regained its former level. While from 1795 to 1807 commerce had declined and many merchants had left the island to settle on others, such as the English Antilles or Danish St. Thomas, at this time a reverse migration took place and many of these returned, to be followed by English merchants from other islands, anxious to share in the good fortune.

As of 1807, Curaçao, now considered British territory, automatically became a part of England's colonial trading system, and relations long proscribed by the Navigation Laws were suddenly and officially sanctioned. In addition, the island was declared to be a free port – a definite asset in the revival of prosperity.

As soon as the news reached Curaçao that England and Spain had decided to set aside their mutual disagreements in order to join forces against Napoleon, Cockburn sent a trade mission to Caracas to inform the local captain-general of the political situation in Europe and to mend relations with the continent. As a result, all Venezuelan ports were opened to British ships and Curaçao benefited directly. The gratitude of her merchants manifested itself in a memorandum of September 1808, addressed to Cockburn, in which they not only thanked him for the support he had rendered to their cause, but also pledged their wholehearted allegiance to the British king. Cockburn, furthermore, was presented with a gift of £ 6000 "as a trivial indemnity."

For reasons of health, Cockburn resigned before long. He was temporarily replaced by John T. Layard, former commander of the garrison. Layard took the necessary precautions for a foreseeable French invasion, calling all free men to arms. However, the French threat failed to materialize.

In 1811, Layard was succeeded by John Hodgson, who soon after taking office, was faced with two pressing problems. The first was of a domestic nature and concerned the chaotic state of finances. The governor was forced to impose new taxes, which, together with a loan, provided temporary relief.

A second dilemma had been created by the rebellion of the nearby Spanish colonies. In 1810, some patriots in Caracas had proclaimed the independence of Venezuela. From the start Hodgson found himself embroiled in the complexities of mainland politics, a situation from which he found it impossible to extricate himself. Yet not only did he maintain strict neutrality in the ensuing civil strife between Spain and her colonies, but, at the same time, he never completely lost sight of the potential benefits which would accrue to commerce in case Spain were to lose her footing in the New World. His biggest problem was, of course, to keep on friendly terms with all parties concerned: Spain, the Venezuelan insurgents, the Curaçao merchants, and Great Britain, Spain's ally in Europe – a task at which he acquitted himself reasonably well.

After the capitulation of Francisco de Miranda, Hodgson offered sanctuary to both Miranda and Simón Bolívar, but only the latter arrived to claim his hospitality. The defeated patriot lived for some time in a house in Otrabanda, where he allegedly prepared his famous Cartagena manifest. His residence became a meeting place for other exiled patriots, of whom approximately fifty were living on the island. Bolívar, who had arrived at the end of August, 1812, left in November of that same year to start the campaign which resulted in the Second Venezuelan Republic.

After the defeat of Napoleon in the Battle of Leipzig, the inconstant map of Europe changed again as the Low Countries became a combined monarchy under the House of Orange. A few months later, Hodgson left Willemstad and was provisionally replaced by John Le Couteur.

The London Convention of August 1814 formalized the relations between Great Britain and the new kingdom, prescribing the return of the six formerly Dutch islands to their erstwhile owners. While the Letters of Kew had guaranteed the restitution of all Dutch territory temporarily in English custody, the Peace of Amiens of 1802 had reversed this decision and the government of His British Majesty now chose to ignore both former agreements. Under the Convention, therefore, England returned their islands to the Dutch, but retained important parts of Guiana: Essequibo, Demerara, and Berbice.

News of this treaty did not reach Curaçao until October, and the prospect of a return to Dutch rule did not generate much enthusiasm. In Venezuela, where the British were held in high esteem as potential allies in the war for independence, public opinion was likewise inclined to view the transition with distrust.

Events in Europe, however, delayed an immediate transfer of power on the islands. Napoleon's escape from Elba plunged the continent into a major crisis with the fate of the new Kingdom of the Netherlands in uncertainty. Not until the French had been decisively beaten at Waterloo could the stipulations of the London Convention finally be carried out and King William I, the new King of the Netherlands, have an opportunity to direct his attention to his overseas domains.

CHAPTER XI

THE DUTCH LEEWARD ISLANDS IN THE SEVENTEENTH AND EIGHTEENTH CENTURIES

When the Dutch first set foot on the Leeward islands they found all three uninhabited, although the fragmentary remains of primitive tools revealed the former occupancy of stone-age Indian tribes.

Just prior to the discovery of these islands by the Spaniards, the resident Arawaks had been conquered and reduced to slavery by the Caribs. Presently the former, who had attained a slightly higher cultural level than the more bellicose Caribs, saw their traditions and customs adopted by the victors. The Arawaks were able to maintain their language and to preserve the ritual of binding and deforming infant skulls. As was their habit they also painted their bodies and inaugurated boys into manhood by covering them with human fat to give them strength and courage. Their dead were buried in a squatting position, although not in burial urns as on the mainland.

When Columbus came to these regions on his second trip to the New World, he christened one of the islands St. Martin, probably because it was discovered on this saint's day. Very likely Columbus' St. Martin is not the present St. Martin but rather neighboring Nevis. Columbus is also said to have discovered Saba and St. Eustatius although he never actually set foot on either island. Spaniards may have derived the name St. Eustatius by onomatopoeia from an Indian word. Saba's name is sometimes attributed to the Arawak word *siba*, meaning rock. Another interpretation points to the biblical Sheba or Seba.

All three small islands are located in a triangle, within 5 degrees of the Tropic of Cancer. Saba is 32 miles from St. Martin and 20 miles from St. Eustatius, while St. Martin and St. Eustatius are 38 miles apart. The three of them are more than 550 miles from Curaçao.

The Lesser Antilles, of which the Leeward Islands form part, were a temptation to English, French, and Dutch trespassers in the Caribbean. English and French occupancy of some islands dates from the first years of the seventeenth century; Dutch efforts at permanent settlement had to await the foundation of the West India Company and the end of the Twelve Years' Truce with Spain.

What finally culminated Dutch interest in these regions were proposals to exploit the salt pans, to cultivate tobacco, and to establish commercial relations with the English and French colonists. Through the Zeelandian Chamber, merchants requested permission from the *Heren XIX* of the West India Company to settle on the islands. These requests were duly granted after an "Order for Colonization" had been drawn up and approved by the States General of the United Provinces. Among the first to take advantage of the new ordinance was Jan de Moor from Flushing, who immediately fitted out several expeditions to the Wild Coast, Tobago, and St. Martin. But the colony he founded on Tobago in 1628 was destroyed by the Spaniards nine years later. Several other Dutch attempts to colonize Tobago were defeated, either by the Caribs or by the French and the English.

Even before the publication of De Laet's *Description of the New World*, the Dutch knew of the existence of rich salt pans north in the Antilles chain. Pieter Schouten had been on the island of St. Martin in 1624, and three years later another squadron under Dirck Simonszoon van Uytgeest had inspected the island's fabled salt pans. However, St. Martin was not permanently occupied by the Dutch until 1631, when a fleet of Dutch salt carriers dropped anchor off its coast, and by that time there may have been as many as fourteen French families already living on the other side of the island.

Rather than having direct Company rule, the new Dutch colony was to be governed by a patron system not unlike the English counterpart of lords proprietors with the patron owing his commission and ultimate responsibility to the WIC. Jan de Moor was St. Martin's first patron; Jan Claeszoon van Campen the island's first governor.

Spain obviously resented this intrusion but was powerless to act. Objection came, however, from another quarter where the Dutch actions were interpreted as a direct violation of sovereign rights. The English kings, James I and his son Charles I, had bestowed grants in the Caribbean to some of their noblemen: James to Robert Rich, Earl of Pembroke, and Charles to James Hay, Earl of Carlisle. To this protest the Dutch correctly replied that they had found the islands uninhabited. Their occupation of St. Martin, thereafter, was never seriously challenged by the English.

Dutch possession had one main motive: salt. They had lost the battle of Punta de Araya and were not doing very well at Tortuga either.

St. Martin's salt was of good quality. In spite of the drawback that the island lacked water, within a year after occupation the garrison consisted of 100 men and the Great Bay was frequented by many salt carriers, not only Dutch but also French and English ones. If the testimony of William Guine, an English captain familiar with the state of affairs, is correct, 90 ships visited the island in the first year of Dutch occupation, 1631, and more than 100 the year after. The salt trade flourished; its profits are said to have paid for two thirds of the expenses of the 6000-man garrison in Pernambuco, which had become a Dutch colony in 1630.

For some time Spain took no action, but Dutch presence was the subject of many heated discussions both in the Spanish War Council and in the Council of the Indies. Puerto Rico's governor, Enrique de Sotomayor, was particularly disturbed by the enemy's thriving salt trade so near by. In an urgent letter he warned the king that the intruders must be evicted before they had time to entrench themselves. Furthermore, a Dutch fleet of more than 200 sails was rumored to be coming from Pernambuco to St. Martin in order to assault both Havana and San Juan de Puerto Rico.

A special committee appointed by Philip IV to study the situation recommended an immediate attack. Whereupon a fleet reinforced with five *galeones* and under the command of the Marquis de Cadereita was fitted out. Cadereita had strict orders not to endanger the treasure ships nor delay their return to Spain in the fall. By April of 1633 everything was in readiness and the Spanish – 53 sails strong – set out for the Caribbean. After first mistaking the island of St. Bartholomew for St. Martin, the fleet arrived at its destination at the end of June. Dutch Governor van Campen was summoned to surrender. He refused. The Spanish thereupon disembarked 1000 soldiers and 300 sailors, and brought several cannons on shore. At the end of the following day, after the Dutch fortress had been cannonaded from both land and sea, the Dutch governor found his position untenable and opened negotiations. Cadereita was under royal orders to be generous: free retreat for the Dutch and transportation back to the Netherlands. By July 1, the Spanish flag was flying from the fort, where it would remain for the next fifteen years, guarded by a direly neglected garrison.

However, the Dutch continued to shovel salt off the small island of Anguilla, which they had occupied at the same time as St. Martin, and they soon found a new base in the Caribbean with the conquest of the Curaçao islands. In 1643, Curaçao's Peter Stuyvesant lost his leg in an unsuccessful effort to reconquer St. Martin. In 1648, for reasons of their own, the Spanish quietly abandoned St. Martin, which was immediately reoccupied – by the Dutch on one side and the French on the other.

Meanwhile, the loss of St. Martin may have been instrumental in stimulating the Zeelanders to launch a new plan of colonization. A company founded by enterprising merchants under the direction of Jan Snouck of Flushing, requested permission of the *Heren XIX* to start a settlement on the island of St. Croix, or, if soil and climate were not convenient, on another island in the area. In 1636, two ships under the command of Pieter van Corselles (who had previously founded a Dutch colony on Tobago) left Zeelandian ports with some 50 colonists. Arriving at St. Croix, the emigrants were disappointed to find an English settlement already in existence, and sailed on to St. Eustatius, which they found deserted and hence more favorable. They called the island New Zeeland. Pieter van Corselles became commander, and with the help of some of the colonists, formed a *Raad* with legislative and judicial prerogatives.

One of the first things to be taken care of was security. On the ruins of a former French bastion overlooking the bay, Fort Orange was built, and stocked with the necessary guns.

Again the English protested, but being informed by the States General of the firm resolution of the *Heren XIX* to keep the island, Charles I did not impose his claims. Thus, St. Eustatius remained firmly in Dutch hands, and, in 1640, its colonists spread to the neighboring island of Saba.

For the next twenty years no important changes took place. On the three Leeward islands, St. Martin, St. Eustatius, and Saba, Dutch settlers turned their attention to tobacco cultivation and salt. In 1648, there was a boundary dispute took place with the French on St. Martin but the problem was settled peacefully with the Dutch retaining possession of the salt pans. In this same year the patronship of the island, exercised by the De Moor company, was appropiated by the well-known Lampsins brothers from Flushing, who also looked after Tobago.

The Peace of Westphalia, ending eighty years of strife with Spain, meant that privateering had to be given up for colonization. The difficulties with Portugal in the fifties, resulting in the loss of New Holland (Dutch Brazil), did not affect the political situation either in the Caribbean or on the Wild Coast. Neither did the first Anglo-Dutch War.

Cornelis Jol's successful exploits on the West Coast of Africa outlined a greatly expanded Dutch Western empire around the Atlantic. This enlarged sphere of influence included the most important slave-providing regions in West Africa, as well as New Holland, the Wild Coast, the Dutch Caribbean islands, and New Netherland. Its expenses were paid by the profits of the budding Brazilian sugar industry, trade in the Caribbean, and the slave trade – the latter monopolized by the West India Company.

This Dutch expansion moved the English, after the Restoration, to the mercantilist policy mentioned above. The Dutch, after suffering initial losses in the ensuing second Anglo-Dutch War, launched a counter-offensive to regain St. Eustatius but were cheated out of victory by their French allies, who, carrying the banner of the King of France and pulling rank over the

Dutch who stood under the command of the Prince of Orange, were the first to enter the island's fort. Once inside the French closed the gates, and it took the States General months of painful negotiations to regain control of the island.

As said before, the new patrons of St. Martin were the Lampsins. Cornelis Lampsins died before the outbreak of the second Anglo-Dutch War but while his brother Adriaan and his son Jan neglected the island, it was kept in Dutch hands by Commander John Simpson. In 1668 the island was plundered by a privateering band of Englishmen. But from then until the third Anglo-Dutch War, St. Martin was allowed to prosper in peace.

As soon as this third conflict exploded, Governor William Stapleton of the British Leeward islands prepared himself to attack the neighboring Dutch possessions. In June, 1672, he arrived with a small squadron in St. Eustatius and occupied the island just before a disappointed French force, arriving too late, would have done the same. Some days later the English also took Saba.

But after the combined Anglo-French attack on the United Provinces had failed, the Provincial States of Zeeland felt strong enough to fit out a force of seven ships under the command of Cornelis Evertsen, scion of that well-known Zeelandian family, to patrol West Indian waters and reconquer whatever the English and French had captured. At the same time, the city of Amsterdam also equipped a squadron of some six ships and put them under the command of Jacob Binckes. The two squadrons met in the Caribbean but their combined operation was not too successful. The planned attack on Martinique failed; and although St. Eustatius was restored to the Dutch, instead of maintaining the island, they demolished the fort, set fire to all the buildings, and left. They did reconquer New Amsterdam, however. With the Peace of Westminster of 1674, the English recognized their loss of St. Eustatius and Saba, but by agreement with the States General, they re-garrisoned the island and stayed for as long as the United Provinces were at war with France. Thus, when Dutch privateer Jan Erasmus Reining tried to reconquer St. Eustatius from the English, he was informed of the situation and relinquished the attack.

No sooner had the outbreak of war become known in the Caribbean than Governor de Maynie of St. Martin occupied the Dutch part. A second expedition of Jacob Binckes, in 1677, again underwritten by Amsterdam with the object of re-occupying the island of Tobago, resulted in another series of offensives against the French islands and St. Martin was subsequently restored to the Dutch. But because Binckes left the island without a garrison, the French overran the Dutch half again immediately after he had left.

With the Peace of Nijmegen in 1678, St. Eustatius and Saba were returned to their former patrons, but St. Martin remained in French hands until 1690.

The last twenty years of the seventeenth century were years of Anglo-French tensions in which the United Provinces played a diminishing role, although Dutch economic power still made them welcome allies. Peace prevailed until the year 1688. But with the advent of King William's War, many of the islands were brought to the brink of ruin. The outbreak of hostilities became known in the Caribbean in March, 1689, and within a month the French were attacking St. Eustatius. Fort Orange soon surrendered and once again the island was French. Saba, however, repulsed the enemy.

Shortly before, in September of 1688, the British Leeward islands had received a new governor, Sir Christopher Codrington. Informed of the French victory on St. Eustatius, the latter immediately sent some ships to protect the strategic island of Nevis; nevertheless the French managed to overrun the English part of St. Kitts largely due to the fact that English loyalties were divided between King William and James II causing their men to waver at the crucial hour. By December, 1689, the English had resolved this dilemna and were ready to assume the offensive. First they turned to St. Bartholomew, which was captured; next they tried St. Martin where they were beaten. St. Eustatius, the object of their subsequent campaign, posed no problem and was easily overtaken. Notwithstanding these mixed results, the English belligerency did result in a general exodus of French colonists from St. Martin, and at the end of the war, in 1697, the Dutch found themselves again in possession of all three of their Leeward islands, prostrated as these were.

The eighteenth century opened with another war between the European powers, and the United Provinces were again involved. Their islands, barely recovered from the previous war's calamities, once more became the target of enemy privateers. However, when in July, 1703, 600 French filibusters landed in St. Martin's Bay of Marigot, they were unable to conquer the Dutch part. A similar attempt to take St. Eustatius equally failed.

A few years later, in 1706, the French tried anew, and this time they were able to pillage Nevis, the English part of St. Kitts, and St. Martin. But the Dutch and the English were soon in control again – a situation buttressed by the Peace of Utrecht. From that year on the island of St. Martin quit changing owners for the duration of the rule of the West India Company.

Although their first effort to capture St. Eustatius had failed, in 1709, the French filibusters made a second attempt – this time with better success. Much booty fell into French hands, although they soon took off and Dutch commander Lamont resumed possession of the island.

There was one more attack to come. In January of 1713, Jacques Cassard – the same man who would also successfully raid the Wild Coast and Curaçao – accomplished the surrender of St. Eustatius. But the island had not yet recovered from the raid of 1709, and there was little with which to satisfy Cassard's greed. He accepted the small ransom of 3400 *pesos* and left within a month.

The eighteenth century contrasts with the stormy seventeenth by a period of almost undisturbed prosperity. Their patronships having expired, the islands became directly dependent upon the new West India Company. Around the middle of the century, with the outbreak of the War of the Austrian Succession, improvements were made on their fortifications. At this time too, John Philips, St. Martin's energetic commander, after whom the town of Philipsburg was to be named, repeatedly advised the *Heren X* to conquer the French half of the island not only for political reasons but also in order to alleviate the Dutch half's overpopulation. In the thirties almost 200 more Dutchmen had come to the colony, increasing its population to over 500, and with the slaves more than twice that number. Although they knew that the French part counted at most 50 people, the *Heren X* had no desire to invite more trouble with the 150,000 guilders the venture would cost, and rejected Philips' suggestion.

Saba and St. Eustatius were also prospering in this period. In 1740 the capital of St. Eustatius, Oranjestad, had nearly 1000 inhabitants and more than 150 houses. After the *Heren X* abolished a one per cent import tax on commodities in 1757, the island's busy commerce soon gave it the name of the Golden Rock. One of the most traded items was sugar, introduced on the Leeward islands after the New Holland debacle of 1654. Even after the London government promulgated the Molasses Act in 1733, many an Englishman continued to smuggle sugar from St. Eustatius to the American colonies in English barrels, pretending that it came from the English Antilles. Sugar exports kept increasing, especially after 1770, when most of this merchandise came from the British, French, and Spanish islands. The enormous scale of Dutch trade and smuggling carried its built-in disadvantages. For one thing, it brought many unsavory characters to the island, and for another, the English were well aware of what was going on and their men-of-war kept up a steady patrol in the Caribbean hunting down all alien vessels trading with the British islands. St. Eustatius is said to have suffered, as early as 1750, losses of ships and cargoes, valued over and above a million guilders, while a few years later this figure was reported at over 1,200,000 guilders. At the end of the fiftees the United Provinces made a pretense of protecting its navigation lines by sending a squadron to the

Caribbean. Its mission was made ineffective, however, when it was ordered to stand by, not to fight – an impossible task. The days of Heyn and De Ruyter were gone, and a war with Great Britain could not be risked.

In the sixties, the French and Indian War, known in Europe as the Seven Years' War, caused another boom in smuggling activities which reached a peak during the American War of Independence. The outbreak of this struggle, in 1774, brought as many as 20 American ships at a time crowding into the small bay at St. Eustatius to buy supplies needed by the rebel patriots. At least 3000 ships seem to have visited the port in 1779, exchanging sugar, tobacco, and other products which brought good prices on the Amsterdam market, for rifles and ammunition.

The United Provinces, at least in the beginning of the conflict, were supposedly neutral, and the Dutch colonists, merchants and planters, enjoyed, for a time, the advantages of this policy. Protests by the English to The Hague resulted in an order emanating from the States General prohibiting the export of war-material to North America – an order which, unenforced was a dead letter, and enforced was anulled by smuggling.

Johannes de Graaf, the Governor of St. Eustatius in those days, also received strict orders to maintain neutrality. The Dutch governor and his *Raad* were merchants. Although De Graaf as commander earned only 500 *pesos* annually, it is known that as a merchant he made at least 30,000 more. He owned a fourth of the island's real estate and more than 400 slaves. Obedience to the new order would have ruined him and his co-merchants, but his ingenuity found a solution: shipping gunpowder as tea!

De Graaf had been commander of the island for seven months when, in 1776, an American brigantine, the *Andrew Doria*, dropped anchor in the bay and lowered the Grand-Union flag in greeting. The garrison's commander answered by hauling down the Dutch banner; whereupon the *Andrew Doria* gave a salvo of eleven shots and De Graaf ordered, as a perfunctory courtesy, a counter salute of probably nine shots. The only unusual detail about this event was that the ship belonged to the rebellious colonies of Great Britain, which De Graaf had not been authorized to recognize. The captain of the *Andrew Doria* had been received, not as a rebel, but as a promising client.

De Graaf's gesture, along with the attitude of the Dutch merchants of St. Eustatius, was brought to the attention of the English governor of St. Kitts who entered an official complaint, but the Dutch governor declined to apologize. The Englishman next informed his immediate chief, the Governor general of the British West Indian islands, of what had happened, adding that after having bought arms and ammunition in the Dutch colony, another American ship had ventured to seize an English one. The complaint was forwarded to London, and in February, 1777, the English ambassador to The Hague peremptorily asked the States General to reprimand its governor.

In spite of its undoubtedly arrogant tone, the States General complied with the British request. The British government was mollified, and in the meantime, back at St. Eustatius, the garrison's commander routinely saluted every ship that entered the bay, including those under the rebel flag.

De Graaf, arriving in the Netherlands wrote a voluminous self-defense and was subsequently sent back to St. Eustatius. Although his actions were not responsible for the outbreak of war between the Netherlands and Great Britain, nevertheless, they had certainly done nothing to promote an atmosphere of understanding. Relations between the two countries rapidly entered a phase of distrust. Before the end of February, 1778, the States General sent a squadron of eight men-of-war to the Caribbean under Rear-admiral Van Bijlandt, who, by choosing the Golden Rock as his base, emphasized the importance of this island relative to Curaçao. During the time they spent in the West Indies, the units of this squadron were repeatedly engaged in skirmishes with British privateers. Van Bijlandt could not stop the British from conquering the French half of St. Martin, but the French were able to reclaim their colony a few months later.

In the beginning of 1780, the British admiralty sent Sir George Bridges Rodney to the Caribbean with a fleet of eight ships, soon to be reinforced with some more line-of-battle units, frigates, and galleons. He was ordered to occupy St. Eustatius without delay, thereby severing the connection between the American rebels and the United Provinces, before another Dutch fleet – the Van Bijlandt squadron had left the area – could arrive in the Caribbean. These orders were issued at the end of 1780 – a month after war was officially declared.

St. Eustatius had just endured a hurricane when Rodney, with 3000 men, appeared at the mouth of the bay to find the small harbor crowded with more than twelve merchantmen, one Dutch warship, and five men-of-war of the rebellious American colonies. The odds were clearly against the Dutch garrison of 50 men. Nevertheless, a few shots were exchanged for honor's sake before the island surrendered.

All the ships in the bay were seized, although the Americans clearly resented having to give up without some show of resistance. A convoy of 24 merchantmen which had left the bay just prior to the arrival of the British, was pursued and seized in an engagement which cost the life of Rodney's rear admiral. By flying the Dutch colors over the fort for more than a month, the English lured many more Dutch and American ships into the bay and were able to carry off around 150 more of these, among them 60 belonging to the American rebels – an almost paralyzing blow to their cause.

From St. Eustatius Rodney sent a squadron to St. Martin which was unprotected and easily taken. The English admiral next pondered the advisability of an attack on Curaçao but wisely judged his forces too weak. He stayed on St. Eustatius, creating such havoc and devastation that the commander of the English troops, John Vaughan, declared in a report to his government, that the Golden Rock was no longer worth the trouble of maintaining it for the king. Indeed, never again did the island recover its former prosperity. The estimated value of the booty, not including captured ships, was between three and four million pounds.

Rodney left after a few months leaving his vice-admiral Hood, to bring back to England part of the enormous booty. Unfortunately, the latter ran into a powerful French fleet under the Count de Grasse; Hood was defeated and lost his gold. Rodney, still in the Caribbean, did not dare to risk an encounter with the superior French forces and sailed home. But in the mouth of the Channel he met similar bad luck when part of his loot was taken by French privateers.

In the Netherlands there was much consternation about the loss of the Golden Rock. The French, allies of the Dutch, made plans to recapture the island, and in November, 1781, a small French force, under the command of the Marquis de Bouillé, disembarked 400 men without alerting the English garrison of 650 soldiers. When the Frenchmen suddenly attacked, confusion reigned; the fort was taken and the island was lost to the English. A few days later another French force seized the Dutch half of St. Martin. When the English also lost Saba, all three erstwhile Dutch Leeward islands had become French.

France and the United Provinces, at this time, were allies against England. Consequently, when peace was concluded in 1783 at Versailles, the islands returned to Dutch control. After the actual change of government took place in 1784, the Dutch West India Company decided to open up the islands' trade to all nations, with the result that prosperity was somewhat revived and many inhabitants who had fled, returned. Before the English assault, for instance, the white population of St. Eustatius had consisted of less than 1400 people. Ten years later the number of whites passed 3000. A similar thing occurred on St. Martin, where the white population increased from 600 to 1200.

Now that there were no patrons, the commander or governor of the most important island, St. Eustatius, had the other Dutch Leeward colonies under his jurisdiction and was represented on St. Martin and Saba by sub-commanders. In 1787, the governmental bureaucracy was further simplified by appointing only one commander, stationed on St. Eustatius, for all three islands – a reorganization too short-lived to prove its worth.

In 1792, the United Provinces became involved in the first European coalition against revolutionary France. In the West Indies, the Dutch population of St. Martin took the initiative, invaded their neighboring half and captured Fort St. Louis at Marigot, which they rechristened Fort Willem Frederik after the oldest son of the *stadholder*. Three years later, the Netherlands were occupied by French forces, causing the demise of the United Provinces and the emergence of the Batavian Republic, and before the end of 1795, when this republic became a satellite of France, the roles of the Dutch and French on St. Martin were reversed. The French also occupied St. Eustatius and Saba.

French rule was unpopular and brief. In 1801, with the cooperation of the Dutch population, the English seized the three islands. But they did not stay long either, for with the Peace of Amiens in 1802, Dutch rule was reinstated.

Soon afterwards, the Council of American Colonies and Possessions, successor to the West India Company, re-organized the lines of command for the Leeward islands. Saba, which had always been administered from St. Eustatius, was now linked to St. Martin. Secondly, on the latter island, the Dutch hold was strengthened by the construction of a new fort, known as Fort Gelderland. In Europe, meanwhile, Napoleon soon liquidated the Batavian Republic and set up instead the Kingdom of Holland, with his brother Louis Napoleon as puppet king. In the hectic years from 1803 to 1810, the Dutch Leeward islands managed to remain free from either French or English control. But in February, 1810, an English fleet attacked the French part of St. Martin, appearing off Philipsburg to demand surrender. In spite of the huge sums just spent on an effective defense system, the island's authorities were disinclined to fight. Saba was included in St. Martin's surrender, and a few days later St. Eustatius followed suit.

The Curaçao islands having been vacated by their Dutch defenders for several years prior to the English occupation of the three Leeward islands, the Dutch flag disappeared from the Caribbean, where it had flown for almost two centuries. Under British rule, trade with the other antilles increased and a strong British fleet protected intercolonial relations.

In 1814, at the London Convention, the English agreed to return the six Caribbean islands to their former masters. When, in the course of 1816, the actual exchange occurred, the Dutch flag reappeared in the West Indies where it was to remain until the present day.

CHAPTER XII

THE WILD COAST FROM PRE–COLUMBIAN TIMES TO 1621

Little is known about Surinam's pre-Columbian inhabitants. Cave sketches, the *timehri*, discovered near the Marowine and Corantine rivers reveal the former presence of Indian tribes whom ethnologists, on ethnic as well as other grounds, have traced to the Arawaks rather than to the more nomadic Caribs. Their *kitchen-mounds* are reminiscent of similar waste mounds foundamong the Toltecs of Mexico, although wether this apparent link is significant has yet to be determined.

In addition to primitive drawings and mounds, excavations in several parts of the country have uncovered axes, clubs, hammers, and spades, all made of stone. In all probability these tools were manufactured by tribes living upstream and were traded to the lowland Indians for food and other commodities, with the Marowine River serving as the main commercial artery between the various tribes.

Besides stone tools, other evidence has been unearthed on the customs of these Indians. Big jars have been found in which the bodies of dead adults, in a squatting position, were interred. Children were buried between hollow plates. Frequently, weapons and other personal objects accompanied the dead into these graves. Ornaments of gold, some in the form of a half moon, have also been discovered and a religious significance proposed. Talismans of so-called Amazon stone, probably worn by the women, may have had some connection with fertility rites, or, on the other hand, have served as amulets to ward off disease.

Toward the end of the fifteenth century, the Guiana highlands were invaded by swarms of Caribs and Arawaks who undoubtedly absorbed the earlier inhabitants, while hotly contesting each other's right to settle in the new country. It is not possible at this time to ascertain which of the conquering tribes was the first to set foot in the territory; it is a known fact that their arrival cannot have preceded that of the Europeans by more than a short period. Arawaks and Caribs kept up a continuous combat with each other until well into the seventeenth century.

The Caribs were by far the more warlike of the two particularly in their methods of killing the enemy and dealing with the vanquished. Rather than assimilate the subjugated tribes, for whom they had only disdain, they made a conscious effort to preserve their own culture and language, and sought to establish a rigid, two-class social structure in which they, the masters, lorded over the subject masses.

The Arawaks, on the other hand, pursued a far different course and one geared to their particular needs. Their expansionism was not so much the result of a militant spirit as a consequence of their agricultural system, by which the land was soon exhausted and they were forced to move on. Upon settling in a new region, the Arawaks traditionally admitted the inhabitants into their social system through exogamy, and since by the Arawak matriarchal system the position of the mother's clan was enhanced, they thus promoted the fusion of the two cultures. This method of colonizing foreign territory was not only peaceful but led to a widespread diffusion of Arawak culture in northern South America – a factor which severely inhibits tribal research, already complicated at the time when English and Dutch seventeenth century travelers, unable to distinguish between the different tribes and confused by the variety of allegiances, indiscriminately labeled all local Indians *galibes* or Caribs.

In his description written in 1668, Major Scott estimates the number of Indians living in the Guianas at 100,000 and locates the various tribes along the many river systems. While his statistics seem highly doubtful, they nevertheless support the theory that before 1492 the majority of the Indians lived in the coastal regions and that the arrival of the white man forced them deeper into the interior.

Surinam, the territory comprising Dutch Guiana, most probably derived its name from the Surinas, an Indian tribe which had migrated from the left bank of the Amazon River, near the Rio Negro, to settle in this area. They called the region Surina or Suliname.

Alonso de Ojeda, passing along the Wild Coast in 1499, dismissed the Guianas as uninhabited and unimportant. The Wild Coast, of course, had been incorporated by the Treaty of Tordesillas into the Spanish colonial empire, but the Spanish government did not grant permits for the colonization of the area until 1531. Portuguese settlers, starting somewhat earlier, moved from the Amazon northward, and after 1580 it is not always easy to distinguish which were Spanish colonizing efforts and which were Portuguese. No one seems to have settled, however, in the Guianas before the English arrived here at the end of the sixteenth century.

Sir Walter Raleigh's description of the Wild Coast, entitled *The Discoverie of the Large and Bewtiful Empire of Guiana,* stimulated the Dutch to follow the English into these regions, although even before Raleigh's propaganda, the *pichelingues* or privateers from Flushing had established two trading posts, Fort Orange and Fort Nassau, up the Amazon River.

Only one report, written by a ship's clerk, has survived with respect to those Dutch expeditions of the sixteenth century. Unlike the exaggeration of Raleigh's, this document tends to give a realistic account of the area. At the same time it reveals, interestingly enough, that the Dutch, although at war with Spain in Europe at this time, were generally well received by Spain's governors and their Indian subjects in the New World.

Unlike their thrust into the Caribbean, aimed primarily at licit or illicit trade and privateering, the Dutch ventures on the Wild Coast were directed toward permanent settlement almost from the outset. Their first forays had produced trading posts; later excursions resulted in the foundation of a fort in the Essequibo region which, according to Spanish sources, was destroyed in 1596, about the same time that the Dutch fortified trading posts on the Amazon were destroyed by the Portuguese.

After 1598, the sight of Dutch ships off the Guiana coast became a regular occurrence, although colonization efforts were temporarily abandoned when the United Provinces and Spain agreed to the Twelve Years' Truce. In 1613, before the Truce was due to expire, two settlements were founded by Zeelanders on the Essequibo and Corantine rivers, but these colonies shortly fell prey to the Spaniards from neighboring Trinidad.

Despite these failures, the Dutch were back in 1615, laying out new settlements on the Cayenne, Wiapoco, and Amazon. In 1616, at least two expeditions fitted out by Jan de Moor left Flushing. One ensconced itself near the Cinipape River, and survived only six years. The other group, under the command of one Aert Adriaanszoon Groenewegen – Llanes in Spanish and Gromwegle in English sources – headed for the Essequibo and settled in an area formerly inhabited by the Portuguese. The ruins of an old fort were restored and called *Kijkoveral,* meaning See everywhere.

Under Groenewegen's effective leadership the colony on the Essequibo River soon prospered. Groenewegen had a way of ingratiating himself with the natives and even earned the hand of the local *cacique's* daughter in marriage. With relationships thus cemented, Groenewegen himself presided over the colony for almost half a century, and died in 1664, at a ripe old age, an extremely wealthy man.

The founding of these and other settlements was a hazardous task, compounded by inexperience as well as the sustained hostility of the Spanish, the Portuguese, and the Indians. Long is the list of those who perished, yet were it not for their courage and perseverance, the history of these regions would have taken quite a different course. In 1615, King Philip III ordered the coast of the Guianas to be cleared of all alien settlements. In the Portuguese bases on the Amazon, an expeditionary force was put together which fanned out toward the north and the west, and carried out the royal command with a thoroughness which only excepted the colony of Groenewegen. It meant the beginning of Portuguese dominion of the Amazon delta.

Not until the foundation of the Dutch West India Company could colonization efforts on the Wild Coast hope to be permanent. And even after the Company took over the responsibility of sponsoring new enterprises, failure, many times, was just around the corner.

CHAPTER XIII

DUTCH COLONIZING EFFORTS ON THE WILD COAST

Prior to 1621, the sporadic Dutch settlements on the Wild Coast had all been undertaken as independent patronships. After that date, although the patron system was not abrogated until much later, all expeditions and colonies were brought under the authority of the West India Company. The *Heren XIX*, determined to make a resounding success of the merger, accompanied its installation with a flurry of activity.

In 1623, the *Pigeon* (Het Duifken), under Jesse de Forest, sailed for the Amazon with French Huguenots aboard. Fearing Portuguese reprisals, the colonists ultimately decided to settle along the Wiapoco (Oyapoc) River at the place where Jan de Moor had established a short-lived colony eight years previously. This enterprise suffered much the same fate as its predecessor and the settlers returned home the ensuing year.

A new expedition, also originating from Flushing, soon followed. It stood under the command of Nicolaas Oudean and Philip Purcell, both veterans of earlier travels to the area. Their colony, augmented by English settlers, was attacked and overcome by the Portuguese and their Indian allies in 1625. The efforts to colonize nevertheless continued. The next year, 1626, saw two expeditions leave Flushing, one under Claude Prevost headed for Cayenne, the other under Jan van Ryen with the Wacogenive River as its destination. Both groups were wiped out by the Indians. Only one settlement at Berbice, sponsored by Abraham van Pere, a rich Zeelandian merchant, did better and managed to survive despite the odds.

Obviously Zeeland had much at stake in the tiny colonies. Except for the abortive expedition of Theodore Claessen in 1615, all Dutch settlements in the Guianas had been founded and nourished by Zeelandian money and blood. Groenewegen was a Zeelander, as were all the others involved in exploring this region. Therefore, there was both alarm and irritation in Zeeland when, in 1635, Amsterdam sent out an expedition of its own. But the *Heren XIX*, who were immediately petitioned to recognize Zeeland's prior "rights" in the area, denied the presumptuous demand.

The Amsterdam expedition in question was led by David Pieterszoon de Vries, and, like the previous one under Claessen, was aimed at Cayenne. It consisted of only one ship with thirty colonists who, upon their arrival in the Wild Coast area, restored an old fort, presumably French, on the small island of Mecoria, and began cultivating the soil. After De Vries' departure, nevertheless, the colony quickly collapsed – a failure which was joyous news in Zeeland.

With the conclusion of a lasting peace with Spain and the renewal of the WIC charter for another twenty-four years, one might have expected rapid development at last in the Dutch colonies on the Wild Coast. The Company, however, now found itself curtailed in its privateering, and bankrupted by the long and fruitless struggle over New Holland. It was not until deep in the fiftees that the WIC finally realized the hopelessness of its Brazilian undertaking. At that time Amsterdam, probably encouraged by a resolution of the *Heren XIX*, renewed its interest in the Wild Coast and approved a request by Jan Claessen Langendyck to settle in the area. Accompanied by thirty or forty colonists Langendyck forthwith took possession of Cayenne and founded a small Dutch colony which, when it ran into difficulties after a few years, was turned over to the Chamber of Amsterdam. Langendyck remained as commander from 1659 until he was replaced in 1663 by Quirijn Spranger, under whom the colony was forced, in 1664, to surrender to the French.

In the early fifties the Zeelandian Chamber once again ventured to colonize the Guianas, this time with the express condition that colonists buy their supplies only from, and sell their produce only to Zeeland, thus monopolizing its pretended "rights" in the area. Between the Pomeroon and Maruca rivers, close to the mouth of the Orinoco, a new settlement subsequently sprung up, drawing people from neighboring Tobago. Prospects for this new colony considerably improved after the loss of Pernambuco by the Dutch, when many Brazilian refugees, mostly Jewish, came to join the settlers.

The exact impact of the first Anglo-Dutch War on the Wild Coast is unknown, although an interruption of communications with the mother country and a certain shortage of supplies may be presumed. Relations between the Dutch and English settlements remained harmonious, and at the end of the war the political situation in the Guianas was unchanged. There were, in 1655, three permanent Dutch settlements, Essequibo, Berbice, and Pomeroon; one English colony on the Surinam River, founded by Francis Lord Willoughby, as well as a few intermittent Dutch and English posts; and not one French foothold.

Zeeland's problems with her Wild Coast enterprises, however, continued, and in June, 1657, the Zeelandian Chamber of the WIC petitioned the Provincial States to assume responsibility for its entire colonial venture. Later that same year, the three great trading towns of Middelburg, Flushing, and Vere offered to commit themselves to the task. The new sponsors took their job seriously, and enthusiastically dispatched many ships to Nova Zeelandia (as the western part of the Wild Coast was now christened) as well as to Africa for slaves. Before long, a new colony was added at the confluence of the Pomeroon and Moruca rivers. Nevertheless, New Middelburg, as it was known, literally never got off the ground, and only the foundations showed where forts and buildings were once planned.

In January, 1658, one David Nassy received a patent to establish a Jewish colony as in Cayenne similar to the one he had founded six years earlier on Curaçao. The new settlement was to be located at the prescribed distance from the older Langendyck colony, and in the end suffered the same fate when the French overran the entire region in 1664. By that time Groenewegen had died and the Dutch settlements were languishing, despite the financial aid provided by the States of Zeeland.

In sharp contrast to these floundering Dutch colonies, stood the thriving English settlement in Surinam, founded in 1650 and brought under the governorship of William Byam in 1663. In that year the colony boasted many plantations and a population of 4000, slaves included. When David Nassy and his followers were turned adrift by the French, they fled from Cayenne to Surinam contributing to the prosperity of Byam's colony.

After the outbreak of the second Anglo-Dutch War, Surinam was used as a base for English attacks on the Dutch settlements, all but one of which fell into English hands. From their remaining outpost in Berbice, the Dutch started a counteroffensive and recaptured Fort *Kijkoveral*, where the starving English garrison were only too happy to surrender to them instead of to the French, who, as allies of the Dutch, retook Nova Zeelandia and the Dutch Pomeroon colony. Thus far, the war had resulted in unmistakable advantages for the French.

The Zeelandian States now launched a vigorous new campaign. As far as the Zeelanders knew, all their settlements on the Wild Coast had been seized by the English, and they were eager to reclaim them before the French could intervene.

In December, 1666, a small Zeelandian fleet of seven ships, under the command of Abraham Crijnssen, left Flushing. Crijnssen was commissioned to reconquer Surinam, to evict the English from Essequibo and Pomeroon, to reestablish Zeelandian authority on the island of Tobago, to attack Barbados, and to hassle the English wherever he could. He was also requested to contact the French and to invite their cooperation.

The Zeelanders arrived in Cayenne in February, 1667, and found the colony in French hands. Since Crijnssen did not wish to antagonize these dubious allies too soon, he proceeded to Paramaribo, Surinam's capital. Governor Byam was invited to surrender, which, after a stubborn show of resistance, he did. Fort Willoughby now became Fort Zeelandia.

The reduction of Surinam to the Dutch flag had been fortuitous. It was succeeded by a strengthening of the Pomeroon settlement in order to make it impregnable. Crijnssen, however, had lost considerable time accomplishing these objectives and was forced to delay his departure for Tobago until the end of April. At that time, finding the island uninhabited, he installed a garrison before proceeding to Guadeloupe, where he joined forces with the French. Due to the incompetency of the French commander, De La Barre, the Franco-Dutch fleet lost the Battle of Nevis to the English under Berry.

The Peace of Breda restored her colonies to the United Provinces and added Surinam in exchange for New Netherland. The Zeelandian States now sent Hendrik Rol as their governor to the Wild Coast. His energetic efforts brought some prosperity to those colonies – especially Essequibo. Rol did not so much concentrate on agriculture as on trade with the Indians, which resulted in the establishment of Dutch outposts as far west as the Barima River. Rol's services were highly appreciated by his Zeelandian employers, who increased his salary and sent him reinforcements.

Of the small colony of Berbice little is known before 1670. One rare source of information is a report written by Adriaen van Berkel, secretary of the colony, in the latter part of the century.

More important than Essequibo, Berbice, or Pomeroon, was Surinam. The colony quickly recovered from the destruction caused by Henry Willoughby, who, in spite of the articles of the Breda peace, had been unwilling to hand back the colony after the English reconquest. In due time Surinam became the center of Dutch power on the Wild Coast. When a new West India Company was chartered in 1674, Surinam kept its special status as a Zeelandian price and was not incorporated into the new mandate. The colony was spared involvement in the Anglo-Franco-Dutch controversy of 1672, and the Dutch expedition under Jacob Binckes which, in 1676, recaptured Cayenne, bypassed Surinam, that colony being firmly in Dutch hands.

After the chartering of the new West India Company, the States of Holland drew up plans for an additional colony on the Wild Coast. The Chamber of Amsterdam, thrilled about the project, urged the States General to place the settlement on either the Wiapoco or the Aprowaco. Both rivers were easy to defend, and neither was, at this point, held by Europeans. In addition, the Indians of the area were peaceful, and the outlook for trade was good. Unfortunately for the Dutch, just as the project was in the process of being realized, two of the new colony's officials – the governor and the Dutch Reformed minister – quarreled. The French from Cayenne (captured from the Dutch by Admiral D'Estrées) were quick to seize the opportunity and razed the settlement. So ended the last Dutch attempt to claim the Wiapoco.

Sixty-five years of Dutch efforts to colonize the Wild Coast thus resulted in firm control of Surinam, Essequibo, Pomeroon, and Berbice. The policy of extending trade to the more remote areas in the interior of the country, initiated by Rol, was pursued for many years by the Zeelanders with most satisfactory results. Their network of warehouses, called *loges*, located on the main rivers and their branches, may have had no great political significance, yet they brought the Dutch what they wanted: profits.

CHAPTER XIV

SURINAM UNDER THE CHARTERED SOCIETY

When the new West India Company was established, the Provincial States of Zeeland were responsible for the Surinam colony. In 1682, Zeeland, tired of this responsibility, sold its rights for 260,000 guilders to the Company. The sale met with the approval of the States General, who gave the *Heren X* a ten-year monopoly to trade with their new acquisition and to import slaves. But the huge expenses of government and defense soon obliged the WIC to take on two partners: the city of Amsterdam, and Cornelis Aerssen van Sommelsdyck, a prominent diplomat of a rich family. The Chartered Society of Surinam, as this partnership was called, existed from 1683 to 1795, with Amsterdam and the WIC holding after 1770, when the Sommelsdyck family sold their part, each half of the shares. According to the charter, which became the basis of governmental policy for the colony, the Colonial *Raad* or Council was to be chosen by all free colonists from among the richest, the ablest, and the most moderate men.

In the same year that he became a shareholder, 1683, Aerssen van Sommelsdyck decided to go to Surinam in order to personally look after his and the colony's interests. He was a strong-willed man, the type of leader needed in a colony where adventurers outnumbered planters and cattlebreeders, and debauchery was widespread among the whites while the slave population lived in the utmost misery.

Severe as he was with respect to drunkenness and gambling, Governor Van Sommelsdyck was tolerant in terms of religion, admitting to the colony Labadists, Huguenots, and even Roman Catholics. The Jews, who had been residents of the colony for almost thirty years, were given even bigger privileges. As a token of the esteem in which they were held, the governor himself attended the inauguration of their synagogue. Religious toleration was accompanied by economic reform. The far-sighted Van Sommelsdyck provided the colonial treasury with a growing source of revenue by establishing a $2\frac{1}{2}$ per cent tax on the export of sugar. He improved irrigation by digging the Sommelsdyck canal. He introduced governmental supervision on measurements and weights and fixed the prices on food-stuffs. Above all, he assured the undisturbed development of agriculture – particularly the cultivation of sugar – and cattlebreeding by ending the many intrusions of Indians and *Marrons* (escaped slaves or maroons) onto plantation grounds. Peace was concluded with the Indians, and, in 1686, the protracted strife between the Caribs and the Arawaks also came to an end. An agreement reached with the powerful *Marron* group at the Coppename River was reaffirmed by the construction of Fort Sommelsdyck at the junction of the Commewine and the Cottica. In addition to all this activity, the governor enlarged and embellished the capital, Paramaribo.

The results of strong rule, abundant fertile land, and unlimited supplies of slaves, soon became evident. During Van Sommelsdyck's term of office, the number of plantations rose from 50 to 200, and the production of sugar from three to six million pounds a year, with the export of tobacco and wood increasing proportionally. Courts for criminal and civil justice were created. Life became normalized, slaves, especially those with Labadist or Huguenot masters, were treated better; and no Indians were molested or enslaved.

All of these improvements were accomplished in spite of the conservative planters on the *Raad* who opposed any innovation. The governor was required to work with this *Raad*, ten members of which were his personal choices from among the twenty candidates submitted to him by the free colonists. Although the latter particularly resented his protection of Negroes and Indians alike, Van Sommelsdyck was able to defend himself, with some success, against their complaints to the Board of the Chartered Society.

In 1688, Van Sommelsdyck's governorship ended abruptly. The soldiers and condemned criminals being used on various irrogation projects mutinied, demanding more food and less work. When the governor refused, he was summarily killed. Briefly, the rebels were masters of the town, until the loyalists regained control, executed some of the offenders while sending others back to the United Provinces.

The year of Van Sommelsdyck's death was also marked by the beginning of King William's War, or Nine Years' War, in which the Dutch sided with the English against the French. Although the French fleet which, in 1689, attacked Surinam left after a few days, the Dutch colony was too close to Cayenne for the peace of mind of Van Sommelsdyck's successor, Governor Van Scharpenhuizen. But the latter's efforts to strengthen the colony's defenses were misunderstood and even opposed by planters and merchants alike, both of whom were afraid of too much executive power. Disappointed, the governor retired in 1696. A year later the Peace of Rijswijk was signed;

Surinam had not noticeably suffered and the defenses of the colony continued to be neglected.

In 1701, the War of the Spanish Succession, or Queen Anne's War, broke out, and again the Dutch sided with the English against the French. Many Dutch merchantmen fell into the hands of enemy privateers who infested the entire Caribbean. One of these, Jacques Cassard presented himself, in the summer of 1712, at the mouth of the Surinam River with two ships. Repelled in July, he reappeared in October within sight of Paramaribo, this time with eight huge men-of-war, a large number of landing craft, and 1000 soldiers under his command. He sailed up the river past the town and attacked the undefended plantations upstream. Panic reigned supreme; women and children took to flight, slaves plundered and killed.

Only after enough havoc had been created did Cassard send his negotiators to Paramaribo. The governor, under pressure from his *Raad*, had no choice. After some stalling the Dutch paid an enormous ransom: nearly half a million guilders in cash, sugar, and slaves.

After Cassard had departed, confusion continued to pervade the colony; everyone blamed everyone else. The planters demanded to have their losses indemnified by the Board of the Chartered Society, but in spite of prolonged litigation nothing was granted. Besides the 700 ransom slaves, valued at 350 guilders apiece, the planters also lost many others who had escaped to join the *Marrons*. It took the colony years to recover.

The other Dutch colonies on the Wild Coast, to which Demerara was soon added, did not fare much better. Berbice endured a French raid in 1689; while in 1712, it was besieged and forced to pay a ransom of 120,000 guilders in cash, sugar, and slaves. Essequibo, attacked twice before, in 1708 and in 1709, in 1712 paid 50,000 guilders to the French in order to keep them from occupying the fort and from ruining the plantations.

In spite of this ominous beginning, the eighteenth century was, on the whole, a booming period for the Dutch Guiana colonies. Recovering from the French raids, they all enjoyed a long period of peace; while their defenses lay in disarray, the number of plantations rose steadily intil by 1740 it had reached 400.

From 1742 to 1751, Johan Jacob Mauricius, a capable man with an excellent record in colonial affairs, was appointed Governor of Surinam, and under his leadership the colony attained peaks of prosperity. Although the first Surinam coffee had made its appearance on the Amsterdam market as early as 1724 and the first bales of cotton ten years later, when Mauricius assumed the govenorship, sugar and wood were still virtually the only export products. Now, however, the narrow economic base of the colony was expanded to include not only coffee and cotton, but cacao and tobacco as well. The slave trade also increased in importance, as more and more laborers were needed. With the consent of the languishing WIC, a new company of Zeelandian origen, the Middelburg Commerce Company, took over this trade and provided the colony and the remaining Dutch Guianas with the requisite number of blacks for many years to come.

Not until the War of the Austrian Succession threatened to engulf the European continent, did the colony's defenses again become a matter of concern. Mauricius restored some of the older fortifications and started the construction of additional ones. He also concluded new agreements with the *Marrons*, although not before his troops had set fire to some of their villages. What angered the *Raad*, however, was the fact that he also procured to broaden the scope of slave legislation initiated by Van Sommelsdyck. The governor had made an effort to be tactful and recognize the *Raad's* prerogatives but being outspoken and straightforward by nature, Mauricius could not help but have made himself several powerful enemies. In particular, he had earned himself the hatred of a group of people known as the *Cabale*, whose accusations reached the ears of the *Heren X*. The difficulties between the governor and this opposition attained a climax when a Jew named Salomon Duplessis, well known as a member both of the *Raad* and the *Cabale*, went to Holland and delivered a list of the *Cabale's* complaints to the States General. A committee appointed by *Stadholder* William IV to investigate the issues came to the conclusion that the charges were based on false premises. Nevertheless, Mauricius, after having been summoned to defend himself in person before the Board of the Chartered Society, and having successfully argued his case, was not allowed to return to Surinam and someone less controversial was appointed in his place.

During Mauricius' tenure, an effort had also been made to exploit gold and other minerals. A certain Wilhelm Hack, having received a twelve-year concession to develop mining, founded the Chartered Surinam Mineral Company which began operations with a capital of 96,000 guilders. But the results of its excavations around the Blue Mountains were not encouraging, and the money was soon exhausted, ending, for the time being, any other endeavors in this direction.

Attempts to encourage white immigration were equally disheartening. The colonial government, faced with an annual increase among the slave population of 2000, not including the huge death toll, actively sought to recruit more colonists, mainly from Germany and Switzerland, even offering attractive enticements of land, tools, and cattle. But the many adversities which lay in wait for the innocent newcomers seemed endless. Tropical diseases afflicted them, and the attacks by the *Marrons* demoralized them.

In spite of these annoyances, the continuously increasing prosperity of the colony at this time can be measured in several distinct ways: by the volume and prices of the export products, by the receipts of the custom offices, by the fortunes made by the absentee and resident planters, by the sales in tropical products, and by the increase in navigation between the colony and the outside world, primarily the mother country.

At the Peace of Breda, when many English planters had left taking their slaves with them, the colony contained only 23 plantations and 560 slaves. Eighty years later, the number of plantations had mushroomed to 430 with more than 50,000 slaves; and in the latter half of the eighteenth century there were over 450 plantations in Surinam with 60,000 slaves. Paramaribo alone had almost 10,000 inhabitants by 1788, with more than 1400 houses. The neighboring Dutch colonies of Essequibo, Demerara, and Berbice grew comparably.

This prosperity was interrupted, from time to time, by falling prices for wood, coffee, and sugar, on the European market, as well as by destructive slave revolts, absenteeism, and other social problems. A depression in the European economy would affect the basically undiversified economy of the colony drastically. Nevertheless, attracted by huge profits that could be made in sugar and coffee in the days before Governor Jan Nepveu arrived, more and more Dutch capital was invested in the colony and loans were acquired without much collateral. It is known, for instance, that in 1751 an Amsterdam banker advanced one million guilders to some Surinam planters, initiating a practice of granting loans of up to 60 per cent of the totally assessed value of the plantations. There were, of course, restricting conditions, the most burdensome probably being the requirement that all produce be sent to the creditor, but the easy way in which large amounts of money could be borrowed led to overinvestment and ended in the crash of 1773 – the first effective blow to Surinam's economy.

One contributing factor to this crisis was absenteeism. When it became easier to borrow money, many planters returned to the *patria*, leaving their plantation in the hands of overseers who were sometimes unexperienced, often dishonest, and almost always brutal. Another factor was the practice common to commercial houses of spreading false rumors in order to bring about fluctuations on the Amsterdam Bourse. In 1773, when the Dutch capitalists and banks refused to invest any further in the colony, this prosperity based on huge loans immediately deflated. Many planters, being hopelessly in debt, lost their plantations when their loans came due and were lucky if they could return as overseers to those same places they had once governed in lofty absenteeism. The plantations changed hands, but the same ills persisted. Of the 500 plantations in Surinam at the end of the eighteenth century, only 80 to 90 had planters in residence; the rest were managed by hired administrators. Similar situations occurred in Essequibo, Demerara, and Berbice. This practice put a powerful drag on production, for an absentee owner could neither tell what needed doing nor see to it that it was done.

Another harmful effect of absenteeism was the rough treatment of the slaves. The pleasures of city life – even of such a small city as Paramaribo – tempted many of the administrators, in turn, to leave the plantation or plantations in their charge to their subordinates, the overseers, and to go and live in the capital. These overseers, respecting neither law nor religion, had the power of life and death over the slaves. In consequence, more and more slaves ran away to join the *Marrons*. If caught they were severely punished, but this did not stop them. In addition to these problems, in 1781, a fourth Anglo-Dutch War erupted. Although the English made no attempt to seize the colony, they nevertheless ruled the sea and all trade with the mother country ground to a halt, bringing Surinam to the brink of ruin and severely curtailing its economic recovery.

In 1795, the Chartered Society was liquidated and the States General appointed a special Committee for the Colonies to take its place. But the Committee's life span turned out to be too short to have any deep influence on the colonial life of Dutch Guiana.

In 1796, Essequibo, Demerara, and Berbice surrendered to a British fleet proceeding from Barbados. Three years later the English appeared on the Surinam River, displaying orange-colored banners. Governor Juriaan F. Frederici, being pro-Orange, was only too glad to hand over the colony, especially as the English maintained him in his position. Although before 1795 a pro-French party had existed, a group of people strongly indoctrinated in the ideas of the Enlightenment, its enthusiasm had rapidly cooled after the excesses of the French Terror. There was no opposition to English occupation, expected to be only temporary. Besides, the larger English market promised greater profits.

CHAPTER XV

SURINAM DURING THE ENGLISH INTERREGNUM

In 1802, France and England concluded peace and, in accordance with the Letters of Kew, the colonies were returned to Dutch rule. The Batavian Republic did not want a pro-Orange governor in her colonies, so Frederici had no alternative but to resign. He was succeeded by Governor Blois van Treslong, who in 1803 was himself replaced, because of his lukewarm pro-French attitude, by the francophile Pierre Berranger. War between France and England had again broken out, and, in 1804, an English fleet appeared at Paramaribo to request the surrender of the colony. Berranger realized the futility of resisting, and Surinam was again in English hands.

The second English interregnum lasted until 1816, during which time there were five governors. Under the second one, William Carlyon Hughes (1805–1808), a good and just administrator, the slave trade was first restricted and then abolished, to the great indignation of the plantocracy. When Hughes refused their request for a suspension of the prohibition there was a considerable increase of slave smuggling into the colony. It was not until 1826 before stiff penalties and a much improved registration of slaves made it virtually impossible to own a non-registered black. But increasing prosperity soon pacified the opposition. Not only did the colonists trade freely with England, but as a result of the efforts of Hughes and his predecessor, commerce was allowed with the United States as well, exposing the voracious American market to sugar, coffee, cotton, and other Surinam products.

In 1809, the British government assigned the governorship to a Dutchman, Baron Charles F. Bentinck, a well-known aristocrat, who, in 1795, had left Holland along with the Prince of Orange. By this appointment, the British hoped to placate the strong anti-English feelings in the colony.

Bentinck received special instructions regarding Surinam's military defense system. Although it must be remembered that the colony was a neighbor to Cayenne, an overland attack was not likely due to the difficulties of east-west movement in the Guianas. Therefore, Bentinck was well aware that defense would be primarily a maritime matter.

The *blocus continental*, proclaimed by Napoleon in 1806, put an end to Surinam's exports to Europe, and what little was sold to American and English markets was not enough to keep the colony going. Merchants and planters were threatened with bankruptcy, and a temporary moratorium had to be declared to ease their distress. But the Dutch governor's rule was also characterized by a more effective enforcement of the slavery laws. Mistreatment of the slaves was punished, and judicial proceedings were initiated against those masters who abused their power – a policy which helped to stiffen the planter opposition.

Bentinck died in 1811 and was succeeded by Benham, who followed the same policy as his predecessor. Especially detrimental to any prospect of progress at that time was the fact that both governors sent all net profits to England, making it well-nigh impossible for Surinam to have reaped the fruits of prosperity if there had been any. In 1813, the smouldering resentment in the *Raad* erupted, when it was announced that one John Bent was to be the new tax collector. Halfhide, a member of the *Raad* and the spokesman for the opposition angrily denounced the governor's policy claiming that it would lay waste to the colony. Halfhide was suspended from his post, but later events proved how right he had been.

Whatever may be said of the English interregnum it did not succeed in anglicizing Surinam contrary to what occurred in Essequibo, Demerara, and Berbice. English capital was never abundantly invested in Surinam, probably because the British never intended to keep the colony. For the slaves the interregnum, as could be expected, was a period of blessed protection although, for a while, smuggling circumvented the anti-slave trade legislation. Records of a mixed English-Dutch court installed, in 1818, in Paramaribo to curb the illegal trade in blacks, show that 2500 slaves were illegally smuggled into the colony annually. But when the registration of slaves became strictly enforced, and severe punishments were handed out which could include loss of citizenship and confiscation of property, the situation improved.

In 1816, the English government ended and a new period began under the Dutch banner.

CHAPTER XVI

ASPECTS OF DUTCH COLONIZATION

Dutch colonization differed in two important ways from any other, whether Spanish, Portuguese, English, or French. While these nations were able to impose, in the West, their religion and their language upon their colonies, the Dutch could neither. Two centuries of Dutch Reformed Church presence failed to make the Dutch Caribbean islands Protestant, and if Surinam did so, other denominations were responsible. Likewise, Papiamento, rather than Dutch, is the popular idiom on the Curaçao islands, on the Leeward islands it is English, while in Surinam the official Dutch has a strong competitor in a *lingua franca:* Shranan.

Papiamento emerged as a slave language adopted, at the beginning of the eighteenth century, by Jewish and Christian masters. It probably has a Portuguese base, but mixed with Spanish, English, African, and – especially in the last fifty years – Dutch words. A literature is in the process of being born, although the language as yet has no written grammar nor established spelling.

Shranan – in earlier days called Negro-English – is a mixture of English and African. Like Papiamento, it is a spoken language.

On the Antilles the Dutch Reformed faith was, in the beginning, the only religion officially sanctioned and observed. When, in 1667, the Dutch occupied Surinam, some proselyting for the Anglican Church continued, but only in a limited sense.

Officials of the West India Company and officers of the army or the navy were required to be members of the Dutch Reformed Church. The religious affiliation of the lower echelons is not known. In the beginning only members of this State Church were permitted to become colonists. But as early as 1651 the Jews received a charter bestowing upon them the same privileges and rights they were enjoying in Amsterdam. In contrast to the small Jewish Savannah community in Surinam, the Jewish community of the Curaçao islands acquired a certain importance as one of the mainstays of the white population. In Curaçao as well as in Surinam the Jews were of Sephardic origin: they came from Spain, Portugal, and Brazil. However, this is where the similarity ends. Whereas in Curaçao the Jewish inhabitants devoted their time and considerable energy almost exclusively to trade, in Surinam they became planters.

In the time of Van Walbeeck the white population on Curaçao stood at around fifty people – not counting the garrison. At the end of the eighteenth century this figure had risen to approximately 4000. Of these only a very small fraction were Roman Catholics. The majority of the non-Jewish whites belonged to the Dutch Reformed Church or the Lutheran Church, organized after the arrival of some German and Scandinavian colonists.

The remaining group of significance consisted of the free blacks. Descendants of slaves set free by manumission or the product of miscegenation, they formed a craftsman class, which, at the end of the eighteenth century totalled probably 3000 people, of whom the majority were Roman Catholic.

The slaves, of course, formed the lowest sector of the population. Around 1650, they numbered not more than 100, but by 1700 their number had increased to 4000 – not including those blacks in transit to be sold elsewhere. A century later, they counted more than 10,000 although for tax purposes this figure was artificially lowered.

The West India Company provided the colonists with Dutch Reformed ministers to take care of their spiritual needs; the Jews paid for their own rabbis. The only group lacking any religious attention were the slaves, and it was the Roman Catholic Church who stepped into this vacuum. Of course, this church being officially proscribed – although the letter of the law was never strictly enforced – any strong missionary effort on its part had to wait until the nineteenth century.

On the Dutch Leeward islands, the Dutch Reformed Church maintained a monopoly of some sort until, in the latter half of the eighteenth century, an Anglican church was built. A few years later a Lutheran congregation was established on St. Eustatius. The Methodists were not long in joining, as was the Moravian Brotherhood, the latter being primarily preoccupied with the conversion of the slaves. There were almost no Roman Catholics.

With the arrival, in 1667, of the Dutch in Surinam, the Dutch Reformed Church became the only officially recognized church, adopting the same indifferent attitude toward missionary activities as it had manifested on the Curaçao islands. Due to the intervention of one of the Count of Zinsendorf's friends, in 1735, the Chartered Society allowed the Moravian Brotherhood to establish a few missions for slaves, *Marrons*, and Indians which, by mid-nineteenth century, had converted close to 17.000 slaves.

The West India Company did little to promote education in its colonies. Whatever was accomplished was mainly the work of a few private schoolteachers, sometimes ex-soldiers, who struggled against public indifference. On Curaçao the first schoolmaster – for white children only – arrived about 1640. In the course of the eighteenth century the number of schools on the islands grew and included, on Curaçao, even a Jewish and a Roman Catholic school. The quality of instruction was poor, but by the end of the eighteenth century most white adult males were able to read and write as were quite a number of mulattoes.

The first teacher to arrive in Surinam after the Dutch conquest came in 1670, and, in order to make a decent living, the offices of sexton, precantor and Bible reader were soon added to his repertoire – functions that accompanied his profession in the Antilles also. However, for lack of schoolmasters, the colonists most often turned to discharged soldiers or foreign adventurers whose meager qualifications were, at the end of the seventeenth century, judged by the ministers and elders of the so-called *Conventus*. A Latin school, which was being proposed in the second quarter of the eighteenth century, never materialized, but another school, destined for the children of free mulattoes and blacks, was opened in Paramaribo after 1760. In the following years, the school system expanded until at the end of the century, there were several schools in the capital. One of the graduated mulatto pupils, Johannes Vrolijk, went to Holland to complete his education and came back to Surinam as a qualified teacher, one of the pioneers in this field.

An interesting development during the second half of the eighteenth century was the brief flowering of a kind of 'planters' literature, completely absent in the Dutch Antilles, but advanced in Surinam by a number of literary societies. A prominent member of one such society was Paul François Roos (1751–1805), who wrote an epic about the conflict with the *Marrons*. Governor Mauricius might be included in this movement, since undoubtedly he had talent as a poet.

Journalism in the Dutch possessions began in 1722 with the *Surinam Wednesday Weekly* (Weekelijksche Woensdagsche Surinaamsche Courant) under the motto of "Justitia, Pietas, Fides." The first daily paper appeared in Surinam two years later, long before the *Courant van Essequibo en Demerary* in 1793, the *Curaçaosche Courant* in 1811, or the *St. Eustatius Gazette*.

In 1787 a Society of Natural History was founded in Paramaribo as was a Surinam Garden, which survived until 1816.

As a result of both intemperance and ignorance, the general level of health in the Dutch colonies was far from satisfactory. Life expectancy was short, and the death rate among children was particularly high. Epidemics of smallpox, chickenpox, and yellow fever were common. The latter illness was described in a letter to the *Heren X* in 1779 as follows: "Strangers and sailors after disembarking are either afflicted with bad fevers and diarrhea, or they come down with the so-called chocolate sickness, called by the Spaniards *vomito prieto* or *chapetonnade*, which is the vomiting of gall, by which the sick person, sometimes in the greatest paroxysm of frenzy, is snatched by death within three or four days."

A less frequent but equally terrifying disease was leprosy, for which a Lazarus Hospital was founded in Surinam. On Curaçao, another hospital existed for slaves brought from Africa. The Company regularly supplied these with doctors, one of whom, David van der Sterre, wrote a biography of the well-known Dutch privateer Jan Erasmus Reining. The Jews had doctors of their own.

Willemstad, founded by Jan van Walbeeck in 1634, was named after William, the son of *Stadholder* Frederik Hendrik. It was a typical fortress town, with very narrow streets, lined with two or three-story houses built within the walls. As the population grew, the town expanded. In 1690, the old wall running from the Waaigat to the sea, crumbled, and in 1703 a new wall was completed. However, by 1700, a new subdivision known as Scharloo, had taken hold north of the Waaigat; houses were also being constructed on the other side of the St. Ann Bay, in an area called Otrabanda; after the Peace of Utrecht in 1713, the Pietermaai section was built up along Willemstad's bayfront.

Paramaribo, place where the paramuru blossom grows, like Willemstad, grew around a fort, Fort Zeelandia, near which the governor's palace was built. Unlike Willemstad, however, Paramaribo had no walls to hamper its growth, which in the eighteenth century directed itself towards the river.

In both of these larger towns as well as in some of the smaller ones on the other islands, samples exist of what may be called the Dutch colonial style, an attractive adaptation of Dutch Baroque and Neo-Classicism to the tropical climate. Scarcity of wood compelled the mansion builders in Curaçao to use stone and coral as building materials; in Surinam, however, that problem was non-existent and wood was pre-eminently used. This style bears a striking resemblance to the colonial architecture of the former Cape Colony, also of Dutch origin.

The income the WIC derived from its monopoly in sugar, slaves, and wood has not yet been completely assessed, and remains subject to much more research. Most local taxes, which provided an important part of the Company's earnings, have already been discussed in a previous chapter (see p. 57). By the end of the eighteenth century the following additional taxes were being collected: an *auction tax* of $2\frac{1}{2}$ per cent on all goods sold at public auctions, an *excise duty* of 3 per cent on all beverages except beer and wine, a *land tax* (akkergeld) depending on the number of slaves used per acre, and the *50 penny*, a 2 per cent tax on real estate sales. The revenues accruing from these and the before-mentioned taxes cannot be definitely stated and consequently it is difficult to come up with a balance sheet of income and debts of the WIC. The small dividends paid in the eighteenth century (an average of less than 2 per cent), stopping completely in the last ten years of the Company's existence, are one indication of its financial situation. With the profits from the slave trade disappearing after 1715, the Company was left without a real core of solid income, but managed to have an extremely slow death struggle ending with its liquidation in 1791.

The Company required a recognition fee from all ships sailing within the limits of its charter. Arriving in its West Indian ports, Dutch ships paid 3 per cent and foreign vessels 8 per cent on the value of their cargoes. Similar taxes were levied in Paramaribo. Dutch ships paid a *ton's tax* of 120 guilders per ton as compensation for the Company's unused right to free freight of up to one tenth of the tonnage. This tax, however, was collected in the United Provinces and did not contribute to the local treasuries.

When the Dutch settled on Curaçao and the neighboring islands, they forced all natives to leave except for 75 Indians whom they needed as laborers. This small group managed, for a long time, to maintain a separate identity; in the eighteenth century, Father P.M. Schabel, a Jesuit missionary, even wrote a catechism in their language. Some of the old Curaçao and Aruba families are probably justified in claiming an Indian heritage but, at the turn of the century, the last full-blooded Indian on Curaçao died, and soon this occurred on the other islands as well.

Negroes were brought to the West Indies in the late thirties of the seventeenth century. Around 1700, the Curaçao islands contained 4000 slaves, most of whom came from the Congo and Angola, although blacks from Elmina, the Dutch fortress on the West Coast of Africa, were considered good house slaves. When, in 1863, emancipation came, there were approximately 6600 slaves to be freed in the Dutch Antilles.

The Dutch Leeward islands were never heavily populated. Charles de Rochefort, a minister of the local Dutch Reformed Church, mentions that in 1658 St. Martin had about 600 people, but this figure included the French half. The number of slaves is unknown. At the beginning of the eighteenth century there is reason to believe that the Dutch part comprised 300 persons of which 250 were slaves. Towards the end of that century there were 1150 whites, 200 freed blacks, and 4000 slaves. For St. Eustatius had were 500 whites and 750 slaves at the beginning, versus 2400 whites and 5000 slaves at the end of the eighteenth century. The small island of Saba, at the end of this century, had only 75 whites and 750 slaves.

Slavery played a much more important role in the economy of Surinam; between 1667 and the beginning of the nineteenth century more than 300,000 blacks were imported – an average of more than 2000 slaves per year. Most slavers were dispatched from Flushing which was the most prominent Zeelandian town to partake in this trade. During the period of its highest prosperity the colony of Surinam in all likelihood held more than 80,000 slaves. Of these less than one third worked on the sugar plantations; more than 30,000 worked as craftsmen: carpenters, bricklayers, plumbers, and blacksmiths; the rest were used less profitably in domestic services. In Paramaribo the average family of some standing had at least ten house slaves. There were, in 1790, more than 8000 slaves in a population of only 2500 whites. After the slave trade had become proscribed by an agreement between Great Britain and the Netherlands, the number of slaves in the colony decreased steadily, until in 1863 the last 32,000 were emancipated.

The institution of slavery was, in the Dutch colonies as elsewhere in the West Indies, an integral part of colonial life. Unlike the Spaniards, the Dutch, however, were completely unfamiliar with this type of human bondage when they made their debut as a colonial power.

The Dutch did not trust the Indians of Curaçao, who, they claimed, were tainted with Roman Catholicism and suspected of being covert allies of the Spaniards, yet there was a desperate need for a strong labor force. It was not long, therefore, before the possibility of importing black labor came under consideration. Even more inviting was the prospect of using the island of Curaçao as a base for the slave trade in the Caribbean, an activity which the West India Company was finding more and more to its liking.

Under Van Walbeeck's successor, Tolck, initial steps were taken to make Curaçao into such a center. The first blacks might have reached the island as early as 1639, although their number remained small and their arrivals irregular until well into the fifties.

In 1640, the *Heren XIX* stipulated in their letters of commission that all privateering ships operating in the Caribbean should bring their captured slaves to Curaçao and sell them to the Company for 65 guilders each, a price which, ultimately, was raised to 150 guilders.

The first known Dutch slaving contract, awarded by the Zeeland Chamber to one Frederick Roeberge from St. Christopher (St. Kitts), expired around this time, and the Company refused to consider its renewal, the reason supposedly being that he had to buy his slaves in Africa, thus encroaching upon the WIC's own monopolistic rights.

In 1611, the Dutch built a small fort at Goree, and in 1637 they captured the Portuguese stronghold of São Jorge da Mina, renamed the Elmina Castle; but, until 1640, the Portuguese controlled the main slave depots on the West African Coast. It was the Portuguese rebellion and its consequences for New Holland (Dutch Brazil) which changed all that. In 1641, Dutch admiral Jol captured São Paulo de Loanda in Angola and the island of São Thomé from the Portuguese, and suddenly it was the Dutch who controlled the slave trade.

The loss of New Holland in 1654 compelled the *Heren XIX* to utilize the potential of the islands in the Caribbean. Curaçao, having lost its former significance as a naval base, developed into the WIC's foremost slave depository, while the trade in blacks became "the soul of the Company, with any decrease or withdrawal apt to cause its ruin." By 1668 the island already had a stockpile of many thousands of blacks.

Understandably, the Company reserved for itself the right to transport slaves from the West African ports to the Caribbean. When private merchants offered to buy them in Africa, as was the case of two Zeelandian merchants who wanted 200 to 300 slaves for independent delivery to St. Croix and St. Eustatius, their requests were summarily denied in favor of the WIC's monopoly.

The capital invested in cargoes of commodities for barter (*cargazoenen*), and those of slaves (*armazoenen*), earned the Company gains which were substantial, if difficult to assess.

Upon arrival at Curaçao, all slaves were sold to the neighboring colonies with the exception of the old or infirm (*mancarrons*) who were relegated to the island's market. It was, of course, not permitted to trade with the Spanish colonies; or, after the reinforcement of the Navigation Laws of 1651 and 1660, with the English possessions; and, after the issuance of Colbert's colonial and mercantilist policy, with the French islands. Indeed, by the end of the Third Anglo-Dutch War, trade with the English and French Antilles had virtually ceased to exist.

In principle, Spain, too, adhered to the prevailing doctrine of mercantilism, but in her case theoretical exclusivity was diluted by economic necessity and political opportunism. After the Portuguese rebellion of 1640, Spain refused to conclude *asientos* with the Portuguese or with anyone else, a situation from which the Dutch, and to a lesser degree the English, indirectly benefited.

In 1662, however, Spain was forced to sign a new *asiento*, this time with the Italian house of Grillo and Lomelino. The new *asentistas* subcontracted with the Dutch West India Company for the delivery of a specified number of blacks, and an agent of the Italians moved to Curaçao.

Under this *asiento*, the Company's trade in blacks rapidly expanded, and in 1668 a special fund was created by her shareholders to provide the necessary financial backing. Over the years the WIC supplied slaves to successive *asentistas* on a fairly regular basis. In 1671, the *asiento* was given to a Portuguese, one Antonio Garcia, who soon lost it. It was next received in 1679, by another Italian, Juan Barrosa, operating in partnership with Nicole Porcio. Ultimately, the *asiento* came into the hands of the Amsterdam merchant house of Johannes Coymans and Brother where the handicap of Protestantism was mitigated by money, so as to permit the Dutchmen to deliver the contracted slaves to the ports of Havana, Porto Bello, Vera Cruz, and Cartagena – although, to be sure, an office of the Inquisition was established in the latter town to protect the Roman Catholics from contamination in their dealings with the heretical Dutch.

These were the golden years for the Company's commerce in slaves. The Spanish government knew very well that merchants and *asentistas* alike were obtaining their black merchandise from the Dutch on Curaçao, but Spain desperately needed slaves for her colonies, and in the face of this pressing reality, closed her eyes to the offensive means of acquisition. It is known that, in the early eighties, there were more than 3000 blacks stored on Curaçao for re-export.

Once the first defense system had been built, the Curaçao islands did not require many slaves. Slavery was virtually unknown on Aruba, and the demand for black laborers to work the salt pans on Bonaire was usually satisfied by a mere 100 to 200. On Curaçao, there were approximately 600 to 700 slaves on the plantations, while an additional 1800 were occupied as craftsmen or as domestic servants.

In the latter years of the seventeenth century, an average of 3500 to 4000 slaves were brought to the New World on Dutch ships annually. However, the role of the Dutch West India Company as the principal supplier of slaves was almost over at the end of the War of the Spanish Succession. After 1715, England received the *asiento*, and by 1730 the trade was hers. Only a handful of Africans continued to arrive in Willemstad, and the Dutch slaver which dropped anchor in 1778, was probably the last to do so in that capacity. After 1730, what was left of the trade was taken over by the Middelburg Commerce Company.

Since the Dutch West India colonies did not have the equivalent of the English indentured servant or the French *engagé*, from the beginning the principal distinction between masters and servants was color. The in-between race, created by miscegenation, was known by several names ranging from mulatto to *liplap* depending upon the approximate mixture of blood. A white man's mixed offspring were not generally used for the heavy field labor but were employed in domestic services instead; hence a lighter color often implied a higher step on the social ladder.

On the Curaçao islands and in Surinam the slave was not without certain theoretical rights – however illusory his legal resource. And these modest rights imperceptibly extended during the colonial period, culminating in the nineteenth century emancipation.

It is doubtful whether the first elaborate precautions of the WIC with respect to her human cargo were wholly based upon humanitarian motives – profit was the principle underlying all Company actions. But as soon as the WIC became active in the slave trade, notices were circulated to Company skippers regulating the treatment slaves were to receive on their journey overseas. In the respresentative "Instructions for the Skippers in the Service of the West India Company Navigating in the Slave Trade," printed in 1675 in Middelburg, the captain was admonished to "give special attention to the religious instruction" of the heathen blacks. "It is intriguing to witness," observed one Dutch historian, "how those concerned with the slave trade did their utmost to stay on a good footing with heaven."

The fact remains that the Company did not think of the slaves as human. Like cattle they were branded, and like cattle they were treated. It was the Dutch Reformed Church, in one of its rare actions on behalf of the blacks, which persuaded the *Heren XIX* to establish medical facilities for the slaves on Curaçao, as well as to employ Dutch ministers for their conversion. Yet the masses of blacks felt more at ease with Roman priests than with puritanical Calvinists.

The conditions under which the slaves lived were without legal precedent under Dutch law, and the few references to Roman law were haphazard and capricious. The least infringement upon the rights of a white person was punishable by death. Yet testimony against a white man by a black carried no weight, not even when several blacks testified unanimously. In the seventeenth century, a white man who killed a slave was merely fined; somewhat later this sentence was increased to a token term of imprisonment. Corporal punishment of a slave usually stopped short of permanent injury. In 1694, for instance, four slaves were condemned: one to be hanged, another to have his right hand cut off, and two to stand under the gallows with ropes around their necks. But the Chamber of Zeeland sent a recommendation to the governor and his *Raad* to refrain from amputation. A slave without hands would become a burden on his master and the community.

In the latter half of the eighteenth century, inspired by the modern ideas of the Enlightenment, the *Heren X* attempted to provide the slave with at least a nominal measure of legal protection, and had Governor Rodier of the Curaçao islands draft a slave code. Yet what practice continued to tolerate, the slave code could not curb.

Even before the code was issued, however, an attempt had already been made to abolish some abuses like whipping, branding, and exile to the Bonaire salt pans. Yet these measures were soon reinstated because of "the brutality of the Negroes and mulattoes." The Dutch colonial slaves were proud and fierce West Africans, who rose up repeatedly against their white masters. Neither whipping nor branding could wipe out their feeling of independence and desire for freedom.

The first slave rebellion on the Curaçao islands, subdued by Governor Faesch, has already been described. In 1771, Governor Rodier issued a decree against those Negroes who disturbed Sunday services with their noisiness. During the next years, more restrictions were circulated against free blacks and *hende di coló* as well as slaves. Grovestins and Boey, in their report referred to on p. 66 devoted special attention to the problem of the Negro, attributing his menial position to a supposed mental inferiority.

The revolt of the blacks on nearby Hispaniola was soon common knowledge on Curaçao, where many a newborn child was named after the famous rebel Toussaint l'Ouverture. The colonial government, sensing the rising unrest, issued a veritable barrage of proscriptive ordinances. In 1795, for instance, it was declared a crime for any person of color to walk the public streets after dark without carrying a light; in addition a slave had to have a permit signed by his master. Despite these precautions, only a few weeks later, a slave revolt was to shake the very foundations of insular society.

The rebellion of 1795, nourished by a multitude of local grievances, was kindled by the ideas of the French Revolution. The French had declared the equal rights of man, and on Hispaniola they had been taken at their word. Also the political arrangement, concluded in The Hague between France and the Batavian Republic, caused much confusion overseas since the abolition of slavery decreed by France was thought to extend automatically to all Dutch colonies.

On Sunday, August 17, 1795, some fifty slaves on one plantation laid down their tools and refused to work. Neither threat nor reward had any effect. Led by a certain Tula, they marched to a neighboring plantation and incited the slaves to join them, under their *bomba* or chief, Bastiaan Carpata. Within a few days, more than 1000 slaves in the western section of the island were in open rebellion.

Governor De Veer summoned the *Raad* to discuss the alarming situation. A small body of troops, consisting of 12 white soldiers, 14 mulattoes, and 31 free Negroes, was dispatched to the trouble spot. However, this force was welcomed with gunfire and had to retreat. The rebellious slaves now stormed the slave prisons, the inmates of which, once freed, unabashedly flocked to the movement. Together they vented their pent-up hostility, running amok, burning plantations, and ruining crops. A priest who had the misfortune of falling into their hands was brutally killed.

After the failure of those first tactics, the government next dispatched a priest who, notwithstanding his colleague's murder, was willing to talk to the insurgents. Although well treated, he failed to reach an agreement. Again the government sent troops, reinforced by marines and the civil militia; and this time, in a bloody encounter, the slaves suffered their first defeat. Closely pursued to the remotest nook of the island, the fugitives gathered at the foot of St. Christopher, Curaçao's highest hill, for a last defiant stand. But by promising pardon to those who would surrender and return to their plantations, the government coaxed away more than a thousand of them, considerably weakening the rebel forces.

Once a price was set upon the heads of the leaders, they were soon betrayed and taken to Willemstad as captives. After a short trial and a procession through the town streets, twenty-nine of them were condemned to death; so ended the second and last revolt of the slaves on Curaçao.

Soon afterwards, a law was passed in which the working hours, rations, and clothing allowances for slaves were specified. But promulgation and observance were two different things. The frequency with which this law was referred to indicates that it was never strictly observed. For example, in the year 1812, a small number of slaves asked to see the governor one Sunday (their only day of leisure), and handed him a list of complaints about their master. The *Raad* was assembled, and after an inquiry the guilty planter was fined, with the warning to be more lenient toward his slaves. In the long run, however, the individual owner had the final word, for the government was no more than the executive committee of the slave-owning class.

Compared with the Dutch Antilles, life on the plantations in Surinam was hellish. Those slaves lucky enough not to have to work a full seven-day week, nevertheless had to utilize their Sundays to cultivate their own little gardens – if they wanted to eat that is. Conditions on the sugar and cotton plantations may have been somewhat better than at the logging plantations, where the big trees were cut, sawn by hand into boards, and carried to the river to be soaked. The opposition of the plantocracy dominating the *Raad* to the reforms suggested by Governor Van Sommelsdyck and some of his successors effectively sabotaged any social legislation.

Like their insular counterparts, the Dutch Guiana slaves had few human rights to speak of. Marriage did not exist; at a whim of their master couples could be separated, their children sold. Dutch Reformed ministers did not deem it worth their while to proselytize them. The Moravian Brotherhood, which rose to prominence in 1734, performed what little christening was done initially before the other Christian denominations had decided to take over. When a slave fell sick he was summarily handed over to the local quack (*loekoeman* or *dressieman*) as a result of which the death rate among slaves, especially small children, was terrifyingly high. An attractive female would become the concubine of the master or overseer as a matter of course, until she became pregnant; after which she was given to another slave to breed her master more slaves. In general, the colored offspring were treated better than the blacks and were employed in domestic services. Conditions were also somewhat healthier for the town slaves.

Mention has already been made several times before of Surinam's runaway slaves who lived deep in the forests of the interior, yet close enough to prey upon the plantations. Many slaves preferred the rough, but free life of a *Marron* to the overseer's whip. Often these *Marrons* would attack under cover of night, robbing, plundering, and killing. Punishment was cruel both for a slave who was recaptured as for a *Marron* caught in action, but even this danger could not quench a brave man's longing for freedom. Under Van Sommelsdyck, the problem of the *Marrons* became so acute that the governor initiated a new method to deal with them. Instead of organizing expeditions – an expense the colonial treasury could ill afford – he entered into negotiations which, in 1684, resulted in an agreement of mutual toleration. However, as this pact implied a tacit recognition of the free status of the *Marrons*, it was unacceptable to the slaveowners and the *Raad*, and hence not honored by them. The result was more raiding and killing, leading to new negotiations, and then to new agreements, which in practice were no more than truces. It may be assumed that until the abolition of slavery a continuous state of civil war existed between the *Marrons* and the ruling class.

It may have been well-nigh impossible to honor these agreements – whatever the intentions on either side. They usually contained a promise of arms, and invariably stipulated that the *Marrons* send back all fugitive slaves in return for a certain price. Mauricius, possibly imitating the English example on Jamaica, may well have been the first governor to incorporate this clause in his dealings with the *Marrons*. In 1757, Governor Wigbold Crommelin faced a serious slave rebellion along the Commewine River. At first strongly supported by the Bush Negroes, as the *Marrons* were called, the latters' proud and defiant spirit is nowhere better reflected than in the reply of one of their leaders to Crommelin's representatives:

We desire you to tell your governor and your court, that in case they want to raise no new gangs of rebels, they ought to take care that the planters keep a more watchful eye over their own property, and not trust them so frequently in the hands of drunken managers and overseers, who wrongfully and severely chastising the Negroes, debauching their wives and children, neglecting the sick ... are the ruin of the colony, and willfully drive to the woods such numbers of stout active people, who by their sweat earn your subsistence, without whose hands your colony must drop to nothing, and to whom at last, in this disgraceful manner, you are glad to come and sue for friendship.

A treaty of alliance was ultimately arrived at, however, which stipulated that the *Marrons* be faithful allies of the Dutch officials, delivering all deserters, and not raid the plantations; in return they were guaranteed a fixed amount of arms and ammunition annually.

Crommelin, realizing the truth of the *Marron's* declaration, endeavored to expand Van Sommelsdyck's modest slave legislation, but found his efforts frustrated by strong opposition in the *Raad*. The plantocracy was disinclined to accept any governmental interference in the master-slave relationship.

In the year 1770 the colony was prospering; the Van Sommelsdyck family sold its shares in the Chartered Society. Amsterdam and the WIC now controlled each half of this Society. In that same year Governor Nepveu (1770–1779) founded the Corps of Free Negroes to deal with the resurging *Marron* problem and to protect the plantations. This Corps resembled a paid militia composed of 150 blacks and mulattoes. Two years later the Corps of Black Chasseurs was instituted: 300 slaves bought by the colonial government and especially trained to fight the *Marrons*. These combined forces, called the Colonial Guides, were reinforced in that same period by 800 soldiers sent from the United Provinces. Preparations for action against the runaway slaves were finally complete. Up the Cottica River a considerable force of *Marrons* under the eminent leadership of Baron, Bonni, and Joli-Coeur, was engaged in battle. They fought bravely but were at last surrounded and defeated. However, victory was not total. Many *Marrons* had managed to escape, and reinforced by fresh runaways from the plantations, continued to be a threat. The colonial government again resorted to treaties. These military expeditions lasted until deep into the nineteenth century, but no permanent solution could be found before the emancipation of 1863.

During the seventeenth and eighteenth centuries, the neighboring settlements of Essequibo, Demerara, and Berbice were outwardly prospering as sugar colonies, especially under Laurens Storm van 's-Gravesande, who arrived in Essequibo in 1738. But in Berbice, where more than 4000 slaves were held in check by a mere 350 whites, the situation was not quite as innocuous. In 1763, matters finally came to a head when the blacks of two plantations rose up in arms forging an insurrection which rapidly grew to critical proportions.

At the request of the local commander, the Governor of Surinam sent help, and somewhat later an additional force of 600 soldiers arrived from Holland. The rebellious slaves – numerically vastly in the majority – were defeated by treachery and lack of discipline as much as by the better organized governmental forces. Coffy, the rebel leader, committed suicide, and his successor tried in vain to continue the struggle. The toll in lives was frightful: besides the 120 leaders who were put to death, more than 1500 slaves had been killed either in action or by disease. Essequibo and Demerara escaped this kind of trauma.

CHAPTER XVII

THE CURAÇAO ISLANDS IN THE FIRST HALF OF THE NINETEENTH CENTURY

On January 27, 1816, the new Governor General of the Curaçao islands, Albert Kikkert, arrived with his staff aboard the *Prince of Orange*, a Dutch man-of-war. Having been Willemstad's harbor commander from 1795 to 1800 and married to the daughter of a prominent Curaçao family, his was a well-known figure to the local inhabitants. In addition, Kikkert's grasp of insular affairs had few equals.

The impressive title of governor-general had been concocted by King William I of the Netherlands in the hope of converting the island of Curaçao into a western Malta or Gibraltar, controlling trade and navigation in the Caribbean. It took the enlightened king several years to realize that he had vastly exaggerated the Curaçao islands' importance.

Upon Kikkert's arrival, there was still one *Raad* or Political Council for the three islands, with the governor-general represented on Aruba and Bonaire by a governor or director and district commissioners. The three Leeward islands constituted a separate governmental unit.

Next to the governor-general the *Raad* consisted of six members, initially appointed by Kikkert himself, and later chosen by successive heads of the government from a list submitted to them by the *Raad*. Each serving for eight years, two were government employees while the remaining four were representatives of distinguished mercantile families.

The governor-general occupied the key position on the *Raad*. No proposal could be discussed without his permission, and in case of a tie he made the ultimate decision. According to a royal decree of 1815, the role of the *Raad* was to regulate all domestic affairs including the supervision of the police magistrates and of those public institutions such as churches, poorhouses, and schools, the maintenance of streets, ferries, and public markets, the guardianship of orphans and minors, and even the manumission of slaves. The administration of Aruba and Bonaire also fell to the *Raad's* advisory prerogatives. All important decisions of the colonial government had to be ratified by The Hague.

The Council of Civil and Criminal Justice, which acted as a court, was created independently of the executive and legislative branches, under the influence of the French Revolution. The rack, abolished in the Netherlands in 1798, continued to be used in Curaçao for another thirty years. The death penalty remained in effect in the Antilles throughout the nineteenth century, although the mother country had ended the practice in 1848.

As part of Kikkert's entourage, a new military commander and almost 300 soldiers replaced the English garrison at Fort Amsterdam and Fort George, now rebaptized Fort Nassau. In addition to this army and to the small police force, the old civilian militia was reorganized into five companies, with Jews, mulattoes, and blacks segregated into units of their own. In Kikkert's time this militia comprised 20 officers and 800 men between 15 and 50 years of age. It was paid by a special tax levied on those who, for one reason or another, were exempt from service.

Government revenues fell far short of expenses. In 1816, income barely exceeded 77.000 *pesos*, and in 1818 reached 100,000 *pesos*, but in that year the cost of the military alone amounted to more than 280,000 guilders (115.000 *pesos*). The new government not only had to cope with a budget deficit, but with heavy debts contracted before 1800 as well. New tariffs were ushered in, and a lottery was instituted, the returns of which were taxed. The mother country made up the remaining shortage.

Relations with Venezuela formed an important part of governmental concerns at this time. From 1816 to 1822, the colonial government of the Curaçao islands, with The Hague's approval, rendered assistance to the Spaniards by convoying their ships in rebel waters and by supplying their troops in Venezuela – a profitable relationship, which made the Dutch slow to render formal recognition to the revolutionary forces. When in March, 1816, the Dutch representative in Caracas informed the Spanish captain-general of the change in government on the Curaçao islands, the latter requested the extradition of a number of Venezuelan exiles who had found refuge under the English flag. This type of request had formerly been refused by the English governors. Kikkert discussed the matter with his *Raad*, who advised him to evict only those exiles who were not contributing to the island's economy. This the governor-general did, setting a reckless precedent for later years.

Of course, in 1816, the rebel cause looked rather bleak. General Murillo's triumphant entry into Venezuela with a huge fleet and a strong army had forced Simón Bolívar to flee before him after the latter's latest efforts to liberate Venezuela had miscarried. But the revolutionists were soon up in arms again. In June, 1816, in plain view of the Dutch forts, the patriots, as the rebels called themselves, captured a Spanish ship leaving St. Ann Bay. Kikkert reacted to this affront by forbidding any ship commissioned by Bolívar to enter his ports. Some time later, a small fleet of patriot ships carrying both Bolívar and Brion presented itself at the entrance to the harbor, yet Kikkert refused to be intimidated and held his ground giving only Brion, who after all had been born on Curaçao, permission to disembark. Brion persuasively argued the rebel cause pleading with the governor-general to recognize the flag of the patriots, and holding out the promise of substantial advantages. Knowing that honoring their flag would be paramount to acknowledging their status as belligerents, Kikkert denied the request, but nevertheless brought the question to the attention of The Hague. There his pro-Spanish attitude was readily endorsed.

However, maintaining an anti-patriot posture in the face of changing odds soon became extremely awkward. The fleet with Bolívar and Brion on board constantly violated Dutch territorial rights by seizing Spanish ships within sight of Fort Amsterdam and by using Bonaire as a naval base. Soon Dutch ships were also attacked by the patriots although men-of-war reinforcements, received in 1817, enabled Kikkert to protect Dutch and Spanish shipping between the island and Venezuela somewhat. As a countermeasure, despite Brion's protests, the Dutch began to board the insurgents' ships and to convey them to Willemstad.

In the midst of these tensions Kikkert died. Governor Pieter R. Cantz'laar inherited only half of Kikkert's title and two-thirds of the latter's 18,000 guilder salary. Cantz'laar remained on Curaçao until 1828, when a governmental reorganization relayed him to Paramaribo.

In his first instructions from The Hague, the new governor was urged to economize, but his subsequent drastic plan to cut expenses and raise revenues was not well received on the island. Several compromises were proposed, but discussions of these in the *Raad* were interrupted by the sudden developments on the mainland.

In June of 1821, the battle of Carabobo freed practically all of Venezuela from Spanish rule. Ironically, Brion was not to share in the glory; having arrived on Curaçao only a month before the decisive battle, he died shortly afterwards. More than 2000 royalist refugees fled across the waters, among them the notorious Spanish generals Murillo and La Torre. In Willemstad, General Murillo made an attempt to collect money from the exiles in order to fit out a new expedition against the patriots. This scheming as well as the mere presence of all these conspiratorial fugitives caused Cantz'laar many headaches.

Yet The Hague continued to point out that recognition of the patriots even as belligerents was still impossible: relations between the Netherlands and Spain were friendly and could not be jeopardized. This partisan attitude of the Dutch government was, of course, bitterly resented by the patriots. Curaçao merchants, indifferent to politics but concerned about profit, were upset over the blockade of the Venezuelan coast, particularly since Spain, which no longer had the power to make such a venture effective, was using outlaws, adventurers, and other riffraff. Cantz'laar protested strongly and let it be known that his government would not tolerate a blockade by a band of hired pirates. The Curaçao population was also aroused: there were riots against the Spanish and royalist exiles, and the house of General Murillo was stoned.

In truth, Curaçao and its trade were virtually defenseless. The men-of-war, recalled when tensions had relaxed temporarily, were sorely needed again. Finally, some insight into the complexity of the situation was gained in far-away The Hague. After Cantz'laar's dilemma had been weighed in the Dutch Cabinet, King William I decided to recognize the patriots as belligerents but to voice this concession in such ambiguous terms as to remain moot on the ultimate question of independence.

A relieved governor immediately informed the revolutionists in Caracas and opened the islands' ports. Piracy against Dutch ships ended and trade with the patriots increased. Relations with Spain understandably deteriorated. General Murillo, still on Curaçao, peremptorily handed Cantz'laar a message threatening to extend the Spanish blockade to the Curaçao islands. But the Dutch did not stand alone, for Spain had previously followed the same line of action against other nations as well. The English, for one, had lost patience and sent a small squadron consisting of five men-of-war to the Caribbean in order to protect their interests. King William I might have done the same, but by that time the Spaniards had had a change of mind. In March, 1822, King Ferdinand guaranteed to respect the rights and property of foreigners as long as the latter did not participate in the fight between him and his American subjects. This signalled the end of the Spanish blockade.

In that same year, 1822, President John Quincy Adams of the United States recognized the independence of Gran Colombia. Great Britain followed suit, in spite of her pro-Spanish attitude during and after the Napoleonic wars. The Hague remained hesitant, but in view of these public avowals, the Dutch government took yet another step toward reconciliation. A representative was sent to Gran Colombia with the purpose of surveying the situation, establishing informal relations, and obtaining commercial advantages for the Dutch.

This reconnaissance resulted in the appointment of commercial agents to

La Guaira, Puerto Cabello, Maracaibo, and other ports. Consuls were also named to several Colombian cities – a *de facto* recognition of the country's independence. The insurrection led by General Páez in 1826, even though crushed by Bolívar, was cited by the Dutch as evidence of the instability of the young republic. No further steps to render formal recognition were taken.

Dutch relations with Gran Colombia were, therefore, of a delicate nature. Difficulties for both governments were created by the geographical proximity of the Curaçao islands to the mainland. Trade, whether licit or illicit, continued to flourish – profits were too high and there was too much at stake for either side to be willing to end this lucrative relationship. Again it was King William I who cast the deciding vote. In return for a treaty regulating navigation, import and export duties with Gran Colombia, he pledged to respect the fundamental fact of independence. However, hardly had this agreement been signed, in 1828, when Gran Colombia split into three parts and negotiations had to start all over again, separately.

King William's fascination with overseas affairs was also clearly demontstrated by the establishment, in 1818, of a new, semi-official West India Company. Primarily intended to encourage trade and navigation in the West Indies, the Company's main office was located in Amsterdam, while Curaçao was expected to play an important role as a storehouse of merchandise. Shares in the new Company sold readily, the king himself buying 1½ million guilders worth. This Company existed approximately ten years, after which it fizzled into oblivion.

William I had soon instituted regular mail and passenger service as well. After 1825, a system was adopted under which every two months a man-of-war would leave Holland with a packet of mail, stay in Willemstad for one month, and return home with the mail from the islands. In addition, a functionary, whose salary derived from fees paid by incoming ships, was appointed to distribute the mail on the islands.

In 1827, the 4000-mile trip of the paddle-boat *Curaçao* from Amsterdam to Paramaribo marked the beginning of a regular passenger connection between the Netherlands and the Curaçao islands and Surinam. It also established the first transatlantic steamship service.

King William's plans included declaring Willemstad a free port. As mentioned before, the colonial budget had shown a huge deficit year after year, especially after the removal of certain import and export duties at the suggestion of Governor Cantz'laar. In 1826, after ample discussion in The Hague, Willemstad followed the example of St. Thomas in the Virgin Islands, which had become a free port twenty years earlier. With this measure it was expected that all trade would be lured to Curaçao and that what had been lost to the Danish would return to the Dutch. William I also hoped hereby to gain exemption from the 5 per cent additional duty levied by Gran Colombia, but this reciprocity never materialized, partly due to the instability of Bolívar's republic.

The multiplicity of King William's activities was truly amazing. In order to get first-hand information on local conditions, he sent one of his most trusted men, one Johannes van den Bosch, to the West Indies and endowed him with far-reaching authority. Van den Bosch had written a study entitled *The Dutch Possessions in Asia, America, and Africa,* in which he tried to show that the colonies could easily be made to turn a profit. The king now sent him to the West to prove it.

Van den Bosch stayed on Curaçao for some time, then paid a brief visit to St. Eustatius, and Surinam, and was back in the Netherlands within a year. His report, presented a few weeks later, effected no miracles and was soon shelved and forgotten. However, he auspiciated the establishment of a Chamber of Commerce on Curaçao which existed for some eight or ten years, after which it shared the fate of the most recent West India Company.

If the advice of Van den Bosch did little to stimulate the lagging economy, it did have one important result which was to alter the relationship between the Curaçao islands and the mother country for some time to come. Until the year 1828, the West Indian colonies had been divided into three groups: the Leeward islands, the Curaçao islands, and Surinam. In his report, Van den Bosch had argued that the colonies would benefit from a unified administration and become not only self-supporting but remunerative. Under the proposed system, which was soon put into effect, all West Indian colonies were to be governed from Paramaribo, thus making Surinam, in fact if not in name the cornerstone of the Dutch West Indian possessions. Henceforth, the governor-general presided in Paramaribo, assisted by a *Hoge Raad,* or High Council, and the first to occupy the high post was Van den Bosch himself. Willemstad merited a mere vice-governor or director. This system lasted until 1845, but the expected boom in prosperity never did come.

CHAPTER XVIII

THE CURAÇAO ISLANDS UNDER PARAMARIBO

No initiative was now expected of the government of the Curaçao islands, only obedience. The first vice-governor to be appointed was Isaac J. Rammelman Elsevier, who had served as acting governor of the islands before the arrival of Cantz'laar. It was a time of drastic economizing, for the Belgian revolution which permanently split the Netherlands into two independent nations, had left the northern one with heavy military debts. Rammelman Elsevier's subordination to Paramaribo also effectively paralyzed any action he would have liked to undertake. Added to this were other grievances, mostly arising from tensions with Venezuela which were not wholly understood in Paramaribo. The mercantile interests of the Curaçao islands had, as a result, to play second fiddle to those of an agricultural colony.

After the separation of Venezuela from Gran Colombia, the colonial administration on Curaçao did nothing to prevent the Venezuelan exiles on the island from conspiring to overthrow their home government, or from buying arms and ammunition and smuggling them into the new nation. There were complaints in the Venezuelan press, and threats to close all Venezuelan ports to the Dutch. Tensions were stopped short of open hostilities by a commercial treaty recognizing an independent Venezuela in which the Dutch obtained some exemptions from incoming duties on a number of commodities as well as on all merchandise imported from the Netherlands.

In the expectation of a revival of the languishing Curaçao trade, a *casa protectora*, or protective house, was established consisting of two members, a Venezuelan and a Dutchman. Trade between the Venezuelan coast and Curaçao would be subject to supervision by the *casa*.

One article of the treaty, in particular, throws light upon the circumstances under which trade relations were to be developed. It was stipulated that in case of any unrest or upheaval in Venezuela, the Dutch were to maintain strict neutrality, abstain from involvement in Venezuelan internal affairs, and not favor either of the parties concerned. Other clauses testify to the prevailing anti-semitic sentiments: e.g., Jews were not to penetrate the country beyond a distance of half a mile from the shores of rivers and lakes or five miles from the sea, and they were forbidden to exercise their religion or to marry Venezuelan women. A few years afterwards, however, these articles were revised to permit complete freedom of religion.

In 1836, Reinier F. van Raders, who had been vice-governor *ad interim* for the last year because of Rammelman Elsevier's illness, succeeded to the latter's office. While his predecessors had always concentrated on trade as the main source of the islands' prosperity, Van Raders – perhaps under pressure from either The Hague or Paramaribo – turned to agriculture. Laudable in themselves, nevertheless his intentions showed great ignorance of the lessons of history. Dutch colonists had been laboring since the beginning, in 1635, to generate some agriculture in the arid soil of the islands, without much success. Governor Doncker's exertions had similarly failed to elicit any marked improvement as had, during the eighteenth century, those by the *Heren X*. In spite of the disappointing evidence so far, Van Raders set out with undisguised enthusiasm.

Part of the plan was to employ soldiers and to buy one of the existing plantations for the experiment. In addition, Van Raders resolved to distribute land to the small farmer – whether white, black, or mulatto. It was on this last account that the vice-governor lost the support of the rich, white merchants, who were week-end planters and dominated the small islands' economy. They were already disgruntled by a 1 per cent tax on the assessed value of their land, although it contributed only a puny 24,000 guilders a year to the colony's treasury. To compound his dejection, when Van Raders left the island in 1842 for a short leave, his temporary replacement openly expressed skepticism about the agricultural plan in the annual Colonial Report.

Van Raders' attempts to revive the government salt pans with the labor of slaves fared no better, partly due to the pleas made to the king by the owners of the private salt pans. Liberalism was at high tide in the Netherlands, favoring a hands-off policy, and private enterprise had emerged victorious over governmental interference. All in all, it was a poor time for government-sponsored projects. While in 1842 Van Raders could still count on a subsidy of 170,000 guilders for his agricultural and other designs, this amount decreased constantly thereafter.

Until 1846, however, there was still some vestige of sympathy in The Hague for the busy governor's plans, even though the benefits accruing from them so far had been minimal. In that year Van Raders was transferred to Surinam – undoubtedly a promotion – a country much better suited to his farming interests. This ended, of course, his participation in the Curaçao projects, which were shortly thereafter scrapped by his successor in Willemstad.

In 1845, The Hague, under King William II, separated the administration of the three colonial groups – Surinam, the Curaçao islands, and the Leeward islands – in view of their divergent interests. At this time, the three Leeward islands were joined to Willemstad in one colonial unit called *Curaçao en Onderhoorigheden,* Curaçao and Dependencies.

CHAPTER XIX

THE CURAÇAO ISLANDS FROM 1845 TO 1900

Major Rutger H. Esser, appointed governor of the six Caribbean islands in 1846, resided on Curaçao and was represented on each of the others by a vice-governor. The Hague, unwilling to subsidize the islands to the same degree as before, instructed Esser to trim expenses and not to imitate Van Raders' forays in agriculture. In the late forties, to wit, the trend of the Curaçao economy was still downhill. Because trade with Venezuela was now the main pillar of the island's prosperity, the slightest fluctuation in that country's political situation was reflected on Curaçao. An era of comparative stability in the thirties under the energetic Páez was followed by a period of liberal-conservative conflict and the rise of the Monagas brothers in the forties. In 1848, it took the new president, General José Tadeo Monagas, several months to stamp out the rebellions against his presidency. During that time, the Curaçao government strove to remain neutral. For instance, only official government men-of-war received clearance to enter the islands' ports while General Páez, leader of one of the revolts, was denied permission to sail into St. Ann Bay. Manuel E. Bruzual, a Venezuelan general conspiring in Willemstad against the Monagas clique, was expelled from the island. At the request of the Venezuelan government, Esser also forbade the export of war materials.

However, if this was the attitude of the colonial government as ordered by The Hague, it was certainly not that of the Curaçao people, most of whom were pro-Páez. Merchants, fondly remembering the profitable years of the Páez regime, continued to support the former president and to supply him with war commodities in open defiance of the regulations. This was made possible by the practice of many Venezuelan ships to fly the Dutch flag on the open seas in times of civil war and to display the Venezuelan colors closer to home in order to be able to navigate the coast without being intercepted.

In June, 1849, another revolution headed by Páez broke out against the Monagas regime. Again Curaçao was accused of being the headquarters of the revolutionary movement. In the *Republicano* (a Venezuelan paper) an article entitled 'La Holanda' demanded that the Dutch envoy surrender his credentials.

The *Curaçaosche Courant* denied the allegations and the Dutch Minister of the colonies in The Hague asserted that neither Curaçao nor its neighboring islands could have given Venezuela any cause for complaint. This was not quite true. The popular feeling on Curaçao as well as the remunerative smuggling of arms and other commodities were no secret to the colonial authorities or any one else for that matter.

The Monagas government expressed its displeasure by seizing various merchantmen from Curaçao which were anchored in Venezuelan harbors – an act glorified in the Venezuelan Senate by a speech insulting the Netherlands. The Dutch representative in Caracas immediately suspended relations and left the capital, and his government, informed of the seriousness of the situation, sent a squadron of six men-of-war to Puerto Cabello and La Guaira. At the same time, the so-called *Ley de Espera*, proclaiming a nine-year moratorium on all debts, including those to foreign creditors, caused Great Britain to threaten Venezuela with a blockade as well.

These actions resulted in a change of attitude on the part of President Monagas and negotiations between the Netherlands and Venezuela soon followed. After the ticklish problem of indemnification for Dutch ships seized by Venezuela had been settled, a better 'rapport' resulted except for the fact that the commercial agreement, canceled by the angry Monagas regime, was not renewed. Consequently trade relations were, for the next few years, hanging in limbo.

In 1855, riots took place in Coro during which some Curaçao Jewish businessmen were mistreated and robbed. Willemstad immediately sent men-of-war, but the Venezuelan government kept cool as a result of which an agreement was reached and compensation promised.

About that same time, a conflict arose between the Dutch and the Venezuelans over the guano-bearing Aves islands. Queen Isabel of Spain, acting as referee, decided in favor of Venezuela.

In the years 1858 to 1863, Venezuela passed through another civil war, in which old Páez was again conspicuous. As the Dutch did not honor his government, friction was bound to occur. The Hague instructed its representative in Willemstad to put a stop to the hatching of conspiracies and not to allow any arms and ammunition to leave the island. This edict, based upon recognition of the Caracas government, lost all meaning with the latter's demise.

In 1863, order in Venezuela was restored by General Juan C. Falcón among whose first actions as president was to conclude an agreement with the commercial house of Abraham J. Jesurun of Willemstad for the delivery of arms and other war commodities. Jesurun was not only a Curaçao Jew but he had actively supported the party of Falcón's opponents; yet, the new president was desperate enough to swallow his natural dislike and to invite the Jew to Caracas in order to arrange a loan guaranteed by 25 per cent of the customs receipts at Maracaibo. This loan, made in 1865, was still not enough to meet expenses and the next year the Jesurun House contracted to hand over 134,000 *pesos* immediately and to supply a daily sum of 5000 *pesos* (or 10,000 Dutch guilders) to the Venezuelan government for a period of eight months. Monthly interest was 1¼ per cent, guaranteed by adding the import duties of the custom house at Puerto Cabello to those of Maracaibo.

By this agreement the Jesurun House became a participant in the unstable politics of Venezuela, speculating, for the time being, on the Falcón government's ability to survive, but always willing to shift and support the more promising party. As a last resort, the House could always invoke the assistance of the Dutch government. This is just what happened a few years later when political events resulted in serious difficulties between Venezuela and the Netherlands.

Towards the end of the sixties, President Monagas, now in his eighties, made a last attempt to take over the government. Immediately shrill complaints were voiced against the colonial government of Curaçao and its pretended neutrality. It was alleged that the Dutch were permitting Falcón, defeated and exiled from Venezuela, to organize a counter movement from Curaçao. Two Dutch schooners loaded with arms, ammunition, and pro-Falcón partisans were captured by their Venezuelan opponents as a prelude to more incidents to come.

In December, 1868, President Monagas died, triggering another wave of violence in Venezuela and resentment towards Curaçao where the revolt against Monagas' successor was being devised. At this point, the new governor of Curaçao and Dependencies, Abraham M. de Rouville, received orders from The Hague to summarily expel all Venezuelan refugees from the island. In January, 1870, therefore, the governor invited four of the most prominent refugees to his office and reluctantly told them that since they had clearly abused Curaçao's hospitality, they must leave.

The Hague's instructions, not showing much insight into the situation, initiated a period of intense conflict, not only with Venezuela but also on the island itself. In an extra meeting on February 2, 1870, the *Raad* requested the governor to suspend the eviction order as being against both Curaçao's tradition and the interests of the colony. The Hague, they said, had made a mistake, being unfamiliar with local problems. The governor, although sympathetic to the *Raad's* advice, insisted that he, as representative of the Dutch government, was under obligation to execute the orders of that government without fail.

The eviction took place as decreed and its consequences were to have a lasting effect on Curaçao-Venezuelan relations. One of those expelled was Antonio Guzmán Blanco, who was to become the next president of the republic. Guzmán Blanco was to harbor a grudge against the Dutch and never quite forgave them the insult. So justified did he feel in his anger that he had no qualms about seizing Dutch ships belonging to the Jesurun House whenever he could. Worse still, when the Dutch representative in Caracas protested, Guzmán Blanco declared him *persona non grata*, suspecting him, probably with reason, of too close an affiliation with the Venezuelan conservative oligarchy.

In the absence of full diplomatic relations, exchanges between The Hague and Caracas were handled by the agent of the Northern German Confederacy. Friction increased, and The Hague sent a man-of-war to Curaçao with instructions to protect Dutch citizens and their interests in Venezuela. Both sides uttered their grievances in a series of notes, and the Dutch Minister of the Colonies was severely criticized for his order to De Rouville. During all these entanglements, commercial relations between Curaçao and the Venezuelan republic continued undisturbed, Dutch consuls carrying on their work as usual. After some time Guzmán Blanco mellowed and expressed a desire to re-establish diplomatic relations, with, however, a different Dutch representative in the Venezuelan capital. Negotiations in The Hague with a special envoy of the president resulted in an agreement indemnifying those Dutch shipowners whose ships had been captured, and arranging payment for debts accrued by the Venezuelan government with Curaçao bankers and merchants. In August, 1872, the agreement was capped by the sending of a new Dutch agent to Caracas. Tensions seemed to relax, for a while, at least.

But the matter continued to have internal repercussions on Curaçao. As mentioned before, the governor had obeyed The Hague against his better judgment. He had been strongly supported in this objection by his friend William Sassen, the attorney general. But The Hague needed a scapegoat and De Rouville was fired.

De Rouville being very popular, the population was naturally shocked to learn of the unprecedented turn of events. Worse yet, his successor was François C. Wagner, an ex-sergeant and the commander of St. Martin. In the opinion of many, Wagner, a man of humble origin must, of necessity, also be a man of few qualifications. Truthfully, he did lack the education and refinement of either a De Rouville or a Sassen.

The dismissal was a bitter pill for De Rouville to swallow. For Sassen it was even more difficult since he now had to work under a man whom he considered his inferior. Besides, it had become customary to step into the governorship from the post of attorney general. De Rouville had done so, and Sassen had probably expected to be next.

From the start there was much ill feeling between the new governor and his highest ranking assistant. When Sassen, as vice-president of the *Raad*, had to present the new governor, his words were poorly chosen, and in Wagner's opinion, even offensive. More incidents occurred in which Sassen's tactlessness was borne by the new governor with patience and restraint. Finally, Sassen was dismissed by The Hague. However, by this time, he had gained a certain popularity among blacks and mulattoes by posing as the defender of the underdog, and for the next two years, and longer, riots disturbed the traditional peace of Willemstad. At length Wagner's level-headedness prevailed. Sassen left the island in 1873, never to return. *Papachi* Sassen, Father Sassen as he was known to the people, may be considered one of the champions of the black man's rights even if his actions were partly inspired by self-interest.

In 1871, the *Hamburg Amerikanische Paketfahrt* began to include Curaçao in its cruise stops, shortening the distance to Europe considerably. Until the first Dutch steamship connection was opened in 1882, the Royal West India Mail Service, it still took four weeks, however, to cross the Atlantic or to receive letters and news from Europe.

In spite of sporadic efforts to promote agriculture or revive salt extraction, for both of which, economically speaking, the emancipation of the slaves in 1863 was a heavy blow, trade remained the main pillar of the island economy. Goat and sheepskins, wood, tobacco, cacao, and a few other commodities of local or Venezuelan origin were exchanged for European goods, an extremely profitable trade, but full of ups and downs because of its dependence on Venezuela and the European market. There was also some trade with the United States, which exchanged provisions and wood for shoes and hats made on the islands, but during their tempestuous sixties the North Americans wanted cash, not barter. Commercial relations with the mother country were few, with, until the latter half of the century, a mere two or three ships arriving any given year.

The main reason for this one-sided relationship, which was somewhat brightened by the highly profitable trade in war supplies was, of course, the fact that the Curaçao islands lacked any native products. Brazilwood, a common cargo in the seventeenth century, was no longer available; only the tannin-producing divi-divi wood was exported to merchants in Hamburg and

Amsterdam. In the early 1800's, there were a few orange groves, but these died in spite of Van Raders' efforts. The salt pans sometimes made a nice profit: Curaçao produced almost 56,000 barrels in 1844, and Bonaire more than 100,000, but too few people were involved to bring general prosperity. The work was done by slaves; as a result emancipation and the competition from rock salt smothered this industry. The number of plantations, 362 in 1828, dwindled to about 100 in 1865; emancipation signalled the end of the 'big houses,' which never had rendered more than the bare minimum to the growing population.

There was, during the nineteenth century, a sizable ship-building industry located near St. Ann Bay. During the hurricane season many ships sought refuge in Curaçao's safe harbor, and used the delay to make repairs. In 1815, four dry-docks existed to handle the demand. Later in the century, new ships, up to 250 tons, were also built. In 1855, for instance, five medium-sized schooners, solidly constructed for fast sailing, were launched in St. Ann Bay. This industry, which gave work to a few hundred men, later in the century expanded into three middle-sized yards and five smaller ones. These operated until after World War I, when one after another closed.

In 1871, John Godden, an English mining engineer, discovered phosphate on Little Curaçao and received a concession to exploit it. Three years later, veins of phosphate were also found on the southern slopes of Table Mountain on eastern Curaçao. During its heyday, between 1920 and 1930, this industry employed an average of 2000 men. After 1930, decline sat in and only 400 to 500 laborers were retained. In the sixties, the veins began to show signs of exhaustion and, today, the phosphate industry too belongs to the past.

Before the construction of the oil refineries, in 1916, more than 1600 women worked in the straw hat industry with exports reaching 350,000 guilders. The business of making cigars from imported tobacco was never significant and had already ceased to exist before the oil came.

In the nineteenth century, fishing was the occupation of many men living along the southern coast of the islands. The oil affected the fisheries less than it did several other industries for, although many young men preferred the security and higher wages offered by the oil, the demand for fish continued to grow. In that same century and well into the twentieth, Bonaire mainly produced salt, which fluctuated in price, while Aruba exported a little gold which did likewise.

CHAPTER XX

THE EMANCIPATION OF THE CURAÇAO SLAVES

When Governor-General Kikkert acceded to the government of the Dutch Antilles after the English interregnum, he inherited a slave system that had survived virtually unchanged from the days of the West India Company. In spite of the slave rebellion of Tula and Carpata, the memory of which was still fresh in 1816, no serious efforts had been undertaken to improve the conditions under which the slaves lived and worked. It was a period of rising liberalism and social legislation was taboo.

As observed before, the ministers of the Dutch Reformed Church were no more inclined to consider the slaves their brethren in the Lord than to proselytize them, an attitude adopted by Lutherans and Jews also. Working under adverse conditions, Franciscans and Jesuits had made some attempts before 1816 to christianize the slaves, but their work had been disorganized and intermittent, with consequent poor results. The slaves, in the first quarter of the century, lived without religion, education, or marriage.

With the return of Dutch rule in 1816, a regular missionary effort was made and subsidized by public funds. The obstacles put in its way by the merchant-planter elite were summarized, in 1818, by a certain Father Stöppel, who had worked with the blacks. He reported that the Protestant masters often refused to allow Roman Catholic missionaries on their plantations, or denied them permission to baptize children, hold services, perform marriages, or comfort the dying. Also, slave families were often broken up by sales.

Father Stöppel implored the king's intercession; instead, William I forwarded the letter to the colonial government for investigation and counsel, thus making known the priest's complaints to the very persons involved. The *Raad*, understandably, reacted strongly by suspending Stöppel from his duties. They probably would have discharged him as well if he had not suddenly died. With this well-meaning but tactless and impatient champion of the slaves out of the way, the *Raad* heaved a sigh of relief, and reverted to doing nothing.

In the meantime, however, some positive steps were being taken by the home government. In 1818, a treaty was concluded with Great Britain in which the slave trade (from Africa) was forbidden. However, the immediate effect of this agreement was not very encouraging. It was extremely difficult to seize the fast sailing slavers and stop the smuggling. In 1821, the treaty was amplified and illicit trade, as far as the Dutch were concerned, ended.

In 1823, a royal decision opened the way for the Roman Catholic clergy to go to the West Indies under government sponsorship. Two priests applied and were accepted. The first, Martinus Niewindt, was given a princely salary of 2500 guilders annually, while the other priest, his chaplain, received 1500 guilders from public funds. In 1824, the two of them set foot on Curaçao and for the first time a regular Roman Catholic mission could be established. Niewindt, a man of humble background, would stay in the West Indies for almost forty years and become the first bishop of the Dutch Antilles. When he came to the island, the emancipation of the slaves could not have been further from his mind. All he wanted was to incorporate the latter into the realm of Roman Catholic christianity. How to reconcile a good Christian with a slaveholder was of no interest to him. As a matter of fact, he did not hesitate to buy a female slave for a housekeeper. But he realized only too well that emancipation was inevitable, and if it were not to end in disaster for the slaves as well as the colony, it must be prepared for, which to Niewindt meant that the slaves must be given a basic education and a Roman Catholic indoctrination. This purpose guided Niewindt's efforts from the beginning, bringing him at times into conflict with the colonial government and even with his own free diocesans.

In those days, all slaves on the Curaçao islands were divided into three groups: domestic slaves, craftsmen, and land-slaves. The domestic slaves were mulattoes fathered by some white merchant or planter. Their lives, rendering service in and around the house, were far from miserable, except that the danger of losing the good will of the master was like a sword hanging over their heads. Pretty young females also ran the risk of rousing the jealousy of their mistresses. The slaves who had learned some craft formed the second group. They were often hired out by their masters or worked independently paying him a certain sum. Not infrequently they were in a position to buy their freedom. The remaining share of the slave population were the ones who tilled the soil. Some of these land-slaves were baptized, most were not. There was some legislation, vaguely restricting their masters' power over them, but in most cases an owner could do with his slave as he darn well pleased – short of killing him, that is.

Niewindt had not been in the colony for long when the government issued a decree making the working hours, meals, and clothing of the slaves the subject of official concern. Although he agreed wholeheartedly with this exercise to improve conditions, as a man of God he felt that his priestly duties must take priority. His first years, therefore, were spent in consolidating the mission. With a small but constantly growing staff Niewindt worked, baptized, preached, and converted, slowly changing the indifferent and ignorant mass of slaves into a coherent, Christian group. One aspect of slavery which he found most galling was the ban against slave marriages. Circumventing this hateful proscription, he introduced a *matrimonium clandestinum*, performed without witnesses by a priest, and, of course, made valid only by the dictates of one's conscience and the Roman Catholic Church.

In 1833, the slaves obtained the right to testify in court – even against whites; the master who put obstacles in the way of this order was threatened with a fine. A year later, a new decree arrived from The Hague insisting that the slaves be protected, yet recommending that the rights of the owners not be jeopardized – an impossible demand. In 1834, Great Britain abolished slavery and substituted an unworkable apprentice system. Niewindt explained this away, proclaiming that the English had not prepared their slaves for freedom, and continued to press for the education and religious instruction of all slaves under Dutch rule.

In 1840, the government gave its official blessing to baptizing slaves. Shortly afterwards, the Curaçao mission was elevated to an Apostolic Vicariate, with Niewindt as its bishop. At this time the idea of total emancipation was very much alive and the subject of many a discussion in the Dutch colonies, as well as in the mother country. The French revolution of 1848 precipitated another emancipation effort without preparation, this time in the French Antilles, with results no more encouraging than the British had been. On St. Martin, the Dutch slaves, looking askance at their French brethren, freed themselves and were soon followed by those on St. Eustatius and Saba, adding momentum to the movement for emancipation on the Curaçao islands.

The first proposals for emancipation were discussed in the Dutch parliament as early as the fifties. One proposal followed another, all to be rejected due to the huge sums involved, for the slaveowners of Curaçao and Surinam alike expected compensation.

Far better than any of his predecessors, Governor Nicolaas van Lansberge (1856–'59) understood the necessity of educating for emancipation and did not allow his Protestantism to stand in the way of an energetic collaboration with the Roman Catholic bishop. In 1857, there were six schools on the island with 1600 pupils, 1400 of whom were children of free blacks or mulattoes.

White children attended separate schools. In that same year, Niewindt and Van Lansberge lobbied for a new government regulation requiring the children of slaves to attend school.

Van Lansberge was also the first governor to insist that better care be taken of the government's slaves working the *salinjas* (salt pans) of Bonaire. The presiding officials were ordered to give the slaves time off to go to church and to allow them to send their children to school. At the same time, the governor amended the ordinance of 1824 regulating food, clothing, and other items for the slaves, greatly improving the living conditions for all.

When emancipation finally came to pass, in 1863, the new freedmen were all Christians. The wisdom of Niewindt's foresight was evident, although he himself did not live to see the peaceful change-over, having died more than two years earlier. For his incessant endeavors, the bishop is known to posterity as the Wilberforce of the Curaçao islands, much the same as Simón Planas is to Venezuela, and Joaquim Nabuco to Brazil. Although there were some slight setbacks – many freed slaves refused, for instance, to work for their former masters, even for fair wages – emancipation did not bring about a recession in the colony's economy. The Curaçao islands, especially the main one, were not planters' but merchants' islands, and slavery was not as vital to prosperity as, for example, in Surinam. In Curaçao, agriculture was a sideline, not a main source of income, and the plantations had become little more than week-end resorts for the merchants. More than before, the island's plantations now became the suppliers of sand (for construction) and water (sand and water 'plantations'), while the salt 'plantation' disappeared; salt produced by paid labor was no longer a lucrative commodity.

CHAPTER XXI

RELATIONS BETWEEN CURAÇAO AND VENEZUELA
TOWARDS THE END OF THE NINETEENTH CENTURY

From 1870 to 1888, Venezuela was ruled by the Great Liberal Party under the leadership of Antonio Guzmán Blanco. In 1874, a rebellion broke out against the self-styled Illustrious American, who, without having any proof, accused the Curaçao commercial house of Jesurun of having financed the uprising. He demanded not only that all Venezuelans be extradited, but also that an indemnification be paid to cover the expenses incurred to suppress the revolt. Curaçao's colonial government, instructed by The Hague, refused to bow to those demands and, in retaliation, the Venezuelan dictator resorted to the old tactic of seizing Dutch ships. Diplomatic relations, restored in 1873, were again severed and, on several occasions, war seemed inevitable. When, in 1877, Guzmán Blanco left his country for Paris, leaving his puppet Francisco L. Alcántara in control, relations improved somewhat, but at the return of the Illustrious American two years later, the situation again deteriorated visibly.

In the early eighties, Guzmán Blanco had his rubber-stamp Congress pass a law introducing differential duties of 30 per cent on goods imported from, but not produced, on the Antilles. Although it is true that this measure also affected the British with whom he was having difficulties over Guiana, the president's main intent was undoubtedly to deliver a mortal blow to the Dutch islands. He had not forgotten his prior eviction from Willemstad and, after his plan to buy Curaçao in order to build himself a new capital there had come to naught, another reason had been added to this animosity.

The additional duty hurt Curaçao bitterly and would have even more, if smuggling had not risen to the task and taken over much of the regular trade before long. Protests by the Netherlands, Great Britain, the United States, and others, did not mollify the attitude of the Illustrious American. The tax was here to stay and, under succeeding presidents, came to play an important role in the relations between Venezuela and the Curaçao islands.

There were other, more persistent causes for tension. Throughout the nineteenth century Venezuela was plagued by continuous unrest and persistent turmoil, and to maintain neutrality was not always easy, although the Dutch colonial government managed as well as could be expected. During General Venancio Pulgar's rebellion against President Joaquín Crespo, for instance, the Governor of Curaçao did not allow rebel ships to enter the islands' ports. Two years later, in 1887, when Guzmán Blanco was in control of Venezuela for the third time, the latter requested that the Dutch governor at Willemstad extradite some pamphlet-writing Venezuelans, threatening to end what little remained of commercial relations between the two countries. But when the American ambassador in Caracas warned that the United States would deplore a break in relations between the Curaçao islands and Venezuela, the Illustrious American managed to contain himself and nothing happened. The Venezuelan refugees stayed where they were.

In 1888, Guzmán Blanco disappeared for good from the Venezuelan scene, but it was not until 1894 that an agreement was reached with The Hague to reinstate diplomatic relations between the troubled republic and the Netherlands. With this agreement, friendship between Venezuela and the Curaçao islands seemed to be assured, even after 1898 when during an insurrection on the mainland, Crespo was killed. In 1900, a new Dutch agent was appointed to represent the Netherlands and her West Indian colonies in Caracas. At the same time, the Dutch archives were made available to Venezuela in order to back up any claims in this country's boundary dispute with Great Britain, and it seemed that the two nations had entered a new phase of good will. In 1901, the Venezuelan government openly declared its appreciation of the prevailing entente cordiale. This announcement was the more remarkable when we consider that it coincided with the rise to power of one of the most capricious men the Venezuelan political scene has ever witnessed, Cipriano Castro, under whose leadership relations with France, Italy, Belgium, and Germany deteriorated rapidly. But the honeymoon with the Dutch was of short duration. Castro soon decided to honor neither public nor private debts to foreigners, a move affecting the Netherlands also and one which not only lost prestige for the republic abroad but almost brought on an economic catastrophe at home.

In January, 1901, the so-called *junta calificadora*, a commission composed entirely of Venezuelans, was installed to investigate foreigners' complaints and demands – but not those dated prior to May, 1899, for which Castro felt no responsibility. Another limitation decreed by the president stated that forthwith debts would be paid not in cash but in government bonds. Germany, Great Britain, Italy, Spain, and the Netherlands collectively refused to accept these terms, indicating their willingness to submit the affair to a court of arbitration, although, to be sure, the Netherlands and Great Britain both reserved for themselves the right of diplomatic intervention if their complaints were not handled satisfactorily. Ignoring all protests, Castro stuck with the *junta*.

Dutch charges of misconduct were many and well-founded. To enumerate, in 1900, two Dutch ships were seized by the Venezuelan coast guard; in March of 1902, a Dutch ship sailing from Curaçao to Coro had been captured. In April of that same year another ship had been boarded but released; in August this same ship was again overmastered. In May, a third ship followed and in August, a fourth. Most often the cargoes had been confiscated without either a word of explanation or compensation, while the ships had been sold.

Besides these accusations concerning ships and cargoes, many inhabitants of the Dutch islands had claims against individual Venezuelans, some dating to before May 1899, others stemming from the span between May and October. Yet, the *junta calificadora* refused to consider these cases, alleging either that they did not fulfill the requirements of the decree of 1901 or that they were too minor.

Feeling ran high on both sides. Dutch citizens living in Venezuela, most of them from the Antilles, were accused of revolutionary activities and imprisoned; some were even drafted into the Venezuelan army and only released after repeated notes from the Dutch envoy and the threat of a Dutch man-of-war on the horizon.

A similar confrontation was brewing with the other countries concerned, among whom Germany undeniably had the most compelling claims. After negotiations with the Castro government had collapsed, Great Britain and Germany lost their patience and determined to use force to bring the Venezuelan ruler to his senses. After informing the United States of their intentions, they still waited almost a year before taking any action. In December, 1902, Germany finally presented the Castro regime with an ultimatum requiring payment of those debt outstanding since the period from 1898 to 1900, and demanding arbitration for successive ones. Great Britain followed suit. Both countries broke relations with the Venezuelan government and announced a blockade of the Venezuelan coast. Soon Italy joined them.

Although Castro's first reaction was to imprison all Germans, Englishmen, and Italians in Venezuela, after his initial anger had cooled, he realized the seriousness of the situation and indicated his government's willingness to accept arbitration. In the talks which followed, an American note seems to have been instrumental in coercing the Venezuelan president into compromising. He gave in to most demands and, in February, 1903, an agreement was reached with the three blockading powers.

In that same month, a treaty was concluded between Venezuela and the Netherlands in which no mention was made of the 30 per cent tax, long a thorn in the flesh of the Netherlands Antilles. But Castro continued to be a whimsical and unpredictable ruler. The agreement of 1903 did not signal an end to all tensions. Indeed, for several years, or as long as Castro was to remain in power, relations grew from bad to worse. Ships continued to be seized for the usual flimsy reasons, namely that they supported rebel movements and carried arms and ammunition to insurgents. This may have been true sometimes; however, in the majority of cases, these allegations were totally unfounded. In 1908, all ties between the Curaçao islands and the Land of Bolívar were again severed and the two sides were perilously close to actual warfare when the Castro government was unexpectedly overthrown and a new ruler came to power. Juan Vicente Gómez, the 'tyrant of the Andes' was to inaugurate an iron-fisted dictatorship which was to dominate Venezuela for twenty-seven years.

Of a different caliber than his predecessor, Gómez immediately moved to improve the rankling relations with the European powers and perhaps the first to benefit from this change in official attitude were the Curaçao islands. Diplomatic relations with The Hague were once more restored, and a new era in the history of the Netherlands Antilles was heralded in. The 30 per cent differential duty, however, did continue to provide a rallying point for future discontent, although never again to the point that both nations were willing to risk war for its sake. Finally, in 1920, this last festering sore, although not permanently removed, ceased to be an obstacle to a mutual good will attitude in an agreement which came to pass as a consequence of the discovery of oil near Lake Maracaibo.

CHAPTER XXII

OIL COMES TO THE CURAÇAO ISLANDS

As early as 1907, the Castro regime had given the British a concession to search for oil in Venezuela. Its successor, the government of Juan Vicente Gómez, betting on oil to alleviate the country's financial problems, freely handed out more concessions, making sure, in the process, that the national treasury cashed in on the demand while Gómez' own pockets were properly lined. In due time, the Dutch-British SHELL, in combination with the General Asphalt Company of the United States, requested permission to exploit the rich oil-fields in the Maracaibo region. Armed with a "fifty-fifty" concession signed by President Gómez – fifty per cent of the profits were to be spent in the country – the new merger was on the look-out for a place to refine the oil it would drill in Venezuela. That country itself did not seem to be suitable, mainly because of its internal turmoil, but also due to the poor facilities characterizing all Venezuelan ports as well as their malarial climate. The Curaçao islands, especially the big one, seemed to provide the answer, in spite of insufficient water and a shortage of experienced laborers. More crucially, the colonial government vouchsafed political stability and the islands had a milder, healthier climate. The distance from Willemstad to Maracaibo was little more than 200 miles. From Curaçao transportation to the most important buyers of refined oil, Europe and the United States, was no problem: Curaçao was 800 miles closer to Europe than Houston, also under consideration, and 200 miles closer to New York. In those days the Panama canal was completed, further promising to turn Curaçao into a relay station for many ships as well as a port of international dimensions.

In 1914, a SHELL agent arrived on Curaçao to investigate the possibilities for a refinery to handle the Venezuelan oil. Discussion in The Hague as well as in Willemstad resulted in a favorable decision, and, in 1915, the SHELL bought three plantations around the Schottegat. In time, almost all the land around this spacious harbor was acquired and in the center, called the Isla because it had originally been an island, the new plant began to take shape.

World War I delayed the construction of the refinery, although in 1916 450 persons had found work on the premises. In 1917, SHELL established a special branch to handle the oil, called the Curaçao Oil Company Ltd., with headquarters in The Hague. A few years later this offshoot was renamed the Curaçao Oil Industry Company (*Curaçaose Petroleum Industrie Maatschappij* or C.P.I.M.) and its headquarters were moved to Willemstad. The name was changed again in 1959 to SHELL Curaçao Ltd.

To move the oil from the Maracaibo fields to Curaçao, a special company was founded, the Curaçao Navigation Company Ltd. (*Curaçaose Scheepvaart Maatschappij* or C.S.M.), and a special type of tanker – the *laker* – was designed to pass the shallow entrance to Maracaibo Lake. The tanker fleet soon grew in number and carrying capacity. In 1929, more than 30 tankers were in operation between Willemstad and Maracaibo, some of them as large as 3000 tons.

After World War I, the refinery grew steadily. In 1919, the amount of oil processed amounted to 14,000 tons; ten years later it had risen to 20,000 tons a day, and in 1959 this amount had doubled. In 1919, the value of the exported oil was only 736,000 guilders as compared to 1929 when it had risen to over 215,000,000 guilders. Taxes on oil, accruing to the colonial treasury, followed the same trend. The importance of the oil tankers to the port of Willemstad can easily be surmised. In 1919, only two small ships of 800 tons each transported the oil from the fields of Maracaibo to the Isla. Ten years later there were 34 *lakers* in the fleet, averaging 2600 tons each, and total tonnage had risen to 85,000 tons.

As the oil industry expanded, the island entered upon a period of prosperity unparalleled even in the eighteenth century. In 1924, for the first time since the Dutch had taken over from the English in 1816, the colonial budget was out of the red, and no subsidy was needed from the mother country. The world depression, naturally, slowed this prosperity down somewhat. SHELL paid out 11 million guilders in salaries and wages in 1927, 15 million in 1928, and over 21 million in 1930, but the amount fell in 1931, and reached its lowest point in 1932 with only $2\frac{1}{2}$ million guilders. Two years later the depression belonged to the past and the curve rose again. In 1935, the wages climbed to $9\frac{1}{2}$ million guilders and soon World War II was to precipitate another boom.

Some side effects of oil were of questionable value. Attracted by the many fringe benefits offered by the SHELL, the Dutch flocked to the island returning to the homeland upon reaching the age of retirement (50 years). Not only was Curaçao's social structure irrevocably altered by this influx of whites, but with the constant turnover in population, established traditions were wont to disappear. The automobile, radio, refrigerator, and television produced something akin to a cultural shock from which the inhabitants emerged with new ideas and different values. Young men were lured away from time-honored professions such as fishing by the higher wages offered by the oil company. For the first time in its history, except perhaps during times of stress, Curaçao had to import food on a large scale, which it did primarily from Venezuela, the Netherlands, and the United States.

In 1934, Curaçao became part of the K.L.M. flight schedule, which some years later was extended to the other islands and Surinam as well. The first tourists soon began to arrive on the island, sparking a new industry. Hotels were built; facilities created and expanded.

The new prosperity was not restricted to the main island. Aruba, until 1924 even less important than Bonaire, was, in that year, singled out for the construction of another refinery. The British Equatorial Oil Company was looking for a suitable place to refine its Venezuelan oil without having to go too far. The best locations on Curaçao had already been taken so the new company wound up in Aruba. The Lago Oil and Transport Company Ltd., the newly created branch of the parent company, settled at St. Nicolaas where the Paardenbaai (Horse Bay) offered protection to the *lakers* from Maracaibo. In November, 1927, the first of these arrived at the bay and a new era began for peaceful Aruba. In that same year, another company, the Arend Oil Company (*Arend Petroleum Maatschappij*), another of SHELL's offshoots, began construction of a refinery in the northeast section of the island at Druifbaai (Bay of Grapes) and by June, 1928, the first barrels of refined oil were exported from this site. Yet Arend lagged far behind both the C.P.I.M. and the LAGO and, in 1960, it was incorporated into the SHELL Netherlands Antilles Sales Company (*SHELL Nederlandse Antillen Verkoop Maatschappij*).

St. Nicolaas, which, before 1927, had been a sleepy fishing village, bustled with life and quickly grew into a medium-sized town. The LAGO Company, taken over by Standard Oil in 1932, became an important industry with more than 7000 employees (as compared to almost 14,000 of Curaçao's SHELL in its top years) in the early fifties – a number which automation had reduced to around 1700 in 1967. The same problems encountered on Curaçao as a result of the spiraling riches occurred, to a lesser degree, on Aruba.

CHAPTER XXIII

THE CURAÇAO ISLANDS FROM WORLD WAR I TO WORLD WAR II

During World War I the Netherlands managed to remain neutral which made for more advantages and fewer problems in the Caribbean colonies than in the mother country. German power, all permeating in the North Sea, was considerably less of a threat across the Atlantic. Although the Curaçao islands were never in any serious danger, nevertheless just prior to the outbreak of hostilities the Dutch government stationed two men-of-war at Willemstad.

Despite the non-involvement, Curaçao did not escape the effects of war altogether. Imports from the mother country often failed to arrive, and after 1917, when the United States entered the war, supplies became a problem. Some South American countries, especially Argentina and Chile, soon filled the gap so that shortages did not occur.

Trade with the rest of the world, of course, stagnated. Whereas in 1913 almost 1500 ships dropped anchor at Willemstad, among them 415 steamships with at total of 2,800,000 tons, by 1918 this number had fallen to 248 steamships and only a little over 680,000 tons. On the other hand, local navigation continued to increase. Sailing ships and coasters, totalling about 122,000 tons in 1913, had reached over 200,000 tons by the end of the war. But this increase far from compensated for the big losses in tonnage from ocean steamers. Only after peace had come again, were navigation and trade restored to their prior highs.

During and immediately after the war, The Hague continued to subsidize its West Indian possessions to insure their survival. In 1919, aid to the Curaçao islands alone amounted to one million guilders annually. In 1924, however, for the first time since 1816, the islands' revenues exceeded the expenses and no subsidy was needed. This was repeated in 1925 and thereafter, except for 1929, when an unusual incident, namely a bold assault on Fort Amsterdam, caused not only a deficit in the colonial budget but temporarily interrupted the island's peaceful development.

This attack was closely related to the political developments in Venezuela,

where, since 1908, Gómez had held sway notwithstanding intermittent in-
surrections and riots. One of these rebellions was headed by Rafael Urbina.
From a well-known Venezuelan family, Urbina, in 1929, was 32 years old.
Due to his involvement in previous conspiracies, he had never completed his
military studies. In November, 1922, he had gone to Trinidad and Curaçao
in order to rally Venezuelans against the Gómez regime, but had failed to
generate much enthusiasm. Three years later, when Gómez proclaimed a
general amnesty for all refugees, Urbina had returned to his country, but by
1926 he could no longer resist the temptation of conspiring against the
dictator.

In 1929, Urbina arrived in Willemstad with a passport issued in Costa
Rica under the name of Pedro Bonilla. He talked to many people, particularly ex-students who had left Venezuela after an attempt to overthrow the
regime in 1928. Together they organized a coup against Gómez, which called
for providing the rebels with weapons from Fort Amsterdam and sailing
from there to one of the Venezuelan ports. Urbina seems to have investigated
local conditions very well; he knew the strength of the garrison, the hours
when the changing of the guard took place and many other important
details.

When all preparations had been made, on Saturday, June 8, 1929, after
sunset, Urbina arrived at the fort with two trucks and 45 men. The gates
were open and he brazenly drove inside. The Dutch guards were not immediately alarmed, although they did report the arrival to their commanding
officer, pointing out that the trucks were driving without headlights. Meanwhile, the conspirators, armed with knives and automatic pistols, jumped out
of the trucks and divided themselves into three groups. One detachment
disarmed the unsuspecting soldiers at the gate, another fanned out to occupy the buildings, fatally wounding one man, while the third group headed
for the barracks. It being the week-end, the majority of the garrison was out
on a pass: no more than 35 men had been left to defend the fort.

Resistance was brief. The attack was spirited and sudden; the Dutch
soldiers, finding themselves without efficient leadership, became demoralized
and quickly surrendered. The Venezuelans entered the ammunition depot,
seizing rifles and other arms. In the meantime, another group, composed of
between five and six hundred men, closed off the pontoon bridge across the
St. Ann Bay and occupied the streets leading to the fort. Within half an hour
Fort Amsterdam as well as a considerable section of Willemstad were under
the control of the assailant. Urbina's men were not only superbly organized,
but a credit to the Venezuelan's outstanding leadership.

At the time of the attack, the Governor of Curaçao, Leonard Fruytier, found himself in his official dwelling, which formed part of the fortress. Hearing the turmoil outside, he had looked down from a window and seen his men taking cover shooting at what seemed to him invisible opponents. As soon as he was told of what was happening, he evacuated his family to another part of the palace and tried to get in touch with the commander of the garrison, who was away from the fort at the time.

It is not quite clear what happened next. It was rumored that the attackers were threatening to level the refinery, but how they could possibly have done so remains a mystery. The director of the oil company, nevertheless, stationed guards at the gates and gave strict orders that no one be allowed to pass. But Urbina showed no interest whatsoever either in following up his conquest or in dismantling the island's principal industry. His one aim was to acquire the means to start a revolution against Gómez, and once he had accomplished this goal, his only object was to get away.

Meeting with the Dutch governor, Urbina solicited the latter's coope-ration in helping him and his men to return to Venezuela. Fruytier, for all practical purposes a prisoner of the Venezuelan, had little choice. He ordered his soldiers to cease fire, and requisitioned a Venezuelan steamer, the *Mara-caibo*, to take Urbina where he wanted to go. The little episode had netted the Venezuelan 4 machine guns, nearly 200 rifles, and some ammunition, as well as 3500 guilders taken from a government safe.

Urbina forced the Dutch governor and a few other high officials to ac-company him as hostages as far as the Venezuelan coast, where sloops were hailed, and he took off on his own. The *Maracaibo* returned to Curaçao and arrived on Sunday afternoon to a silent welcome.

In Fruytier's absence, Adriaan Berger, the garrison commander, had hur-riedly assumed control of the government forming a civilian militia composed of members of the dissolved Defense Corps. As soon as the governor was back, however, Berger relinquished his command. Fruytier immediately called a meeting of the Colonial *Raad*, the members of which, prodded by the nagging fear that the Venezuelans would return, voted to request reinforce-ments from the Dutch and Surinam governments. On the advice of The Hague, martial law was subsequently declared, the daily papers were cen-sored, and restaurants and cafes closed.

In the Netherlands, feelings ran high and the unwarranted reaction was not surprising. News of the attack had arrived just as Dowager Queen Emma's birthday was being celebrated and the country was steeped in festivities.

Displeased with the course of action Fruytier had chosen to follow, the Dutch government ordered the governor to keep silent, "in the interest of the country," and relieved him of his duties. In July, Fruytier left the colony convinced that he had acted in the best interest of the inhabitants. Upon his arrival in The Hague in September, he was made the scapegoat for the Dutch government's negligence to provide the Curaçao islands with an adequate defense system. A commission appointed to look into this grievous omission failed to publish any report. Instead of putting out some feelers as to how the Venezuelan government had fared in the revolt, the Dutch forthwith apologized for Urbina's attack on Venezuelan territory. However, President Gómez was unmoved by these friendly overtures. Not only did he accuse the Dutch government of siding with the rebels, but he launched an investigation to determine the extent of collusion. Requests for Urbina's extradition went unanswered. The revolt had been a dismal failure and Urbina himself had been killed at the outset.

Appointed to succeed Fruytier was Bartholomeus van Slobbe, a soldier *par excellence*, who had to deal, not with repeated Venezuelan invasions, but with the Great Depression. The refineries on Curaçao and Aruba stopped their growth and began to lay off employees until, within two years, their number had dwindled to half of what it had been in 1929. In 1931, there were close to 1300 unemployed laborers on Curaçao in addition to the 5000 people who, in that same year, had left the island. With the backing of a progressive Dutch bishop, some tentative efforts had been made to unionize the laborers, but they had met with little success. In 1929, the Roman Catholic Church again attempted to be in the forefront of social reform when another priest, Petrus I. Verriet, launched a Roman Catholic Laborers Association. Van Slobbe might not have been the right man under the circumstances, but whatever his personal feelings, he did see the need for social legislation. This is more than can be said for the Colonial *Raad*, where outdated ideas of old liberal resistance to government control and supervision in the field of labor continued to prevail.

Around 1935, the worst of the depression belonged to the past and the economy was slowly recovering. The oil refineries on both Curaçao and Aruba had already increased production and the improvement showed no sign of abating. Another indication of better times was the growing importance of immigration.

Things being so, the governor's legislation now had a better chance of being accepted. Van Slobbe's accident and health insurance, amended and supplemented several times, in time became the basis of the government's social welfare program. In 1939, for instance, child labor was prohibited – thirteen being the minimal age. As a military man, Van Slobbe also paid close attention to the defense of the islands, a matter which, after Urbina's easy conquest, had attained top priority in The Hague. Until then almost nothing had been done except to maintain a garrison, while both fortresses and guns were hopelessly outdated. Van Slobbe vigorously pushed for reforms in this area, not forgetting Aruba and Bonaire.

In 1936, Van Slobbe was succeeded by Guilliam Wouters, a man experienced in civil as well as in military affairs. Two months after the new governor had assumed command, the English government devalued the pound, creating a precedent for the successive devaluations of other currencies including the Dutch guilder. To stop the outflow of bullion to Venezuela and other countries, Wouters immediately prohibited the export of Dutch and Antillian gold and silver, coined and uncoined. Shortly afterwards, despite the opposition of the business interests dominating the *Raad*, he promulgated a law fixing prices at a set level.

At this time it was realized in The Hague that now that the colony had become self-sufficient financially, it would want a greater degree of self-government. Consequently, the Colonial *Raad* was made more representative and its name was changed to States. At the insistence of Wouters, the franchise was extended to include every adult who could satisfy the minimum educational requirements. Even so, the new law doubled the number of eligible inhabitants to only 3 per cent of a total population of 90,000.

The political events in Europe after Hitler came to power forced the Dutch government to re-examine its national as well as its colonial defenses and, in 1937, Wouters' designs for the Dutch Caribbean islands were debated at length in The Hague. Forthwith the States voted to allocate an additional 100,000 guilders towards the 1939 defense budget of the Netherlands Antilles – 656,000 guilders in total – with the mother country underwriting other needed outlays. The volunteer corps, founded after Urbina's coup, was also revived and reorganized. In August, 1939, just before Germany invaded Poland, mobilization of the Royal Dutch Navy was decreed and, a few days later, all Antillian draftees were ordered to report. At the beginning of September, a board was set up to regulate the supply of food imports and similar measures soon followed. The government was girding itself for a long siege.

In March of 1940, the German consul left Willemstad accompanied by some of his nation's ships which had been anchored in either Curaçao or Aruba waters. Others delayed and, after May 10, when the Germans invaded Holland and the Dutch government fled to London, were summarily seized.

Curaçao's strategic value was obvious and, before long, the governor extended an invitation to the British and French governments to station troops on the island. Not only would the allies contribute significantly to the defense of the Curaçao islands, but the coalition itself was to be bolstered by this overt display of solidarity. When, in 1941, the United States entered the war, the Curaçao islands became part of the so-called Caribbean Sea Frontier, and in February, 1942, American soldiers took the place of the British and the French. Allied headquarters were in San Juan, Puerto Rico, and the commander of the military forces on the Curaçao islands was a member of the general staff.

The Curaçao islands now formed an essential link in the American defense periphery. The gold reserves of the Bank of Curaçao, about eight and a half million guilders, were shipped to the United States for safe-keeping. The Americans modernized the airports and made them feasible for bombers. Blackouts became mandatory and iron nets were lowered in St. Ann Bay and some others to prevent the German U-boats, which seemed to be everywhere, from entering. Although there was never any overt danger of German occupation, many tankers sailing to and from the islands were torpedoed and sunk by the enemy. In February, 1942, a refinery was even bombed. For some time in 1941 and 1942, these attacks came close to paralyzing the transport of oil. Oil, of course, was too important to allied warfare for any chances to be taken. In February 1942, the officers and crews of the Curaçao Navigation Company were brought under military law, forced to sail whenever ordered. Those who opposed the measure were imprisoned and court-martialed. The refineries on both islands increased production, with the SHELL reaching 30,000 tons daily. Curaçao and Aruba provided the allied forces with 80 per cent of their high octane fuel needs. It is no exaggeration to say that the war was fed by the gasoline refined on Curaçao and Aruba.

With the German occupation, relations between the Netherlands and her oversees territories were severed. All reliance on imports from the mother country came to an abrupt halt, causing some discomfort but no real shortcomings. Food, once brought from Holland was now again provided by the United States, Argentina, Venezuela or Colombia. Workers no longer available from the Netherlands were replaced by Antillians. In these various ways the war contributed to the development of another, more independent status for the islands. When, after five years, in May, 1945, The Hague reasserted her authority, the relationship had irrevocably shifted and demands for autonomy could no longer be denied. Thus, after 1945, the struggle for self-government commenced.

CHAPTER XXIV

THE DUTCH LEEWARD ISLANDS IN THE NINETEENTH AND TWENTIETH CENTURIES

In 1816, the three Leeward islands, organized into one governmental unit as the result of the Regulation of September, 1815, returned to Dutch control. The governor's seat and a central Council of Justice were located on St. Eustatius. That island, St. Martin, and Saba all had their own *Raad*, of which the governor was president.

Because of the high expenses, this system was abolished in 1828 and the Western colonies were henceforth all governed from Paramaribo. There was a chief deputy for St. Martin, and another for St. Eustatius and Saba. These were responsible to the governor-general in Paramaribo, who, in turn answered to The Hague. By 1845, the Dutch home government realized the unwieldiness of this system and a further reorganization occurred. At this time the three Leeward islands were joined to the Curaçao group forming one unit: Curaçao and Dependencies (*Curaçao en Onderhorigheden*). The governor in Willemstad and the deputies on the other islands were all appointed by the king. On all islands, advisory councils were chosen by restricted electorates reflecting property and education.

During the first decades of the nineteenth century, the Leeward islands passed through a severe depression. Their productive capacity had never been great, even for their small size, and their trade had never fully recovered from Rodney's attack in 1781. Governor-general Van den Bosch, hoping to stimulate trade and navigation, had suggested improving the bays on both St. Martin and St. Eustatius, but the hurricane of 1829 completely demolished the changes, modest as they had been. Legal commerce never did as well as smuggling anyhow! The illicit traffic in slaves was a thriving business as was the trade in arms and ammunition for which customers abounded. How to deal with the smugglers, most of them of creole origin, was always a delicate problem. Officially, they were not admitted to Dutch ports, but practice differed from the directives issued by The Hague.

In 1848, the French slaves on St. Martin were freed, and their counterparts on the other half of the island took the helm in their own hands. Official emancipation followed in 1863 with compensation for the owners. As a result of the lack of labor, agriculture became even more unprofitable. The plantations were deserted and, before long, overgrown by tropical vegetation.

Throughout the nineteenth and twentieth centuries all three islands' budgets were running in the red, with the mother country covering the deficit. Since economic conditions on the islands were so bad, men had no alternative but to go as seasonal migrant workers to cut sugar cane in Cuba and Puerto Rico, to work in the salt pans on St. Kitts, or to labor in the phosphate mines in French Guiana. During the Boer War many of the islanders, especially those from Saba, worked as guards in British concentration camps (for prisoners-of-war) in the Bermudas.

World War I had little impact in this area until 1917, when the United States entered the war and there was a sudden abundance of jobs. The boom, however, was of short duration.

When oil brought new prosperity to the Curaçao islands, the emigration of men from the Dutch Leeward islands began to flow that way. At first many of them sent their paychecks back to their families on the home islands, causing an apparent increase in prosperity, but when it began to look like the oil jobs would be permanent, these families followed their husbands and fathers. Comparing the census of 1920 with that of 1929 one can see the extent of the exodus:

	St Martin	St Eustatius	Saba	Total
1920	2633	1315	1661	5609
1929	2180	965	1408	4553

World War II affected the Leeward group even less than World War I. One response to the war was increased emigration to the oil islands, in spite of German U-boat activities, which, for some time, prevented all travel to Curaçao. Although American planes occasionally landed on St. Martin or St. Eustatius, these islands were considered too unimportant for permanent bases. In 1943, however, the K.L.M. initiated a regular flight service between Curaçao and St. Martin from which one could take a boat to the other two Leeward islands. Telephone and radio ended their total isolation in the late twenties and early thirties.

When the Dutch Antilles became an autonomous part of the Dutch monarchy, the two main Leeward islands were represented by one member apiece in the eighteen-member States. Reforms introduced in the States were also applicable to the Leeward group. On the budget of the Antilles, the Leeward islands were still a liability. At this time, however, the two prosperous islands of Curaçao and Aruba carried the load of the less fortunate ones.

There have been many plans to aid the islands and bolster their economies. Even before autonomy a sociological study had been made to find a solution to their problems. In 1954, Antillian Prime Minister Efraim Jonckheer suggested a remedy for the situation by promoting agriculture. But none of these efforts to lift the islands out of their economic morass was very effective. In 1959, a commission of the States visited them and reported "great social, economic, and political neglect."

One of the proposals under discussion since 1956 to ameliorate the conditions of some Leeward islands has been the so-called MABES project, which called for a cooperative of the three Dutch islands together with Anguilla, and St. Bartlomew (MABES is an acronym for St. Martin, Anguila, St. Bartholomew, St. Eustatius, and Saba). With a united economy of fishery, agriculture, and cattle breeding, it was hoped that the 15,000 inhabitants of the five islands might jointly prosper. The costs of this project would be divided among the countries involved according to population: France 60 per cent, the Netherlands 30 per cent, and Great Britain 10 per cent. The plan failed to curry favor, one possible reason being the local animosity between the Dutch, British, and French islanders.

Another proposal for prosperity called TERNA (Technical and Economic Council of the Netherlands Antilles) does not concentrate on agriculture but on the development of fishing, mining, tourism, and industry on the Leeward islands as well as on Bonaire. In 1960, the first steps were taken towards its realization when the Dutch government put up nine million Antillian guilders, one third of the capital for a Three-Year Plan.

When project TERNA was conceived, the Caribbean was already in the throes of a tourist boom. The first hotel on St. Martin, the Little Bay Hotel, has been operating profitably for several years. For the three Leeward islands tourism appears to be *the* solution to end their budget deficits.

In contrast to the Curaçao islanders who are mostly colored and Roman Catholic, the majority of the people on the Leeward islands are white and Protestant, not belonging to the Dutch Reformed Church however, but to English and American denominations. On St. Martin the Methodists are particularly strong; on St. Eustatius and Saba most people belong to the Episcopalian church. The common language on all three Dutch islands is English.

CHAPTER XXV

SURINAM IN THE NINETEENTH CENTURY

King William I, whose ideas about the importance of the Curaçao islands were vastly exaggerated, was also overly optimistic about Surinam. He did not have to wait long to be disappointed.

The capital, Paramaribo, on the banks of the River Surinam, had, in 1816, between 1100 and 1200 houses all of them well furnished and almost all made of wood. There were two Protestant churches: one Dutch Reformed and the other Lutheran. The number of white inhabitants was estimated at 1200. The entire colony probably had no more than 2000 whites, to some 3000 free mulattoes and blacks, and over 50,000 slaves.

In the nineteenth century, the Surinam economy was based on sugar, coffee, cacao, and cotton. Sugar had been the basis of the colony's prosperity in the eighteenth century, but for internal and external reasons its cultivation had suffered severe setbacks. Crop diseases, the attacks of the *Marrons*, unpredictable weather, were only part of these. The collapse of the Amsterdam Bourse in 1773, the end of the slave trade, the abolition movement, the *blocus continental* of Napoleon, and the growing competition of beet sugar hurt the colony's prosperity likewise. Sugar production, up to now the economic mainstay of Surinam, was declining without being replaced.

The slaves, for some time, had formed a riotous and rebellious part of the population. Many plantations were terrorized by the escapees, or *Marrons*, and not even Paramaribo was safe from their raids. In 1819, the sugar harvest collapsed after a terrible smallpox epidemic in which 15,000 slaves died. Two years later, fires attributed to slave arsonists began breaking out in Paramaribo. Since most of the construction was wood, and no fire brigades existed, in 1821 four hundred houses were gutted. After the fires of 1832, three black suspects were tortured to obtain confessions and publicly burned alive, but fires continued to occur from time to time and it was not always possible to determine whether slaves were at fault.

Under the first governors during this century, Van Panhuys, Vaillant, and De Veer, the colony's monetary system, education, and administration were reorganized. A Court of Civil and Criminal Justice, similar to the one on Curaçao, saw to the people's legal rights and processes. De Veer introduced measures against the smuggling of slaves, and those planters who did not register their blacks were heavily fined and even threatened with imprisonment. This, of course, caused even more tension between the plantocracy and the government. The former had already lost much of its political clout because of the newly founded Court, and soon another one of King William's decrees followed introducing far-reaching changes in the *Raad*. Henceforth this body's members were to be appointed by the governor and allowed to discuss only what he sanctioned.

As part of his campaign to promote the prosperity of his West Indian domains and to simplify their administration, in 1828, William I sent his personal representative, Johannes van den Bosch, to the Caribbean to visit first the islands and then to proceed to Surinam. It was one of Van den Bosch's conclusions that the slaves were no asset to the colony. He predicted that there would be a shortage on the labor market once Great Britain abrogated the institution of slavery, as blacks in bondage did not reproduce fast enough to replace themselves. Following Van den Bosch's suggestions, the king, for reasons which have been explained before, merged the Dutch Antilles and Surinam into one governmental unit under Paramaribo. The Surinam town thus became the capital of all Dutch colonial possessions in the West. The first governor-general was Cantz'laar, the same who had previously served on Curaçao.

But the administrative reorganization did not produce the results anticipated by Van den Bosch. Agricultural Guiana contrasted too sharply with commercial Curaçao, making centralized legislation extremely difficult. Communication between the two parts was slow, and Curaçao's proximity to the Venezuelan coast as well as its embroilments in Venezuela's struggle for independence and in this republic's internal affairs, added to the confusion.

One of Cantz'laar's successors, Governor-general Elias, attempted under the benign but watchful eye of The Hague to improve conditions for the slaves, one of the many attempts in this field, and to introduce other much needed reforms. He was, as could be expected, opposed by the still powerful plantocracy, who enlisted the support of the Amsterdam merchants. The latter were disgruntled with William I for a number of reasons. They felt that the king had not insisted strongly enough on the return of the former Dutch colonies of Essequibo, Demerara, and Berbice, where they had vested interests. In addition they thought that some of the duties he had proposed hampered their trade.

During the period of the Batavian Republic, that is during France's domination of the Netherlands, many markets had been taken over by competitors from North America, Great Britain, and the city of Hamburg. Dutch businessmen saw their radius of action shrink to the East Indies and grumbled. The orthodox solution of William I, to found another Dutch trading company for the West, was not met with enthusiasm.

But the Hollanders were interested in exports – not in the humanitarian problems evoked by the peculiar institution of slavery. In giving the plantocracy their support, they ignored the important fact that Governor Elias had acted with The Hague's tacit approval. Twice the plantocracy and their Amsterdam allies addressed themselves to the king, pleading that he abolish Elias' measures, which they saw as obstacles to trade and development. Both times they failed.

The opposition from the merchants and the planters probably inclined to disillusion the king with centralized government for all the West Indian colonies. Statistics show that in spite of Van den Bosch's predictions, the colonies still made no profits. In 1845, Surinam and the Dutch Antilles were separated, and Dutch Guiana returned to its own local rule.

During the governorship of Elias, The Hague approved a European colonization project suggested by three ministers of the Dutch Reformed Church. In 1845, this Saramacca project began to take shape with the arrival, in Surinam, of 180 people from the Netherlands. A few weeks later, a second group composed of 180 immigrants presented itself. The plan was ill-prepared, however, and worse executed. Many of the pioneers died within a few months, and the survivors returned to the home country, a disillusioned lot.

In that same year a new governor arrived in Paramaribo. He was Van Raders, the former vice-governor of the Curaçao islands, where as we have seen, he had done all he could to promote agriculture in spite of the arid landscape. To him, Surinam represented another chance to test out his theories of developing agriculture. But, soon, Van Raders' Society for the Promotion of Agriculture had to be dissolved for lack of funds, while the failure of the Saramacca scheme represented another serious setback for the governor. A third pet project, to connect the Saramacca river area to the capital via a canal, failed due to the fact that a thrifty home government was unwilling to invest money. On top of these frustrations, Van Raders had to contend with the stubborn opposition of the plantocracy, who resented his efforts on behalf of the slaves. Charity and profits were not meant to be partners and one or the other had to give. The only lasting improvement that the hapless official was allowed to make, on orders of The Hague, was to open the colony to free trade.

The defeat of these grand designs was largely due to the constricting policy of the parsimonious, liberal-controlled, Dutch government whose attention was concentrated almost exclusively on keeping subsidies and grants to the colonial treasuries to a minimum. There was no boldness in planning, and, as a result, conditions in the colonies deteriorated visibly.

Other rebuffs were not long in appearing. In 1853, Kappler, a German and long-time resident of the colony who had been engaged in trade with the Indians and *Marrons* at the Marrowine river, resolved to go into the wood-cutting business instead. With the help of some 30 woodcutters from Würtemburg he founded the Alpina settlement, the prosperity of which was based on cutting and exporting wood. However, before long, the lack of funds caused the project to be abandoned. An effort in 1853 to employ a hundred Portuguese immigrants in agricultural designs met with a similar fate. These, and the preceding flop at Saramacca, led the authorities to believe that Europeans as settlers were doomed to failure.

To counteract the anticipated labor shortage after emancipation, in 1858, 500 Chinese from Macao were brought to Surinam. After many initial hardships, these immigrants adapted to the different environment and became industrious and productive citizens. Their number, however, was far from sufficient to absorb the effects of emancipation.

When, in 1834, slavery was abolished in British Guiana, unrest spread among the Surinam slaves, many of whom fled to freedom across the border. Similar discontent occurred in 1848 when the French emancipated their slaves in Cayenne. In Surinam, legislation concerned with slavery proceeded on a parallel line to that of the Dutch Antilles, but friction between the planters and the government, trying to execute orders from The Hague, was more intense in plantocratic Surinam than on the Curaçao islands, where the oligarchy was strictly commercial. To these tensions was added the repeated disappointment of the slaves, for whom freedom was continuously delayed by legislative and financial red tape.

In 1853, a State Commission was appointed to discern the best way of eliminating slavery in Surinam and on the Dutch Antilles. The Dutch Parliament rejected several of the Commission's proposals outright mostly for monetary reasons, namely the huge cost of compensation. The number of slaves on the six Antilles did not exceed 6700, but Surinam had close to 33,000.

In those days, the Surinam colony had the good fortune to be ruled by some far-sighted men who were opposed to slavery. One of them was Governor-general Elias, who had previously incurred the planters' wrath by trying to extend slave legislation. Elias also supplied The Hague with detailed information concerning the treatment of slaves. The grim contents of these reports released a hurricane of indignation and raised anti-slavery feeling in the mother country to a high pitch.

In 1851, new regulations for slave owners were decreed for the colony, but in practice actual improvements in the slaves' conditions were slight. Five years later, when the liberals again enjoyed a majority in the Dutch Parliament, the way was prepared for eventual emancipation by creating special kinds of bailiffs, called *landdrosten*, and appointing as attorney general a Mr. Gefken, a warm advocate of abolition. These new officials were assigned to report on the treatment of the slaves. A foundation of earlier origin, the Society for the Promotion of the Abolition of Slavery, was now encouraged to make open propaganda for total emancipation, with which the popular consensus agreed. The only difference between the champions of abolition and the more conservative-minded was the "how" and "when" of the event. Even the planters were resigned to the inevitable. Most of them had sold off their crops and equipment, and were retaining their slaves only to collect compensation. Nevertheless, many slaves lost patience with the slow bureaucratic process and ran away. In 1861, for example, the slaves of one plantation all disappeared to join the *Marrons* under Broos, the leader, preferring to harass the planters than to wait and hope. A promise of amnesty, promulgated in October, 1862, had no effect: the fugitives did not trust the whites and did not dare return.

In 1862, after endless debates in the Dutch Parliament, a proposal for the compensation of the slave owners was finally accepted and at last, on July 1, 1863, the guns of the Zeelandia Fortress at Paramaribo announced the end of slavery. That the new order could be established without violence or serious disruption was, due largely to the untiring efforts of the Moravian Brotherhood to prepare the slaves and to christianize them. Governor Van Lansberge, the same warm advocate of abolition who had collaborated with Bishop Niewindt on Curaçao, with great satisfaction freed the slaves in Surinam.

Soon, however, rejoicing gave way to resentment when the former slaves discovered that they were still bound to the same work – for wages and under State supervision – in a system comparable to the unsuccessful English plan of apprenticeship. It seemed to the freedmen that their new status was nothing more than slavery in disguise. On many plantations, the men laid down their tools and refused to work. At the same time, the planters were dissatisfied with the low efficiency of the new free labor as well as with the low compensation received. A drop in production after emancipation also caused discontent among the merchants.

The diplomacy of Van Lansberge, and an easing of the regulations making it possible to shorten the supervisory period, relieved the apprehension of the former slaves. With the planters it was different. Many of them had already suffered years of economic depression before emancipation became a fact, and their main object had been to keep the plantations going long enough to cash the indemnity. This compensation was set by the government, the same as on Curaçao, at 300 guilders per slave, regardless of sex and age. A strong male between eighteen and thirty-five could easily be sold for two or three times that much. With some 33,000 slaves freed in Surinam (plus over 6600 on the Dutch Antilles) the emancipation cost the Dutch taxpayer almost 12 million guilders, of which close to 10 million was paid out in Surinam.

After cashing their compensation, most of the planters sold their plantations and liquidated their business. There was, they thought, no future in Surinam, and nothing more for them to do. There were a few courageous and optimistic men whose money did not leave the colony but who invested in the development of their land, but these were in the minority. Speedy relief for the deteriorating economy was requested by a number of prominent citizens in a petition of 1870, addressed to King William III. Plantation agriculture found itself in a severe crisis of survival, being slowly absorbed by small farming (*kleine landbouw*).

Within the restricted scope of its budget and politics, the government made more or less successful efforts to reduce the upsetting consequences of emancipation. The supervision of the former slaves was entrusted by law to commissioners, sixteen in all. Although these men at first met with great distrust from the former slaves, the system did not work as badly as in the English colonies, thanks to these commissioners and Governor Van Lansberge. Old slaves immediately received pensions from the colonial treasury.

In spite of attempts to keep the freedmen on the land, a drift soon began towards the capital. Former slaves had no desire to stay in those places that had witnessed their disgrace for generations. Besides, in the beginning better wages were being offered in Paramaribo than could be made on the plantations. The consequent labor shortage was disastrous for the planters. Of the four hundred plantations operating in 1860, not even a hundred were left in 1900.

In the irresistible capital city, meanwhile, the unemployment situation worsened, especially when the freedmen were released from State supervision.

The government, anticipating this trend even before 1863, had followed a policy of granting small plots of land to encourage family farms, and promoting immigration as the only way to restore agricultural production and to ameliorate the economic stagnation. In the fifties, Portuguese workers from Madeira and Chinese farmers from Java and other places in the Far East had been encouraged to settle in the colony. Immigrants from Java followed. But many of the newcomers could not resist the magnetic pull of Paramaribo and left their acres to seek their fortunes in crafts and trade. As a result, Paramaribo grew like wild fire.

British Guiana, wrestling with the same problems after its slaves were freed in 1834, had done well with laborers from India. The Surinam planters pressed their government to solve their labor shortage in the same way. Accordingly, The Hague concluded an agreement with Great Britain in 1870 in which it acquired the latter country's permission to promote Hindustani emigration to Surinam.

The Hindustani were hired on a five-year basis by a particular plantation at stated wages. They received free transportation, free medical care, and were under the supervision and protection of an agent appointed by the British government. When the contract expired, they could either renew it or return to their country – at government expense. They could also choose to remain in the colony and become permanent residents.

In 1873, the first Hindustani of a long line of immigrants arrived – a movement which continued until 1917. The plantations prospered again, and so did small farming, for many Hindus, after their first contract expired, elected to stay in the colony and use their transportation money to purchase a small lot from one of the parcelled-out plantations. The colonial government encouraged this trend toward small-scale agriculture by making it possible to buy lots on easy terms.

In 1917, this Indian immigration (about three fourth were Hindus and the remainder Moslems) was abruptly ended by the British, due to the growing influence of Mahatma Ghandi and his demands for the independence of India. Between 1873 and 1917, 34,000 Indians had entered the colony as contract laborers. Of these one third, around 12,000, had returned home; the rest had stayed. The Indians quickly recognized the importance of a Western education and children of theirs often went to the Netherlands to study. The descendants of this group form the most numerous sector of the Surinam population today.

In the last decade of the nineteenth and the beginning of the twentieth centuries, another type of immigrant appeared on the scene in Surinam: the Javanese. Governor-general Van den Bosch had once proposed the use of deported Javanese criminals on the sugar plantations, but the Dutch government fortunately had not heeded that part of his suggestions. When the Indian independence movement gained ground, however, and threatened to cut off immigration, The Hague reconsidered the idea of Javanese laborers. In 1890, the before-mentioned Dutch Trading Company (*Neder-landsche Handel Maatschappij*) initiated the immigration of Javanese workers to its plantations in Surinam.

The Javanese, like the Hindustani, were accustomed to work in the tropics; they were industrious and adapted easily to the new environment. And Javanese immigration offered several advantages over the Hindustani. In the first place the Javanese were already Dutch subjects, a fact which circumvented international agreements and difficulties. At the same time, they were also acquainted with the Dutch system of government and labor, and some even knew the Dutch language. Seeing that the experiment of the Dutch Trading Company was a resounding success, the home government turned its attention to this type of immigrant. Again, as with the Indians, the main goal of bringing the Javanese into the country was to save the plantation system (*grote landbouw*) from total destruction.

In 1894, the first group of Javanese laborers arrived under government sponsorship. Like the Indians, the Javanese received a contract with conditions and provisions. They worked five years at a certain wage, medical care included, then had a right to a free return trip home. If the laborer wished to stay, he could either sign on for a second term or establish himself permanently. In return for his transportation money, he received a premium of one hundred guilders and the option to buy a small lot on easy terms.

After some time the penal provisions for non-fulfillment of contract were dropped, introducing a period of free immigration. The results were excellent: Surinam obtained a steady supply of willing and competent laborers, and Java's population explosion was somewhat alleviated. In 1939, the so-called Welter Plan was conceived to facilitate immigration on an even larger scale, but the outbreak of World War II arrested this project and Javanese immigration altogether.

In conclusion, Surinam in the nineteenth century presents a rather gloomy picture. True, some failures were due to circumstances beyond anyone's control, such as changes in the world market, crop diseases for which no cures had been discovered, disappointing mining projects, and the reluctance of freed slaves to work on the plantations. But the liberal policy of restricted government involvement – *versoberingspolitiek* – annihilated the efforts of men like Van Raders to improve the situation. The experiments in immigration, once started, were indeed highly successful, but the benefits did not begin to be felt until the turn of the century and did not save the plantation economy (*grote landbouw*). The changes in Surinam's society did not become obvious until after World War II.

CHAPTER XXVI

THE EARLY TWENTIETH CENTURY IN SURINAM

The twentieth century began ominously for Surinam. Large-scale agricultural production (*grote landbouw*) was declining despite the massive influx of laborers from abroad. The slump was mostly due to the fact that after the expiration of their contracts most of the Hindus and Javanese preferred to leave the sugar plantations and start their own little farms. Whereas during the first half of the nineteenth century an annual output of over 10,000 tons of sugar was no exception – in the peak year of 1850 it reached 17,200 tons – after emancipation this amount decreased steadily. After 1860 especially, ever-increasing wages, which were absorbed in the price of sugar, made competition prohibitive. At the same time, the opening of the Suez Canal in 1869, by drastically reducing the distance between Western Europe and the Far East, eliminated Surinam's advantage on the European market and precipitated a serious crisis in the colony. Although sugar continued to be the mainstay of Surinam's economy for a while longer, exports to Europe virtually ceased.

In the twentieth century, the situation went from bad to worse. Only three plantations, laboring in the face of ever-increasing odds against which mechanization proved to be helpless, continued to grow sugar cane. Under the system of "imperial preference" adopted after World War I, Great Britain would buy sugar only from its dominions. In addition, the world price of sugar was falling relentlessly, dropping ever faster after 1929 and reaching its lowest point in the mid-thirties. Measures to deal with the situation were characterized by a lack of imagination as well as an absence of long-term planning. Today sugar is no longer important to Surinam's economy.

As early as the eighteen hundreds coffee had been introduced in Surinam and had flourished. At the end of the nineteenth century, the Dutch Trading Company had brought new seeds from Africa to replace the old Arab species, and, by 1930, 12,000 hectares were planted with the new coffee known as Liberia. Not as sweet as the Colombian or Brazilian variety, it nevertheless became very popular in the Scandinavian countries and

Germany. Consequently, during World War II, coffee experienced a sharp drop in exports which lasted until the end of the war when coffee resumed its former importance to the country's economy.

Cacao is another of Surinam's ranking products. Highly profitable during the early colonial period, after emancipation the new freedmen took to its cultivation with the same enthusiasm as their former owners on the plantations. Not only is cacao very well-suited to small farming but it brings a good profit and requires little attention or professional knowledge. In 1860, Surinam exported 6000 bales of cacao which, by 1890, had increased to 30,000 bales. Three years later, however, the plants were attacked by a disease, and it was many years before the cause – a mould – could be discovered and eradicated. After World War I, cacao culture slowly recuperated and, in the last two decades, new species have found their way to the plantations and small farms. In 1953, cacao was back on the export list.

When, during the twenties, the end of cacao seemed to be near, efforts were made to find a substitute to take its place and, for some time, *bacobas* filled the vacuum. The United Fruit Company itself supervised the planting of the banana trees, pledging a guaranteed export quota to the United States. When the so-called Panama sickness devastated the entire crop, other types were tried, among them the Congo *bacoba*, but before the new plants could get a good start, World War II intervened, blocking exports.

The story of cotton follows a similar pattern. Various difficulties, f.i. a shortage of labor, diseases, and other calamities, caused its ultimate decline. Soon after 1863, its significance as an export product disappeared.

Rice had been grown in Surinam long before the arrival of the immigrants from India and Java, but it was only after they settled in the colony that its cultivation became an indispensable part of Surinam's economy. Between 1895 and 1915, over four million kilos of rice were imported annually, but since that time imports have decreased at a steady pace. The economic significance of rice is enhanced by the fact that it is almost exclusively grown on small and medium-sized holdings.

Some mention has already been made of efforts to foment mining and other industries such as woodcutting. Sir Walter Raleigh, in his well-known description of the Guianas, dwelled on the huge quantities of gold to be found on the Wild Coast, but all subsequent quests to locate El Dorado failed. An Englishman, Rosenberg, who, in 1862, had participated in a Dutch expedition into the interior of the colony, was convinced that there was gold in some of the regions he had crossed. He was able to talk some Americans into founding the "New York and Surinam Company" and, in 1870, was given a mining concession by the colonial government. Two years later, the first miners were sent to certain areas on the right bank of the Surinam River, but the adventure was a dismal failure and, in 1874, the company's concession was annulled.

Cornelis van Sypesteyn, who had served the colony in several capacities before becoming its governor (1875–1882), believed Rosenberg to be right. After all, gold was being found in French-Guiana – in 1872 alone more than 1400 kilos. The governor, therefore, fitted out an expedition to the Marrowine River. In some areas, the soil did prove to contain traces of gold and, within a short time, mining claims were being sold at ten cents per hectare. Success encouraged the government to construct a railroad to the Marrowine River. Explorers and miners poured into the area, and soon a local government office was set up in Albina to handle the many problems of an incipient gold rush.

During the following years, until 1902, gold digging operations were enlarged and, to a certain degree, mechanized. Once this mechanization proved to be unprofitable, it was abandoned for a return to a simpler system. At this time, the corporations involved decided to take on individuals as partners for 10 to 15 per cent of the gross returns. This became known as the "pocknocker system."

The amount of gold mined between 1876 and 1960 came to around 45,000 kilos. The peak period fell between 1905 and 1910, when the average annual output rose to more than 1000 kilos. Later production, has dropped to barely 200 kilos. Because of his initiative to harness the industry Van Sypesteyn has been called the "father of Surinam's gold-mining."

Complicating the development of the industry was a border dispute with the French – the so-called Lawa question. The latter had always considered the Tapahony River to mark the frontier between the Dutch colony and their own while the Dutch claimed the more eastern Lawa River to be the boundary. A binational commission of French and Dutch members decided, in 1861, in favor of the Lawa boundary, and, as a result, the disputed area became Dutch. In 1885, however, when gold was found in the Lawa district, the issue was revived and looked at in a new light. A second commission, international in composition, was put together and presided over by Czar Alexander III of Russia. The matter was again debated and decided, in 1888, in favor of the Dutch, thus ending the matter.

A similar problem arose with Great Britain. The London Convention of 1814 had established the Corantine River as Surinam's border with British Guiana, although, at the time, nothing was known about the upper course of this river. In 1843, Robert Schomburgk, the well-known explorer, was commissioned by the British Government to follow the Corantine to its

sources. A similar exploratory journey was made in 1871 by Charles Bar-
rington, who suggested that the New River and not the Cutari Curuni River,
was the continuation of the Corantine. As a result, the New River became
the border between the two colonies and Surinam lost a substantial slice of
its territory.

In 1902, the Dutch colonial government undertook the construction of a
railroad to the Lawa district. It took five years to complete 120 kilometers,
and another five to connect the region with the capital. Costs ran as high
as 9 million guilders, whereas few expectations were ever fulfilled, mostly due
to the decline, after 1910, of the gold-mining industry here as well as along
the Marrowine.

There were many false starts in the development projects for Surinam's
agriculture and industry during the first half of the twentieth century. One is
inevitably led to the conclusion suggested in the preceding chapter that the
government was at least partly to blame for the many failures which occurred. Certainly it lacked the far-sighted policy needed to overcome the serious
problems of underdevelopment and, in the thirties, of depression. The two
commissions, appointed in 1911 and 1916 to study causes and to come up
with suggestions, had no effect, because their reports were filed away and
forgotten. Liberalism dominated the mother country's policies, and to the
liberal point of view a balanced budget was the ultimate goal. Any interference with the market mechanism was frowned upon. The possibility that
the colony's economy might be totally different in structure from those of
Western Europe and the mother country, was ignored. The Hague was
haunted by the fear that the colony would cost more and more, and was
unwilling to increase its subsidies. This line of thought which has been defined
as *versoberingspolitiek* – the policy of restriction – effectively eliminated both
expansion and constructive planning, and prevailed up to the Second World
War.

This attitude had its repercussions as far as the population was concerned.
The capital was overrun by thousands of small farmers and plantation
workers, who had left the land and moved to Paramaribo looking for better
paid jobs, a trend started by freed slaves and repeated by former contract
laborers. They soon formed a discontented and restless group living in
abject poverty on the outskirts of town, whose desperation culminated in a
conspiracy to overthrow the government: the Killinger plot of 1911.

Killinger, a Hungarian of middle-class origin, had fled his country after
wounding a man in a fight. Consequently, he signed up for the Dutch
colonial army and was sent to Surinam in 1899. There he caught the attention
of his superiors and was rapidly promoted to inspector of the police depart-

ment. Somehow the plight of Paramaribo's underdogs deflected Killinger onto another road. In him the freed slaves and their descendants, reinforced by immigrants, found a champion able to organize them into a solid group. Killinger's objectives have never been quite clear; yet the plot – if there ever was such a thing – was discovered. Killinger was imprisoned, and condemned to death, though never executed. His imprisonment ended the movement.

The economic situation worsened during World War I when exports to Europe were drastically cut and unemployment rose. Food shortage became critical. Governor G.J. Staal (1916–1920) personally traveled throughout the colony to encourage planters and small farmers to cultivate more foodstuffs. He also made an attempt, with some success, to stimulate the importation of food from other countries in the hemisphere. Once peace was concluded, ships again dropped anchor off Paramaribo and the food crisis was a thing of the past.

Staal's successor, Governor Arnold Baron van Heemstra (1921–1928), tried, with discouraging results, to interest Dutch private capital in investing in the colony. Under Abraham Rutgers (1928–1933) mechanized rice culture was introduced, but due partly to the reluctance of The Hague to underwrite the project, this innovation did not meet with immediate success. These were the years of the Great Depression which struck the colony hard. Yet in spite of the vast unemployment and underlying misery, the mother country continued to show little concern for the problems of Surinam.

For the first time, popular movements arose against the existing order and power structure – Killinger's plot not having been a popular movement. In 1931, a socialistic Committee of Action, under the leadership of L. Doedel, presented the governor with an extensive Plan of Labor. An aggressive, extreme leftist Popular Front (*Surinaamsche Volksbond*) publicly criticized all efforts by the government to solve the urgent problems, and welcomed riots and violence. Shops were plundered, buildings were wrecked, and traffic was paralyzed. On several occasions, the police were forced to intervene while people lay wounded or even dead. In this atmosphere of tension, communism found a fertile soil.

In 1932, the Surinam Laborers Organization (*Surinaamsche Arbeiders en Werkers Organisatie, or SAWO*) was founded by some of those who had been active in the disturbances of the previous year. SAWO soon received the support of A. de Kom, a Dutch schoolteacher, who was instrumental in the organization of a League against imperialism and for colonial independence, which found much sympathy among the unemployed immigrants and penniless blacks. After a few demonstrations, De Kom was arrested by the authorities. Some of his followers, protesting the arrest, were wounded or killed, and order was not resumed until De Kom was sent back to the Netherlands.

While the movements of Doedel and De Kom were important as the first popular protests against the prevailing social order, they never really threatened the stability of the government. On the contrary, the Doedel Plan of Labor reflected a demand for a solution of pressing problems to be approached and alleviated on the basis of an officially sponsored welfare plan. Nevertheless there was a growing uneasiness in the air. It had finally dawned on the population as a whole that it was the *laissez faire* attitude of the mother country which had been, to a high degree, responsible for the stagnation and lack of progress in Surinam. Underlying this dissatisfaction was the deepening resentment regarding the subordinate role of the colonists within the Dutch monarchy. For example, up to 1922, all important positions in Surinam had been held by native Dutchmen, as they were the people with the brains, the power, and the qualifications. The level of colonial education was still low and in order to obtain a college or even a secondary school degree, a student had to go abroad – an undertaking possible only to the very rich. Scholarships and grants for the less well-to-do did not yet exist.

Dutch colonial governors as well as officials in The Hague were well aware of the growing demand for better education and self-government. Long before World War II the necessary steps were already being taken toward these goals. But it was really this war which would give the region what it desired.

CHAPTER XXVII

POLITICAL DEVELOPMENTS IN THE DUTCH WEST INDIES IN THE TWENTIETH CENTURY

Up to 1848 the Dutch West Indies were ruled by the king without the interference of the Dutch parliament, a two-chamber representation of the people who, at that time, had the franchise. Hence, the colonies were in reality Crown colonies.

For the Antilles this meant that the governor was an appointee of the king and responsible to him only, either directly or through the Minister of the Colonies. The *Raad* or Political Council was a strictly advisory body appointed by the governor subject to approval from The Hague. In 1828, when the Antilles were linked to Paramaribo, the always minor importance of this *Raad* dwindled to none at all.

In Surinam, the political situation differed slightly. Ever since the institutions of the Chartered Society in 1682, the *Politieke Raad* or Political Council had represented the planters, aiming to defend and promote their interests. In 1816, this *Raad* was superseded by a new Political Council similar to the one in the Antilles except for one difference: the planters retained the right to draw up the slate of candidates for the Council, the members of which were, in the final instance, chosen by the governor. In 1828, even this token participation by a small number of franchised, wealthy colonists disappeared when the king, heeding Van den Bosch's suggestions, centralized the West Indian government in Paramaribo.

As colonies of the Crown, the colonial governments in the West operated under regulations (*regerings reglementen*) which were, in reality, royal decrees. It was not until 1848 that a thorough overhaul of the Dutch constitution made the ministers responsible to the States General (the two-chamber parliament) and, in turn, put this body in charge of all legislation, thus potentially limiting the Crown's almost absolute control over the colonies.

Parliament was slow to use its new authority. Seventeen years passed before it made any change in the government of the West Indian dependencies. Yet, the apparently unobstrusive measure introduced in 1865, the substitution for the *Raad* of a new Council, the Colonial States, was to be anything but insignificant. Although composed, like its predecessor, of the governor's appointees, it had the rights of initiative, amendment, petition and budget. This last prerogative, however, did not amount to much in practice: as the colonial budget was constantly in need of subsidies from The Hague, the States General always had the last word.

In spite of several efforts to acquire the right to vote, the islanders still had no universal franchise. In 1892, for example a group of more than 200 citizens of Curaçao petitioned the States General to this purpose, only to have their request turned down. One of the most prominent champions of voting rights, the Jewish lawyer Abraham M. Chumaceiro, publicized his ideas in pamphlets, brochures, and in the daily papers.

Surinam enjoyed a degree of franchise not known in the Antilles. Perhaps there was more concern in The Hague for Holland's "twelfth province," as Surinam was sometimes called, whereas international complications could easier occur with the Antilles due to their geographical location. Surinam's Colonial States signalled a return to the *Politieke Raad* of the Chartered Society. Composed of thirteen members, only four were appointees of the governor, the other nine being elected by the tightly-knit group of planters and well-to-do merchants. Before 1900, the plantocracy numbered no more than 500; in 1921 it had reached almost 1000. This plantocratic oligarchy was absent in the Antilles.

Until 1910, the interests of the plantocracy prevailed in Surinam. In 1911, the Dutch government appointed the Surinam Commission to examine the political and economic situation of the colony. Its well-documented report was soon forgotten and its suggestions never followed. Five years later, the so-called Study Commission did the same, urging the home government to abandon its policy of restriction and to invest more freely in the lagging economy. Nothing ever came of this laudable advice either. And where the government was reluctant to invest, it is understandable that private capital would be even less willing to venture.

In 1922, a step forward was taken when the mother country suggested a new relationship by amending its constitution. The term "colony" was henceforth to be replaced by the word "dominion." Fourteen years later the Dutch Parliament again took notice of the West Indies in a new regulation containing the following items: the name Colonial States was changed to the States of Curaçao and the States of Surinam. The number of members was fixed at fifteen for both bodies, ten of whom were to be chosen by popular vote while the remaining five were to be appointees of the governor. The governors of both dominions were given the power to approve any proposed legislation without consulting the States and an Advisory Council was set up in both the Antilles and Surinam for their assistance.

In the Antilles, a strong feeling prevailed that in reality nothing had changed and that the mother country continued to be in control. Yet it was in the same year, 1936, that the organization of political parties began. The Roman Catholic Church was the first to enter the political arena, founding Catholic parties in Curaçao and Aruba.

The Second World War interrupted this political development in the Antilles for several years. In 1944, however, the Democratic Party was founded under the leadership of the Jonckheers, a prominent family of the island. In 1948, three years after the Democrats had won their first election, one of the leaders of the Roman Catholic Party branched off to found the National Popular Party, which, like its Democratic counterpart, was not based on religious principles. A fourth party, the Independents, also founded the same year, attested to the growing political awareness of the population. Similar parties sprang up on Aruba and the other islands.

In Surinam, the Progressive Surinam Popular Party, the National Surinam Party, the Hindustani-Javanese Party, the Negro Political Party, and the Christian Socialist Party were the more important political entities to be established at this time. After 1952, some changed names and programs. All participated in the first general elections of 1948; whereas in the Antilles the Democratic Party gained a resounding victory in Surinam this feat was accomplished by the N.P.S. (National Surinam Party).

This development was accompanied by other significant innovations in the political arena. One of these was a growing demand for autonomy which was not only endorsed by most parties but greatly contributed to their popularity. Though it had been a declared ideal of the older Roman Catholic Party, it had not generated much appeal until the forties, when Queen Wilhelmina, from her exile in London in 1942, broadcast a speech promising self-government to the Dutch East and West Indies once the war was over. The United States welcomed the project, which the Queen envisaged as a commonwealth embracing the Netherlands, Indonesia, Surinam, and the Caribbean Antilles, as a constructive effort to achieve the goals of the Atlantic Charter.

The year before, in 1941, the States of the Dutch Antilles had proposed that Governor Wouters appoint a commission to study the political future of those islands, but events rendered its conclusions obsolete before they were presented. A new commission, appointed by Wouters' successor, Petrus A. Kasteel, and known as the Ellis Comission after its president, in 1946, made a new report which became the basis for future discussions. In that same year, a deputation from the islands' States, composed of three members, two of them high officials of the Antillian government, arrived in The Hague to present the Queen with a formal request for autonomy. This request was studied in the Dutch Parliament and resulted in startling developments.

Similar political events took place in Surinam where the fear of abuses by the executive had caused the changes of 1936 to be coolly received. This mistrust was shown to be justified during the stormy governorship of Johannes C. Kielstra (1933–1943). An undiplomatic governor, the latter twice bypassed the States to issue decrees while the legislature retaliated by not approving his budget for 1937. What enraged the Surinam States even further was the fact that the governor would not enlist the educational system to promote the integration of Surinam's many races into a homogeneous nation. On the contrary, it often appeared that Kielstra wanted the different groups to remain apart. Finally the States turned to the Crown, which decided in their favor, rendering Kielstra's position, of course, impossible. He was subsequently appointed ambassador to Mexico. Under his successor, J.J. Brons (1944–1948) the conflict between executive and legislative power ended and a forward-looking constructive policy took its place.

Brons was no stranger to Surinam, having been in that country for years before reaching his exalted position. He now had the distinction of being at the helm while the cause of autonomy was enormously advanced. As Van Lier puts it, the exploitation colony now became a plural society, four years after Queen Wilhelmina's message had evoked a resounding response in Surinam. In February, 1946, a Dutch mission arrived in Paramaribo to inquire into the desires and aspirations of the population. Autonomy was not yet, at that time, as much on everyone's mind as it was to be later on and there was no recognized political party or group working towards that goal. But before long the political field was to become alive with aspirations and in June, 1946, the States of Surinam appointed a commission under Lim Apo to submit a list of requests to the Queen, and to exchange thoughts about Surinam's future relationship with the Dutch government. Coincidentally, at the beginning of 1947, another parliamentary mission arrived in Paramaribo to study problems *ad loci*.

Pending the planned Round Table Conference between The Hague and the Dutch dominions, and the adoption of a new amendment to the constitution of the Netherlands, in 1948, an interim solution was introduced for both the Antilles and Surinam. A Committee of General Government (*College van Algemeen Bestuur*) was installed in both Willemstad and Paramaribo and charged with executive power while the governor's role was reduced to one of supervision. In both dominions the difficulties arising from this temporary measure were amiably solved by governors Kasteel and Brons.

As a result of the activities of these Committees for General Government, several reforms were introduced, one of the more important being universal suffrage for men and women. In both dominions the States were dissolved and a new membership was elected by popular vote. The Antilles and Surinam were each represented in the Netherlands by an agent appointed by the new States.

These far-reaching innovations nevertheless did not proceed fast enough for some of the more radical-minded. In Surinam, a group under the leadership of one Simon Sanchez lost patience and started a movement to overthrow the government, which failed.

In January, 1948, the first Round Table Conference was held in The Hague after the Dutch constitution had been amended to allow for sweeping changes in the relationship between mother country and dominions. The meeting took place under the leadership of Dutch Prime Minister L.J.M. Beel. Surinam as well as the Antilles were represented. Although for some time the discussions were not very fruitful, in March the decision was finally reached to base the new relationship among the three parties on the equality and autonomy of each as partners in a "new style monarchy," also called the "tripartite kingdom," with equal participation in all matters of common interest and close collaboration in the economic, social, and cultural fields.

In September, 1948, the Dutch constitution was again revised, this time to allow for the transition to final and complete autonomy within the framework of the "new style monarchy." Military intervention in the East Indies resulting in the permanent loss of Indonesia delayed final agreements with the West, but in 1949 *ad interim* solutions were adopted for both the Antilles and Surinam, wich, in the course of 1950, were introduced in both regions. Thereafter the monarchy was to consist of three partners: the Netherlands, the Antilles, and Surinam. This was the "tripartite kingdom of the Netherlands." The Crown reigns over each of the three partners while a Council of Ministers was set up, composed of Netherlands Ministers together with the two Ministers Plenipotenciary of the Antilles and Surinam, to discuss all matters concerning the three partners of the kingdom.

The final framing of the "new style monarchy" necessitated two more Round Table Conferences in which the so-called Statute (*Statuut*) was drafted, discussed, amended, and finally adopted as a permanent basis for the relations between the three partners. It was in great measure the work of Moises F. da Costa Gomez, the able Prime Minister of the Netherlands Antilles from 1951 to 1954. In the latter year this Statute was endorsed by all members of the realm and signed by Queen Juliana. Under it, the overseas

Government Councils (*regeringsraden*) which had replaced the Committees for General Government in 1950, were renamed Cabinets or Councils of Ministers. Both the Antilles and Surinam were now each represented in The Hague. The governor continued to be appointed by the Crown.

Thanks to the Statute, the Netherlands have the opportunity of rendering the social and economic assistance that will prevent Surinam and the Antilles from becoming a ready quarry for communism. While the internal reorganization did not alter the existing situation in Surinam, on the Antilles far-reaching consequences were the result. Previously, of the six islands only Curaçao and Aruba had had balanced budgets; the other islands were haunted by permanent deficits. This situation had fostered a strong separatist movement in Aruba. To promote cohesion the Statute gave the smaller islands an advantage over Curaçao even though this island contributed 70 per cent of the total budget. Of the eighteen members of the Antillian States, Curaçao elected only eight, Aruba six, Bonaire two, and the three Leeward islands two.

The new organization for the six islands required an expensive bureaucracy, with each island having its own vice-governor (*gezaghebber*) and island council (*eilandsraad*). With their responsibilities in local affairs verging on the absolute, the Antilles and Surinam were still far removed from complete independence. Foreign affairs and defense remained kingdom matters, although through that ingenious and subtle constitution, the Statute, they had an excellent chance of influencing the wealthier and more powerful partner in The Hague at the highest level.

The National Popular Party of Curaçao and its allies on the other islands lost the 1954 elections and Premier Da Costa Gomez had to give way to Efraim Jonckheer, the leader of the Democratic Party. After more than ten years as Premier, in 1964, the latter was succeeded by Ciro Kroon. It was in the sixties that, for the first time, the governorship went to a native-born Antillian, Cola Debrot, who, in time, was succeeded by another Antillian, B.M. Leito. Political maturity did not eliminate tensions, however, especially between labor and management. The final eruption came in 1969 when in the ensuing disorder many stores in downtown Willemstad were looted before order could be restored.

In 1949, the National Surinam Party carried 13 out of the 21 seats in the new States, a comfortable majority. But, the next year, the N.P.S. split over some issues involving the *ad interim* regulation and effective government became impossible. As The Hague was unwilling to interfere, the governor dissolved the States. New elections again gave the N.P.S. 13 seats and a new cabinet was formed to deal constructively, this time, with the pressing problems of government. But soon internal differences and other difficulties forced the resignation of this cabinet also, along with its Prime Minister, J.A.E. Buiskool. Stepping into the vacuum, in 1955, was a coalition government called the United Front.

The failure of Buiskool's cabinet can be related to the peculiarities of a plural society. While Antillian society is characterized by relatively little racial variety, the composition of Surinam's population had changed radically in the course of the nineteenth century. A majority of the inhabitants are Creoles, that is, descendants of Africans in various shades of color as a result of miscegenation. In the mid-sixties this group contained around 115,000 people. With about 112,000, the Hindustani, in the middle fifties, were a close second and gaining, having a higher birthrate than the Creoles. The third place was occupied by the Javanese with over 48,000. The future will witness a power struggle among these three main groups with the Javanese holding the balance of power. The remaining population groups are unimportant either numerically or politically. The Amerindians live outside the economy and number at the most 5,000. The more than 4,000 Europeans maintain a certain degree of economic influence but have lost their political clout. There are over 5,000 Chinese, while the number of former *Marrons*, now called Bush negroes, probably amounts to around 30,000. The co-existence of all these groups forms the central theme of the Surinam flag: a circle with five stars: one white, one black, one brown, one yellow, and one red.

The essential difference between the Antilles and Surinam is not, however, the racial composition. It is rather the political perspective. The road towards complete independence will be easier for Paramaribo than for Willemstad. True, the Statute has worked reasonably well during its first fifteen years in spite of the many problems arising from both the new arrangement and today's complicated realities. Now, however, there are voices calling for a complete overhaul of this document, while more extreme groups will only be satisfied with total independence. This was the goal of the National Surinam Party, for example, whose leader, J. Pengel, was one of the prominent politicians of the country and its prime minister on several occasions. It was not until 1975, several years after Pengel's death, that Surinam reached this goal.

This clamor for independence can also be heard in the Antilles, although in a more subdued way. The political structure of the Antilles differs sharply from that of Surinam. The two islands of Curaçao and Aruba are not only economically independent, but politically more mature than the others. Besides, the Antilles lack the common interests and group mentality prevalent in Surinam. Instead the political problematic is decided by island individualism. There are island interests and an insular mentality. Arubans, for instance, will not tolerate decisions made by Curaçao.

Then too, there is a geographical factor. The islands' location inspires fear that the consequence of a total break with the Netherlands would be the increasing influence of Venezuela. Annexation by this country lurks just around the corner, and would probably occur as soon as the Dutch marines leave, or a time of international crisis evolved. Surinam, on the other hand, is safe between Guyana and Cayenne, with the high Tumac Humac Mountains protecting the country's southern border. Its autonomous ambitions merely had to await the right moment to be realized.

Never in complete sympathy with independence, many Creoles, Hindustani, and Javanese preferred to throw their lot with the mother country. The enormous exodus of many inhabitants to the Netherlands on the eve of independence – around 100,000 or probably more than 25 per cent of the population, many of them from the ranks of the educated – is a disturbing omen for a country ready to begin a new life. Time will show how well Surinam's problems will be solved by those who stayed behind.

CHAPTER XXVIII

ECONOMIC DEVELOPMENT OF THE DUTCH ANTILLES AND SURINAM

For another decade after World War II the oil refineries continued to provide job opportunities for the inhabitants of the Dutch Antilles. But for several reasons, 1958 signalled a decline in those very factors which had promoted prosperity to such a high degree during the previous forty years. After the fall of Marcos Pérez Jiménez in that same year, the Venezuelan government embarked on an extensive program of refining its own oil, although scrupulously observing existing contracts with SHELL and LAGO. Yet, a tacit understanding was reached with these companies not to expand their refineries on the islands. Concomitantly, both SHELL on Curaçao and LAGO on Aruba initiated a process of automation which, for the first time since the Great Depression of the early thirties, caused a downward trend in the labor force. In 1952, before the automation program, the refineries were employing 13,000 laborers on Curaçao, and over 7,000 on Aruba. Within a mere fifteen years this picture was to change drastically. In 1967, SHELL was employing less than 4,000 men, and LAGO not quite 1,700. The impact of this sharp drop in employment on the islands' economy was even greater than it would seem at first sight, coinciding as it did with a population explosion. It so happened that during the same period the population of Aruba increased nearly 20 per cent, while on Curaçao the gain came close to 35 per cent.

These two converging currents – the lay-off from the oil refineries and the tremendous increase in population – put the government under great pressure. Without a satisfactory compromise, the existing social order was sure to collapse – as some leftist extremists were indeed betting. Several ways were devised to deal with the situation. In the first place, the government made a serious attempt to create a favorable climate for investment. At the same time, effective legislation was passed to attract new industries, for example, by offering temporary monopolies. Trade and tourism were likewise assiduously courted. Last but not least, an appeal was made to The Hague – on the basis of the Statute – for aid in building up the infrastructure of the economy which resulted not only in loans from the Dutch government but brought the islands into the sphere of the European Common Market.

It cannot be denied that these various approaches have had some degree of success. Capital investment has increased rapidly, in spite of a setback in 1964 when tax agreements between the United States and the Netherlands eliminated most of the incentives offered to the investor. Since 1965, a steadily expanding tourist industry has both stimulated development and reduced the unemployment rate.

One of the leading thoughts behind the framing of the Statute had been the idea that the three partners of the "new style monarchy" would be of mutual assistance to each other – primarily in the economic field. In an addendum to this agreement, it was further emphasized that each of the members should bear each others' demand and supply in mind. These stipulations proved to be of the utmost importance, both for the Netherlands Antilles as well as for Surinam.

In spite of the oil industry which, after 1920, casts its huge shadow over every activity on the islands, trade, ever since it was spearheaded in the middle of the seventeenth century by Portuguese-Brazilian-Dutch Jews, had always been of great importance to the Antilles. The government's new projects to fan prosperity kept this tradition of commerce in mind when laying out trading zones and creating free port facilities. In addition to this historical factor, the geographical situation further guaranteed commercial success. The islands once again reaped the benefits of their proximity to the continental coast, the Panama canal, and their location at the crossroads of the principal navigation routes for the tourist cruises. In the thirties, moreover, KLM chose to designate them as stop-overs on its transcontinental flights and a net was set up to link the Dutch Antilles not only with the other Caribbean islands but with the mainland coast as well. With the coming of the jet age in the sixties, Curaçao lost its significance as a flight stop; yet as a tourist center it remained unrivalled. The KLM, meanwhile, under the pressure of growing competition and in order to keep a foothold in the area, has founded branch companies such as the ALM, the Antillian Airlines, and has become a shareholder in some of its very rivals, the Venezuelan VIASA, for instance.

With the close collaboration of the mother country, in 1961, an Advisory Council was established to promote industry on the island and, for the time being, tourism seems to hold out the best promise. Indeed, temporary tax exemptions encourage the construction of luxurious hotels, while an extensive propaganda campaign in other countries – notably the United States – appears to be paying off. Tourists are flocking to the Caribbean in ever-increasing numbers and the Dutch islands are included in more and more cruise itineraries.

This tantalizing outlook has been made possible by the close cooperation between the authorities on both sides of the Atlantic. Collaboration between Willemstad and The Hague unfolded in three clearly defined phases. First, the Dutch government made known its willingness to underwrite a development program for the Leeward islands and Bonaire. It set apart a sum of 16 million guilders for several projects: water distillation, electric power, and the construction and enlargement of airports, harbor facilities, and roads. The Leeward-Bonaire phase has now been completed.

The second phase of the program, which is now being carried out, bears upon the islands of Curaçao and Aruba, for the development of which the Dutch government, in the so-called Urgency Plan, has earmarked 114 million guilders. A third phase is still in the discussion stage. The Netherlands Antilles have proposed a Ten Year Plan with a budget running into hundreds of millions of guilders. Dutch involvement will probably amount to 185 million guilders.

The islands' participation in the European Common Market, dating from October 1964, is of great importance, in that it makes the Antilles eligible for the Common Market Fund for Countries Overseas – a program of economic assistance which may reach 15 million dollars.

Thus it appears that tourism, trade, and industry – for the immediate future at least – will be the main pillars of subsistence for 250,000 Antillians. Although their problems are staggering, in their struggle for survival, the islanders have the full support of the Netherlands. In spite of all mutual efforts, however, unemployment is still substantial. In 1964, it was officially estimated at 18 per cent of the labor force of 55,000, while 73,000 people made up the labor force in 1970, of whom an estimated 20 to 25 per cent were out of work. What these figures boil down to is that between 3,000 to 4,000 new jobs have to be created a year in order to keep the economy solvent. This is not an easy task and both wisdom and courage are required to cope with the situation.

Autonomy and independence might never have been achieved for Surinam were it not for the development of a completeley new industry which, like the refineries on the Curaçao islands, brought about a balanced budget. For the first time since the emancipation of the slaves, subsidies from The Hague were no longer needed and with financial security political independence was not long in coming. Surinam's redeemer has been bauxite, aluminum's main component.

In 1865, the government of Surinam came into possession of an abandoned plantation, located close to the capital, the soil of which contained an unknown substance which was soon used to construct roads. In 1898, a Dutch engineer sent samples of these rocks to Holland requesting an analysis which revealed that the mysterious matter was known in academic circles as bauxite. The discovery meant little at the time: no market existed and, besides, Surinam lay far beyond the world's trade routes. It required two world wars to get bauxite mining off the ground.

During World War I, aluminum steadily increased in importance at a time when European bauxite became more and more difficult to obtain. Demand rose and, before long, the Guianas and Jamaica became the principal suppliers of this essential ore to the United States. In Surinam, hitherto worthless lots were bought and sold at fabulous prices upon the slightest rumor that they contained bauxite.

In 1917, the Surinam Bauxite Company (SBM), an American undertaking, initiated the leasing of land on a long term basis. Bauxite deposits were marked out and, in 1922, the first shipments were dispatched to the United States. Mechanization soon replaced manual labor, and production climbed steadily, reaching higher and higher levels during World War II. In 1943, two years after a second company, the Dutch Billiton Ltd., was given a concession, bauxite production totalled 1,600.000 tons, and revenues from the industry had just about balanced the colonial budget. Soon afterwards production tripled to over 4 million tons.

Although before emancipation, Surinam's balance of payments had been favorable, after 1863 there was an almost permanent deficit – except for some years during and after World War I – and The Hague had to supply the funds to make up the difference. Between 1900 and 1946, the Dutch government subsidized the colony with almost 90 million guilders. But bauxite changed all this and, after 1930, replaced coffee as the country's primary export. Several attempts to stimulate the country's reviving economy now followed in a revolutionary tempo, totally reversing former lackadaisical and blundering approaches and creating an atmosphere of expectation and hope. A Ten Year Plan, for instance, was announced as a determined effort to "sow the bauxite" and to provide the base for an all-round economy. One major aspect of the Plan was concerned with the availability of sufficient energy to maintain or increase the level of production in order to build aluminum plants and to diversify the country's industrial output.

Undeniably, Surinam's prospects are bright. With a surface of 55,000 square miles of which only $\frac{1}{2}$ per cent is under cultivation, the country's resources remain virtually untapped. There are various reasons for this. The one-crop economy of the seventeenth and eighteenth centuries, for instance, seriously hampered the extension of arable land. After agriculture was diversified, the frequent occurrence of crop diseases, causing kaleidoscopic changes in the quality and quantity of the national output, loomed as another enormous obstacle to agricultural expansion. The official *laissez faire* attitude and the government's otherwise restrictive policy were additional factors in the underdevelopment of the country. Furthermore, Surinam's internal market being small and poorly distributed, not even the demand for precious woods had been pressing enough to force people up the rivers into the interior. Even today the country has fewer than 400,000 inhabitants (not counting the 100,000 who left in the seventies), and of these, 40 per cent are concentrated in and around the capital with another 50 per cent living along the coast on a stretch of land 30 miles wide at the most. It is hoped that industrialization, which in the last analysis means bauxite, will change all this also.

In 1947, the Dutch Parliament established the Prosperity Fund (*Welvaart Fonds*) allocating 40 million Dutch guilders for the colony's development. When it became evident that this sum was not enough, more was promised. The administrators of the Fund were also charged with carrying out the development projects, to take inventory of the country's natural resources, and to prepare studies for a long-term plan to promote prosperity.

Within eighteen months sixteen such projects were being studied. One of the first was concerned with aerial surveys; others dealt with immigration from the Caribbean islands, housing, road construction, mining, logging, fishing, small and middle-sized farming, various industries, and education. Their execution was taken up with vigor, despite the devaluation, in 1949, of the Dutch guilder to almost 50 per cent of the value of the Surinam and Antillian guilders.

What was urgently needed was for someone to take a hard look at the colony's resources and to prepare a long-term, balanced plan for its development. In 1952, this Ten Year Plan, mentioned above and encompassing 250 million guilders, one third of which was to be carried by Surinam, was announced. Its basic aims were to broaden the country's economic base, to achieve independence by eliminating the weak spots in the balance of payments, and to promote the socio-cultural conditions necessary for physical and intellectual development.

The Plan relies heavily upon the cooperation of the other two partners in the monarchy. It envisions exchanging Surinam's agricultural exports in the markets of the Dutch Antilles and the Netherlands. Future economic growth will also require, however, the investment of risk-bearing capital. The Plan is aware of this factor and provides for it. Although agriculture was given a large slice of the Plan's budget, several other schemes, including the Broko-pondo Project, also ran into the millions.

One possibility for economic cooperation, mentioned in the Plan, was the migration of labor, such as resettling in Surinam those who had been laid off by the Antillian oil refineries in the sixties. However, so far emigration from the islands has not been too successful.

As important as the creation of new markets, the transfer of capital, or the migration of labor, are knowledge and experience – the exchange of know-how. Of the three partners, Surinam is the one most in need of this give and take, especially after the emigration to the Netherlands of more then 100,000 of its inhabitants, a loss of over 25 per cent of the population, who feared the effects of independence. Many of those who left were profes-sionals and this brain-drain multiplied the shortage of skilled laborers, aggravating the situation for many years to come.

The Brokopondo River Basin Development was one of the most ambitious projects ever to be undertaken in Surinam, holding out a heady promise of future riches for the country. Although its main purpose was the genera-tion of cheap electricity, accompanying results were a better navigation of the Surinam River as well as increased possibilities of irrigation for agriculture. The main focus, however, was concentrated on the creation of hydroelectric power and the construction of an aluminum factory which was to use almost 90 per cent of the new electricity. The increased government revenue expected from these sources was to finance further development.

It has always been one of Surinam's pet projects to start her own aluminum industry rather than to export the ore. The basic raw material is present in almost unlimited quantities but a lack of coal and oil to provide energy precluded its processing hitherto. The manufacture of one kilo of aluminum requires 22 kilowatt hours of electricity making it an absolute necessity that power be cheap. A factory with a planned capacity of 40,000 tons aluminum produced from 160,000 tons of bauxite requires 880 million kilowatt hours yearly.

One look at the map of Surinam with her many rivers makes it abundantly clear that adequate power is only a matter of planning. After extensive topo-graphical, geological, and hydrological research, it was therefore decided to construct a dam in the neighborhood of Brokopondo, 90 miles south of Paramaribo, creating a lake with a surface of 400 square miles. Expecta-tions ran high. It has been calculated that the hydroelectric power from this one power plant will amount to a billion kwh a year.

In the selection and study of this and other sites, aerial surveys have been invaluable, replacing the time- and money-consuming charting expeditions of earlier years. In the period between 1860 and 1880, a map on a scale of

1:200,000 was drawn from explorations made by Cateau van Roosevelt and Van Lansberge. A later map, based on a survey done in 1913 by F.E. Spirelt and on a scale of 1:800,000 was, consequently, less accurate. Another one dating from 1930, and in Mercator projection by L.A. Bakker and W. de Quast, was on the same scale as the first mentioned map.

The crude methods with which such maps were drawn up, made it well-nigh impossible to mark out concessions for prospecting, exploitation, or cultivation. The solution was an aerial survey, begun in 1947 and financed by the Prosperity Fund. Within a few years, thousands and thousands of photos had resulted in a map of the most important northern half of the country on a scale of 1:40,000.

Many other important items listed in the Ten Year Plan, besides the Brokopondo Project and the air surveying, were realized. Irrigation methods were perfected; dams, roads, and bridges were constructed. There has also been a certain degree of success in agricultural planning: schools were founded, scientific research initiated, and the quality of many crops improved. Credit banks made financing easier for the small as well as the middle-sized farmer. Fishing was encouraged, cattle breeding expanded. More than 80 per cent of Surinam is covered with dense forests – a source of immense wealth if well handled – and the Plan, therefore, emphasized forestry. Industry and mining also received their share of official attention. So far the results have been encouraging but far from conclusive.

In 1968 the Ten Year Plan expired. Its achievements had exceeded all expectations, but development, of course, was far from complete, a ten year period being too short to accomplish the country's ever expanding goals. The Surinam government, therefore, readily announced a second Development Plan closely modeled after its predecessor. There is, for instance, the Kaba-lebo-Avanavero hydroelectric project which, like the Brokopondo under-taking, is meant to increase the power production of the country and thus promote its industrialization.

At the same time, the government is endeavoring to develop a sound fiscal climate which will attract investors. Current projects have placed a heavy load on the treasury, and ultimately on the taxpayer, with no promise of alleviation in sight. The impetus of a sustained growth of employment, local production, and national income, must now be provided primarily by private enterprise. Implied in this hypothesis is the corollary of stimulating invest-ment – a problem shared with the Antilles. A special ordinance for both regions attempts to meet this need by lowering taxation and import duties. As in the Netherlands Antilles, lately much attention has also been directed to the tourist industry, and plans are under study to construct several hotels and centers of recreation. However, unlike the islands, Surinam suffers the disadvantage of being isolated from the main routes of travel.

Programs of social legislation and labor organization fit into the framework of all efforts to bring the Netherlands Antilles and Surinam to a higher level of prosperity. Labor unions in both regions are still in the developing and organizing stage, trying to define realistic bases for action and growth. There are a number of trade organizations but their membership is generally limited and their financial power non-existent. Employers, on the other hand, better educated and stemming from the higher echelons of Antillian and Surinam society, realize the importance of presenting a united front. Thus, for example Surinam has its Surinam Trade and Industry Association (*Surinaams Bedrijfsleven*), an organization which represents the employers' point of view.

Social legislation is also still in its infancy. But there is a growing awareness of the country's social ills and of the government's responsibility in this area. The Antilles and Surinam each have a Department of Social Affairs (*Sociale Zaken*), which proposes legislation and takes care of labor and safety inspection, labor arbitration, and welfare. Both governments also subsidize rehabilitation, have instituted old-age pensions, and contemplate further projects in the interest of the workingman.

In spite of all these energetic attempts of the part of the governments of the Antilles and Surinam, unemployment is still rampant. Surinam, though, has more assets to counteract this problem: an abundance of fertile land, minerals, woods, and other raw materials waiting for investment and exploitation – assets the Antilles lack while their status is much more profoundly influenced by international developments and political complications.

In summary it cannot be denied that, in the last half century, the political and economic development of the Dutch regions in the West has gone through some remarkable phases. Up to 1940, the Netherlands had full political and economic control over her dependencies. With oil in the Antilles and bauxite in Surinam came prosperity and the desire for autonomy and independence. They were granted. But political retreat of the metropolitan power often coincided with an even firmer hold of private Dutch interests over the economic sector, especially in Surinam. Many Dutch companies and corporations have invested in the former dependencies overseas although this input is still far from adequate. The present recession, after the long fat years, leaves both the Antilles and Surinam with political self-determination, but without economic and financial sufficiency – exactly the reverse of their former situation, before 1954, when the "new style monarchy" was created. Nobody knows if this is a coincidence or the result of a consistent, although not conspicuously purposeful, policy of the former mother country.

CHAPTER XXIX

SOCIETY AND CULTURE IN THE NETHERLANDS WEST INDIES IN THE NINETEENTH AND TWENTIETH CENTURIES

The Curaçao islands were never plantation territory. The white upper class, composed of merchants and government employees, did not merge into a plantocracy as in Surinam; neither was the insular society characterized by cultural affinity since the Protestant and Jewish communities shied away from any intermingling.

The absence of a genuine plantation economy might account for the historically mild relations between the races. Contacts were usually on a much more personal basis than on the plantation, although social distance was maintained by a code of conduct crystallized into what a prominent sociologist has called the "master and slave" pattern of behavior.

Although it is true that, in the eighteenth century, a small group of mulatto merchants and craftsmen did become prosperous, most of the *hende di coló* (colored people), along with the blacks, belonged to the weakest economic sector of the population both before and after emancipation. Among the three groups of whites, mulattoes, and blacks, sexual relations were not uncommon – these being most often extra-marital as marriage was usually reserved for members of the same group. There did exist, however, a mutual cultural exchange whereby whites absorbed the influence of blacks and vice versa.

This slightly patriarchal society existed right up to the arrival of the Royal Dutch SHELL on Curaçao and the Standard LAGO on Aruba. It was profoundly altered first by industrialization and next by the autonomy the islands acquired under the Statute.

The coming of the oil caused an influx of immigrants, Dutch and others, the majority of whom left at retirement or upon expiration of their contracts – even if their stays had lasted for more than twenty years. One cannot help but be reminded of the similarity with the Dutch government employee under the WIC in the seventeenth and eighteenth centuries. Among the newcomers, the *macambas* (Dutchmen born in the Netherlands as opposed to the white natives of Curaçao) generally wound up occupying the white-collar positions in government and industry; the remaining immigrants, many of them Portuguese speaking Madeirans, filled the blue-collar jobs joining the ranks of Antillians of colored and black skin. As the governmental bureaucracy grew and educational facilities expanded, the islanders, white, colored, or black, soon saw themselves as secondary citizens of their own country. Thus the *macamba*'s prominent position in the island's budding society could not help but create a certain ill-feeling against the recent arrivals. Patriarchal feelings of good will and an inherent gregariousness faded in the face of the demands of a highly complex confrontation.

With autonomy the picture reverted and the *macamba* was replaced wherever possible by the native Antillian, the *landskind*. At first, the white *landskind* was able to maintain a firm hold on the white-collar jobs. The founder and leader of the Democratic Party, Efraim Jonckheer, was a white Antillian who, for many years, headed the government of the islands as Prime Minister. However, the large majority of colored and black inhabitants, many of them well-educated with degrees from Dutch universities, were rapidly becoming dissatisfied with their subordinate positions. In 1964 Jonckheer was succeeded by Ciro Kroon, and the colored or black man finally took full possession of his prerogatives.

Surinam's society underwent even more drastic changes. The plantocracy, which had ruled the country for two centuries before emancipation, remained a powerful influence until 1910. Yet as a consequence of the unabated influx of contract laborers from the Far East, a far more heterogeneous society resulted than on the Antilles.

Much more so than on the islands, in Surinam the premise of supposed white superiority went virtually unchallenged. Plantation slavery did not permit the degree of personal master-slave relationship common in the Antilles. Extra-marital relations could not be avoided, of course, although the so-called Surinam marriage was a respected bond between a white man and a colored or black girl, usually ending when the white returned to the home country.

The whites, numerically small and long isolated at the top of the social pyramid, were a culturally homogeneous group. But this solidarity also existed among the Creoles (those Surinamese having Negro blood), the Hindustani, the Javanese, and the Chinese. In contrast to what happened in the Antilles, Surinam's social classes evolved according to color values, scaled from black to white. Today, the whites still find themselves in the upper levels, not so much politically as economically; the colored are, in the real sense of the word, the middle class people, while the blacks are at the bottom of the ladder. Between these extremes move the Hindustani, the

Javanese, and the Chinese, straining to move upward while the Amerindians and the Bush negroes still exist outside the economy. Surinam has become, without any doubt, a very plural society.

Of the original Indian inhabitants barely 5,000 (some say only 3,000) are left, divided among the Arawaks, the Caribs, and the Waccaus. The history of the Bush negroes, formerly known as the *Marrons*, dates back to the days of the Chartered Society. Many of them remained in the country's interior even after emancipation, and today they number between 20,000 and 30,000. Living under a matriarchal system in which Christianity has made few inroads, the Bush negroes, like the Indians, continue to live almost completely isolated, although their chiefs or *granman* are subsidized by the government. *Rebel Destiny* by M.J. Herkovits, was the first in-depth study of their society. More recently, Silvia de Groot and Richard Price have added to our knowledge of these people.

The former slaves, ill-prepared for freedom as opposed to those on the Curaçao islands, were slow to find their places in this changing world. Ultimately they merged with other elements of the population to form the so-called Creole group, the racial composition of which incorporated the Negro-Chinese, the Negro-Hindu, and the Negro-Javanese. Poor and almost always belonging to the lower classes, the Creoles have been anxiously searching for an identity of their own. In Pengel, they found a powerful champion who propelled them into becoming a politically conscious group.

In number, the Hindus or Hindustani, approach the Christian Creoles. Politically coherent, they are religiously divided among 70 per cent Hindu, 18 per cent Moslem, and 12 per cent Christian. Many have prospered being able to send their children to schools in the Netherlands or the United States.

The 50,000 Javanese today form about 16 per cent of the population. Initially at odds in a strange country, partly because of strong ties to their homeland, by the 1940's, this feeling of separateness was beginning to wane as successive generations born in Surinam were coming of age. Although clinging to their colorful traditions – the gamelang (Javanese xylophone) is still to be heard alongside the rivers – there is a growing receptivity to Western education, and the problems of Surinam now take priority over those of Java. Nevertheless, when in 1949, Indonesia became independent, the vast majority of the Surinamese Javanese elected to adopt their new nationality and become Indonesians. Some actually preferred to return to Indonesia but the great majority stayed in their new fatherland where a special law enabled them to apply for Dutch citizenship. Today they belong to either the Indonesian Party or to the People's Party of Indonesia.

The Chinese, the Lebanese, the Portuguese, and the Dutch are all numerically much less important. Chinese immigration took place so long ago, between 1850 and 1870, that the Chinese of today are completely westernized. They speak Dutch and most of them are Christians. The few hundred families of Lebanese or Syrian descent are active in trade. The Portuguese, migrants from either Madeira or Brazil, are mostly government employees, teachers, or soldiers. So are many of the Dutch. When autonomy came to Surinam, there was a small group composed of old-time resident planters and newly arrived farmers, but since then the Dutch factor has been decreasing. There are also some Jewish planters and merchants, of importance to the society's economy, but without any political significance.

Economically, this heterogeneity, or segmentation of Surinam's society, is usually viewed as an asset. The different groups supplement each other to form a coordinated and well-functioning whole. The Creoles are not attracted to agriculture, for instance, but the Hindus and Javanese are. In a way, this situation works to everyone's advantage: the Creoles specialize in mining while the other two groups till the soil, breed cattle, and busy themselves with crops. One enormous drawback to farming, however, is the fact that the plots are much too small. In a way small farming (*kleine landbouw*) still suffers the effects of the old policy of restriction.

The distribution and sale of food is almost exclusively in the hands of the Chinese while the Bush negroes participate in the logging of Surinam's many fine species of precious wood, which is floated in rafts down the numerous rivers.

When, in 1816, the Antilles and Surinam were returned to Dutch rule, there was a small number of schools in operation in both colonies. The next year, King William I nominated a school commission to supervise the instruction and examination of students. Pioneer educators under this system were Johannes Vrolijk and Cornelis A. Batenburg in Surinam, and Gerrit van Paddenburgh in the Antilles.

The regulation of 1817 was amended several times to conform to the school system as it developed in the mother country. The number of schools grew with the population, but until well into the nineteenth century only the children of the free citizens received instruction; children of slaves were excluded.

In the latter half of the nineteenth century, nevertheless, the government became more aware of its duties. Under the progressive Governor Cornelis van Sypesteyn, compulsory primary education was introduced in Surinam – twenty years ahead of the mother country. In 1877, the governor also encouraged the establishment of a teachers college, although it was closed a year later on orders of The Hague as being too expensive for the colonial budget. Soon afterwards, however, Surinam was fortunate enough to secure as Inspector of Education the well-known H.D. Benjamins, whose pioneering efforts are still well remembered.

Education in both colonies continued to expand, despite the mother country's restrictive policy. Real improvement only came after the Dutch constitution was revised in 1922, ending the *schoolstrijd* (school struggle) in the Netherlands. From now on parochial schools were to be sponsored by the government – a principle which likewise applied in the Antilles and Surinam. In the Antilles, financially independent because of oil, the expansion of education did not encounter any great obstacles. But in Surinam, education did not flourish until after World War II.

Thus the Antilles, and now Surinam too, enjoy a good system of education structured after the Dutch master-plan. Secondary school diplomas are fully acknowledged and guarantee admission to Dutch institutions of higher learning. Grants and scholarships enable many Antillians and Surinamese to pursue the professions they choose and their countries need. Besides the primary and secondary schools there are technical schools, trade schools, teachers colleges, a law school on Curaçao (now a University), and a medical school in Paramaribo (also now a University).

In both the Antilles and Surinam the official language is Dutch, but the *lingua franca* on the Curaçao islands is Papiamento, on the Dutch Leeward Islands, the "island English," and in Surinam, Shranan or Negro-English. This linguistic polarity has greatly hampered literary development in these areas.

Both Papiamento and Shranan are relatively new languages which, until recently, existed only in spoken form. Papiamento, originally a slave lingo, was, in time, adopted by the Dutch and Jewish masters of the blacks. But a proper literature did not emerge until after the Second World War.

Shranan likewise is primarily a spoken language, but written samples have been found dating from the eighteenth century. It first appeared in print in 1718 when J.D. Herlein published a little book entitled *Description of the Surinam Colony* (*Beschrijvinge van de Volks-plantinae Zuriname*). More than a century later, in 1829, the Moravian Brotherhood issued the first Bible in Shranan. Until recently, the language has not been too highly regarded. Governor Mauricius referred to it as *jabber* and Benjamins, Inspector of Education, said "that a poorer vehicle of expression was hardly thinkable." All colonial literature, however, was still written in Dutch. In 1782, a Society for the study of Dutch History was founded, followed two years later by the establishment of a Society of Surinam Literature. Both were typical of the Enlightenment as it penetrated the colony, yet the language used was Dutch.

Cultural development in the nineteenth century was extremely laggard. A few clergymen ventured into the literary field, and a transient schoolteacher, Hermanus J. Abbring, was among the first to write down his feelings about his stay on Curaçao in a booklet called *Weemoedstonen* (*Songs of Nostalgia*). During many years another teacher, Pieter Poel, wrote a historical column for the *Curaçaosche Courant*, a weekly paper founded in 1811 during the English Interregnum, and, in the 19th century an important vehicle of public opinion.

With economic development, Antillian literature has become linguistically diversified: Spanish and Papiamento have been added to Dutch as vehicles of expression. A native of Curaçao, John de Pool, wrote a delightful book in Spanish, *Del Curaçao que se va*, in which he worded his sentiments about the modernization of insular society. It was published in 1935. Among those who have written in Dutch, mention must be made of David M. Chumaceiro, a Jewish lawyer. Since World War II the best Dutch writers have been: Cola Debrot, whose short novel *Mijn zuster de Negerin* (*My Sister the Negress*) is on its way to becoming a classic; Boeli van Leeuwen with *De Rots der Struikeling* (The Rock of Stumbling); Tip Marugg with *Weekend Pelgrimage*, Oda Blinder with *Een handvol leegten* (*A Handful of Emptiness*); and more recently Arion F. Martinez with *Dubbelspel* (*Double Game*). The native tongue is well represented by Pierre Lauffer, Elis Juliana and others.

Two nineteenth century Antillian painters of good standing who followed established European trends were Cornelis Gorsira and Johnny Ecker. Along with oil prosperity came the new fads. Abstract art found an energetic sponsor in Christiaan Engels, a local physician, who, it can be said, was the Father of the Curaçao Museum. Some local artists like Elis Juliana and Hipolito Ocalia were influenced by the Haitian School. Gil Hagedoorn was a fine representative of the impressionistic current.

While the Antilles produced no novels of great value before World War II, Surinam was fortunate enough to have, in this period, a novelist of exceptional qualities, Albert Helman, a pseudonym for Lou Lichtveld. His *The Silent Plantation* (*De Stille Plantage*) and other novels are fascinating interpretations of Surinam society during and after slavery and merit a wide readership. Dutch novelists do not easily get the fame of a Mittelhölzer or Naipaul of the British West Indies. Interest in the theatre manifested itself in Surinam at a much earlier date than in the Antilles. By 1840, Paramaribo had its first amateur theatre which put on such well-known tragedies as *Joseph in Dothan* by famous Dutch poet Joost van den Vondel and Shakespeare's *Merchant of Venice*. But popular plays like *Charley's Aunt* or *The Little Room* were more successful.

The Statute of the "New Style Monarchy" included a paragraph dealing with cultural interchange among the three partners. As a result of this, the Foundation for Cultural Collaboration (*Stichting voor Culturele Samenwerking, Sticusa*) was created in 1948 and reorganized in 1956, with branches in the Antilles and Surinam. This foundation has both stimulated and directed many of the cultural activities after World War II.

In this respect, the situation in the Antilles nowadays is quite different from that in Surinam. On the islands, society is racially less complex with no Indian or Asiatic groups to complicate matters, but there are more foreign-born workers, and much more contact with the outside world. For instance, there is a strong Latin American influence which is completely absent in Surinam.

The fact that all cultural centers of the Sticusa in the Antilles as well as in Surinam promote the use of the Dutch language – financed as they are by Dutch subsidies – may introduce an element of discord. True, the goal of the Sticusa is not Dutch cultural penetration but collaboration on the basis of equality, each partner freely developing within its own environment. Competition with the Dutch language makes it hard on Papiamento and Shranan to survive and carries, undoubtedly, the seeds of inequality.

Cultural collaboration encompasses such areas as the organization of all types of exhibits, the presentation of musical performances, theatre plays, sports, and many types of contests, and, in particular, the establishment of libraries and the distribution of publications. Tens of thousands of books and magazines from the Netherlands – in many languages but mostly in Dutch – are sent to the Antilles and Surinam, with special emphasis on books for children.

A similar organization in the scientific field, the *Wosuna* or Foundation for Scientific Research, filled a parallel role by stimulating and promoting research in this field in the West Indies. In 1964, its name was changed to *Wotro*, Foundation for Research in the Tropics. In 1955, a Marine Biological Institute, called the Carmabi Institute, was established on Curaçao.

There are several daily papers in the Antilles and Surinam, most of them in Dutch. Radio and television, however, often use the local vernacular.

As a result of international tension, the United States came to realize the importance of the Caribbean area to its own defense and, in 1941, organized the Inter-American Caribbean Union, which included the countries of the circum-Caribbean. After Pearl Harbour, the Union became known as the Anglo-American Commission representing the U.S.A. and the independent islands. In 1946, it changed names again and was called the Caribbean Commission. As it now stands, the Caribbean Commission is composed of 16 members: four apiece from the U.S.A., the British, the French, and the Dutch islands. Its purpose is to promote collaboration and prosperity by providing the various governments with advice in agriculture, education, fishing, health, housing, industry, labor relations, etc. The members come together twice a year at West Indian Conferences to hear reports and to discuss the issues. The central secretariat is located in Kent House in Port of Spain, Trinidad. A monthly bulletin in published in four different languages: English, Spanish, French, and Dutch. The Caribbean Commission is financed in the following manner: the U.S.A. pays 38,4 per cent of the annual budget, Great Britain 34,3 per cent, France 16 per cent, and the Netherlands 11,3 per cent. Of the contributions from the Netherlands The Hague pays half; the Antilles and Surinam at first divided the rest evenly between them, but these amounts were altered in 1960 so that the Antilles now contribute more and Surinam less.

Lately, the Dutch have put out some tentative feelers toward participation in the CARICOM or Caribbean Common Market.

The independence of Surinam, after long deliberations between The Hague, Willemstad, and Paramaribo ended the "New Style Monarchy" based on the Statute and opened a new phase in the history of the three former partners. Many problems have to be solved and a few relationships will be affected, not the least being Surinam's share in the European Common Market, economic cooperation with the erstwhile partners, the interests of Dutch companies, e.g. KLM, and other corporations investing and working in Surinam, cultural collaboration, etc. The Netherlands have expressed their continuous interest in the development of the former colony and are willing to conclude an agreement for economic cooperation. The new Surinam government is bound to take into account the Dutch commitments in the country.

In spite of the many problems facing the autonomous Antilles and independent Surinam, the future looks rather rosy. Both are progressing under sound democratic systems of government anchored by constitutional freedoms. That they should be wrestling with the growing pains of young nations is not surprising.

SELECTED BIBLIOGRAPHY

Because I have added no notes to the text, acknowledgment must be made to some sources which give information on the topic.

Works on the Caribbean and the Guianas pay only scant attention to the former Dutch colonies. A outdated but good introduction is the work of Ph. Hanson Hiss, *A Selective Guide to the English Literature on the Netherlands West Indies With a Supplement on British Guiana* (New York, 1943). For more and detailed information knowledge of the Dutch language is necessary.

General works on the Netherlands Antilles and Surinam exist almost exclusively in Dutch. They include J.H.J. Hamelberg's pioneering study *De Nederlanders op de West-Indische eilanden.* I. *De Benedenwindsche eilanden Curaçao, Bonaire, Aruba.* II *De Bovenwindsche eilanden St. Eustatius, Saba, St. Maarten* (Amsterdam, 1898, 1908); the two works of W.R. Menkman: *De Nederlanders in het Caraïbisch zeegebied* (Amsterdam, 1942), and *De West-Indische Compagnie* (Amsterdam, 1947), and the very detailed work of J. Hartog, *Geschiedenis van de Nederlandse Antillen.* I. *Aruba,* II. *Bonaire,* III and IV. *Curaçao* I and II, and V. *De Bovenwindse eilanden* (Oranjestad, 1953–1964). For Surinam we can only refer to J. Wolbers' *Geschiedenis van Suriname* (Paramaribo, 1861).

In addition to these general works we mention H.D. Benjamins and Joh. Snelleman eds., *Encyclopaedie van Nederlandsch West Indië* (Leiden, 1914), H. Hoetink ed., *Encyclopedie van de Nederlandse Antillen* (Amsterdam, 1969), and C.F.A. Bruyning and J. Voorhoeve, eds., *Encyclopedie van Suriname* (Amsterdam, 1977).

As of yet no study has been published on the pre-Columbian inhabants of the former Dutch possessions. We can refer to the outdated work of W. Ahlbrink, *Encyclopaedie der Karaiben, behelzend Taal, Zeden en Gewoonten dezer Indianen* (Amsterdam, 1931). Valuable information given by C.H. de Goeje, J.P.B. Josselin de Jong, P. Wagenaar Hummelinck and others is scattered in some of the reviews mentioned at the end of this summary. One should also look into the anthropological studies of Venezuelan authors as well as Irving Rouse's *An Archeological Chronology of Venezuela* (Pan American Union Soc. Sciences Monographs, 6 vols. 1958–1959).

The presence of Spain on the A.B.C. islands, especially Curaçao, is the topic of C. Felice Cardot's book *Curaçao Hispánico* (Caracas, 1973). It is also found in some articles by Menkman and C.Ch. Goslinga in the *West-Indische Gids* (WIG). The early Dutch activities and colonization in the Caribbean are well related by Ioannes de Laet, *Historie ofte Iaerlijck Verhael van de Verrichtingen der Geoctroyeerde West-Indische Compagnie* (S.P. L'Honoré Naber ed., 4 vols., 's-Gravenhage,

1932–1937), and G.J. van Grol, *De grondpolitiek in het Westindische domein van de Generaliteit* (3 vols., 's-Gravenhage, 1934–1947). Goslinga discusses the period between 1580 and 1680 in *The Dutch in the Caribbean and on the Wild Coast* (Assen, Gainesville, 1971). Dutch privateering and piracy is the topic of John Exquemeling's *The Buccaneers of America* (many editions) while David van der Sterre wrote the biography of a Dutch privateer in *De seer aenmerckelijcke reysen van Jan Erasmus Reining* (Amsterdam, 1691).

Eighteenth century Curaçao is depicted by J.H. Hering's *Beschrijving van het Eyland Curaçao* (Amsterdam, 1779). L. Knappert did the same for the Dutch Leeward islands: *Geschiedenis van de Nederlandsche bovenwindsche eilanden in de achttiende eeuw* ('s-Gravenhage, 1932). The turbulent days of the end of this century are chronicled in N. van Meeteren's *Noodlotsdagen* (Willemstad, 1944).

In the nineteenth century several authors of more or less genuine scholarly purity put their Curaçao histories on the market: G.G. van Paddenburg, *Beschrijving van het eiland Curaçao en onderhoorige eilanden* (Haarlem, 1819), S. van Dissel, *Herinneringen en schetsen* (Leiden, 1857), G.J. Simons, *Beschrijving van het eiland Curaçao* (Osterwolde, 1868), and A.T. Brusse, *Curaçao en zijn bewoners* (Curaçao, 1882).

For Surinam, the earliest period has not yet been put into a framework of good research. Mention should be made of Vincent T. Harlow, ed., *Colonizing Expeditions to the West Indies and Guiana 1623–1667* (London, 1925). The eighteenth century is well represented by J.J. Hartsinck, *Beschrijving van Guiana of de wilde kust in Zuid-Amerika* (2 vols., Amsterdam, 1770), and the two works of Ph. Fermin: *Description générale et politique ... de la colonie de Surinam** (Amsterdam, 1769), and *Tableau historique et politique ... de la colonie de Surinam** (Maastricht, 1778). J.F.E. Einaar explored the English interregnum in *Bijdrage tot de kennis van het Engels tussenbestuur in Suriname 1804–1816* (Leiden, 1934). M.D. Teenstra's *De landbouw in de kolonie Suriname* (2 vols., Groningen, 1835) is valuable for the early nineteenth century, R.M.N. Panday discussed Surinam's agricultural experience in *Agriculture in Surinam 1650–1950* (Amsterdam, 1959), while A. Kappler's *Holländisch-Guiana. Erlebnisse und Erfahrungen während eines 43-jährigen Aufenthalts in der Kolonie Surinam* (Stuttgart, 1881) covers the middle half of that century.

Dutch participation in the slave trade is the topic of modern continuing research. A good outline is given by A. van Dantzig, *Het Nederlandse aandeel in de slavenhandel* (Bussum, 1968), while additional information is provided by Johannes Postma, *The Dutch Participation in the African Slave Trade* (Univ. of Michigan Microfilms, Ann Arbor, Michigan, 1970), and the articles of S. van Brakel and W.S. Unger (in *Economisch Historisch Jaarboek*), and B. de Gaay Fortman and Goslinga (in *West-Indische Gids*). The special problem Surinam had with the Marrons is eloquently told in the classic work of John G. Stedman, *A Narrative of a Five Years' Expedition Against the Revolted Negroes in Surinam* (2 vols., London, 1796), and in Silvia de Groot's *Van isolatie naar integratie. De Surinaamse Marrons en hun afstammelingen* ('s-Gravenhage, 1963). Other studies on Dutch slavery and its emancipation are Goslinga, *Emancipatie en Emancipator* (Assen, 1956), J.F. Zeegelaar, *Suriname en de opheffing van de slavernij in 1863* (Amsterdam, 1871),

---

* Where this asterisk appears, the title has been abbridged.

Teenstra, *De negerslaven in de Kolonie Suriname** (Amsterdam, 1853), and A.D. van der Gon Netscher, *De opheffing van de slavernij en de toekomst van Nederlandsch West Indië* ('s-Gravenhage, 1862).

Numerous authors have given their views on the ABC islands' local vernacular, the Papiamento, in a variety of articles and other publications spread over many years. Some familiar authors on the subject are W.M. Hoyer, *Papiamentoe, su manera di skirbié* (Curaçao, 1918), and M.D. Latour (in *WIG*). Similar is the case with Negro-English or Shranan in Surinam which is researched by J.J.M. Echteld, *The English Words in Sranan* (Groningen, 1961), R.D. Simons, *Het Neger-Engels* (Paramaribo, 1941), Ch.H. Eersel, *De Surinaamse taalsituatie* (Paramaribo, 1970), and several studies by J. Voorhoeve.

The twentieth century has witnessed an avalanche of authors and publications from which a choice necessarily becomes difficult and seemingly whimsical. Basic works on society are those by M.J. Herkovits, *Rebel Destiny* (New York, 1934), R.J. van Lier, *Samenleving in een grensgebied* ('s-Gravenhage, 1949), a study of Surinam's segmented society, and H. Hoetink's *Het patroon van de oude Curaçaose samenleving* (Assen, 1958), and *De gespleten samenleving in het Caribisch gebied* (Assen, 1961). Curaçao's elite is the subject of A.J.C. Krafft's *Historie en oude families van de Nederlandse Antillen* ('s-Gravenhage, 1951). On the Jews we have the excellent work of I.S. and S.A. Emmanuel, *History of the Jews of the Netherlands Antilles* (2 vols., Cincinnati, 1970). Several articles by R. Bijlsma, J. Zwarts, Ph.A. Samson, J.H. Adhin, and F. Oudschans Dentz on this topic have appeared in *WIG* and *Schakels*. The history of other population groups in Surinam is recorded by C.J.M. de Klerk, *De immigratie der Hindustanen in Suriname* (Amsterdam, 1953), J. Ismael, *De immigratie van Indonesiërs in Suriname* (Leiden, 1949), A. de Waal Malefijt, *The Javanese of Surinam. Segment of a Plural Society* (Assen, 1969), J.D. Speckman, *Marriage and Kinship among the Indians of Surinam* (Assen, 1965), and W.F. Buschkens, *The Family System of the Paramaribo Creoles* ('s-Gravenhage, 1974).

In the field of international relations which affected the Antilles more than Surinam we recommend K.H. Corporaal's contribution *De internationaalrechtelijke betrekkingen tusschen Nederland en Venezuela 1816–1920* (Leiden, 1920), and Goslinga's *Curaçao and Guzmán Blanco* ('s-Gravenhage, 1975). More locally oriented are Surinam's relations explained in G.J. Kruyer's *Suriname en zijn buurlanden* (Meppel, 1960).

The industrialization of the Dutch Antilles and Surinam is more a topic of numerous articles than of in-depth studies. For the importance of the oil we have J. van Soest's extensive study *Olie als water* (Willemstad, 1976). For Surinam J.F. van Kersen, *Bauxite Deposits in Surinam and Demerara* (Leiden, 1955), and A.L.R. Smit, *Surinaamse bauxiet maskerade* (Paramaribo) deal with bauxite and the dealings around it. Some contributions in this field are found in the articles of Ph.H.A. Zaalberg (in *Erts*), L.C. Panhuys (in *WIG*), J. Kuiperbak and D. Hillen (*in Schakels*) on bauxite, and of R.H.D. Debrot (*Schakels*) and reports of the *Caribbean Commission* on oil.

Political development has witnessed drastic changes. A good general review is given by A.L. Gastman, *The Politics of Surinam and the Netherlands Antilles* (Puerto Rico, 1968). H.W.C. Bordewijk wrote at an early stage of this development in *Ontstaan en ontwikkeling van het staatsrecht van Curaçao* ('s-Gravenhage, 1911), followed by M.F. da Costa Gomez, *Het wetgevend orgaan van Curaçao* (Amsterdam, 1933). W.H. van Helsdingen published two studies: *De staatsregeling van de Nederlandse Antillen* ('s-Gravenhage, 1955), and *De staatsregeling van Suriname* ('s-Gravenhage, 1955). De Gaay Fortman, well-known for his numerous articles on the Dutch West Indies (in *WIG*), wrote *Schets van de politieke geschiedenis der Nederlandse Antillen* ('s-Gravenhage, 1947), and A. Kasteel, *De staatkundige ontwikkeling der Nederlandse Antillen* ('s-Gravenhage, 1956).

Surinam's economic and political development is the topic of A. Van Traa's *Suriname 1900–1940* (Deventer, 1946), J. Brons' *Het rijksdeel Suriname* (Haarlem, 1952), and J.A.E. Buiskool's *Suriname nu en straks* (Amsterdam, 1946). Recent developments are analyzed in C.E.M. Mitrasing, *Tien jaar Suriname* (Leiden, 1959), and F.J. van Wel, *Suriname. Balans van een kwart eeuw opbouwwerk* ('s-Gravenhage, 1975). The Sticusa published *Tien jaar Statuut* ('s-Gravenhage, 1964), a summary on the constitutional role of the Statute.

Cultural life in both the Antilles and Surinam is depicted in many publications. C. Debrot published an outline for the Antilles in *Literature of the Netherlands Antilles* (Curaçao, 1964), while two reviews, *De Stoep* and *Antilliaanse Cahiers* became the mouthpiece of blossoming Antillian poets and novelists. R. Boskaljon contributed to the musical history of the islands with *Honderd jaar muziekleven op Curaçao* (Assen, 1955), John de Pool wrote a delightful impression of pre-war Curaçao in *Del Curaçao que se va* (Santiago de Chile, 1935). M.D. Ozinga discusses Dutch colonial architecture in *De monumenten van Curaçao* ('s-Gravenhage, 1959), Y. Attema contributed to this field with *St. Eustatius. A Short Story of the Island and its Monuments* (Zutfen, 1975) and S.L. Temminck Grol et al. did the same for Surinam in *De architektuur van Suriname* (Zutfen, 1973). M. Brada and A. Euwens wrote on the Roman Catholic mission of the Antilles in numerous booklets and articles, while M.D. Latour wrote the history of this subject: *Geschiedenis der missie van Curaçao* (Curaçao, 1945).

Concerning Surinam J. Voorhoeve and U.M. Lichtveld published *Creole Drum, an Anthology of Creole Literature in Surinam* (New Haven, 1975), while many articles found their way to *Schakels*. The Sticusa published, in 1972, a *Bibliografie van Suriname* and a *Bibliografie van de Nederlandse Antillen*. J. van Raalte gave an outline of Christian denominations in Surinam in *Cultureel mozaiek van Suriname* (Sticusa, 1977), J.W.C. Ort wrote a history of the Dutch Reformed Church: *Vestiging van de Hervormde Kerk in Suriname 1667–1800* (1963), and M.F. Abbenhuis did the same for the Roman Catholic church: *De Katholieke Kerk in Suriname* (Paramaribo, 1959).

Some reviews about the Netherlands Antilles and Surinam are: *West Indische Gids* (and *Nieuwe West Indische Gids*), *Oost en West*, *Schakels*, *Vox Guyanae*, *Christoffel*, *Neerlandia*, *Economisch Historisch Jaarboek*, *Indische Gids*, *La Prensa*, *Beurs en Nieuwsberichten*, *Amigoe*, *De West* (the last four daily papers of the Antilles and Surinam). Scattered in many other publications and in the *Koloniale Verslagen* (Colonial Reports) one may find more information available for the interested researcher.

GENERAL INDEX

absenteeism, 100, 101
admirals and naval commanders, 22, 29, 30,
38, 41–43, 45, 46–49, 64, 65, 71–73, 79
80, 83–85, 94, 95
aerial surveys, 179–181
agriculture, 54, 55, 79, 97, 100, 125, 152–
158, 162, 164, 179, 180, 187
airlines, 143, 151, 176, 191
Alpina settlement, 156
Amerindians, 173, 186
Ampués, Juan de, 10, 14–18
Anglo-Dutch wars, 33, 36, 38–40, 43, 45–
47, 65, 79, 80, 83, 92, 93, 101,110
Apo, Lim, 170
Arawaks, 4, 87, 88, 97, 186
asiento, 51, 63, 110, 111
audiencia, 14–16, 18

Baas, Jean Ch. de, 45–47
Bastidas, Rodrigo de, 13, 18, 19
Batlle of Nevis, 42, 94
bauxite, 177–180
Berbice, 91–95, 98, 100–103, 116, 117, 154
Black Chasseurs, 116
Bolívar, Simón, 74, 119, 120, 122
boratio, 4–6, 17
Bosch, J. v. d., 123, 150, 154, 159
Brion, Pedro L., 70, 71, 120
Brokopondo project, 180, 181
Bush negroes, 3, 115, 173, 186, 187
Byam, William, 42, 93, 94

cabale, 99
cacique, 4–6, 15, 17
Caiquetíos, 4, 11, 14, 15
Campen, J. C. van, 30, 54, 77, 78
Cantz'laar, P. R., 120–122, 154
Caribbean Commission, 191
Caribs, 14, 87, 88, 97, 186
CARICOM, 191

Casas, Bartolomé de las, 10, 14
Cassard, J., 61, 62, 82, 98
Cayenne, 2, 43, 45, 89, 91–95, 97, 102
Charles I, 77
Charles II, 37, 38
Charles V, 15, 16, 18
Chartered Society, 96–99, 101, 105, 116, 168
Chinese, 173, 185, 187
Claessen, Th. 91, 92
Colbert, 37, 41, 44, 110
Columbus, 8, 10
compensation, 157, 158
conquest, 20, 23, 24, 26, 31
Corps of Free Negroes, 116
Cosa, J. de la, 8, 10, 13
Costa Gomez, M. F. da, 171
Creoles, 173, 174, 185–187
Crijnssen, A., 42, 93, 94
cultural development, 106, 184–191
Curaçaosche Courant, 128, 189

Debrot, Cola, 172, 189
Demerara, 75, 98, 100–103, 116, 117, 147,
154
Doedel, L. 165, 166
Dutch Trading Company, 160, 161
Dutch Billiton Ltd., 178

economy, 69, 175–182, 189, 191
education, 105, 106, 153, 187, 188
emancipation, 131–136, 151, 156–158
Engels, Chr., 189
English period, 68, 69, 72, 102, 103
Essequibo, 75, 89, 92–95, 98, 100, 101, 103,
116, 117, 154
European Common Market, 176, 177
export, 96–100, 102, 103

Fajardo, G., 31, 32
Ferdinand VII, 121

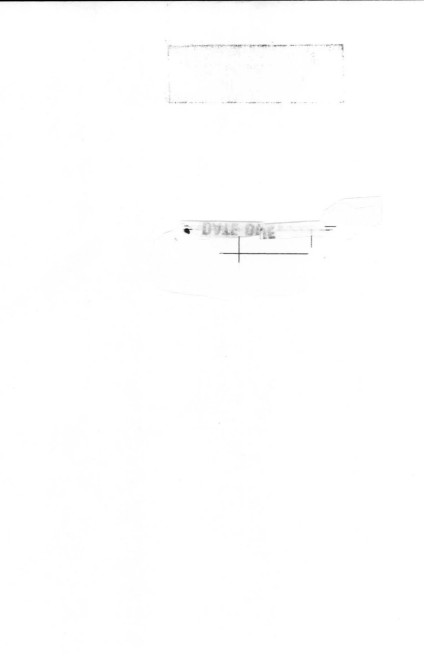